A SOCIAL HISTORY OF ENGLISH ROWING

A SOCIAL HISTORY OF ENGLISH ROWING

NEIL WIGGLESWORTH

FRANK CASS

First published 1992 in Great Britain by
FRANK CASS AND COMPANY LIMITED
Gainsborough House, 11 Gainsborough Road,
London E11 1RS, England

and in the United States of America by
FRANK CASS
c/o International Specialized Book Services, Inc.,
5602 N.E. Hassalo Street, Portland, Oregon 97213

British Library Cataloguing in Publication Data

Wigglesworth, Neil
  A social history of English rowing
  1. Great Britain. Boating, history
  I. Title
  797.1230941

ISBN 0-7146-3399-2

Library of Congress Cataloging-in-Publication Data

Wigglesworth, Neil
    A social history of English rowing / Neil Wigglesworth.
      p.   cm.
    Includes bibliographical references (p.   ) and index.
    ISBN 0-7146-3399-2
    1. Rowing—Social aspects—England—History—19th century.
    2. Rowing—Social aspects—England—History—20th century.
    3. England—Social life and customs. I. Title.
    GV795.W54   1992   91-3481
  797.1'23—dc20   CIP

For my mother and father

Contents

Illustrations

Acknowledgements

In collecting information for such a wide-ranging survey, I can only echo the sentiments of the new editor of the *Rowing Almanack* in 1870 who commented that 'no conception can be formed of the labour of such a task by those who have not undertaken it'. Fortunately, I have been helped in my task by fellow-oarsmen throughout the country whose assistance I gratefully acknowledge here: Keith Osborne, the present editor of the *Rowing Almanack* who loaned me precious back numbers of the publication, and the following who helped me with their club histories: Graham Pointer (Royal Chester R.C.), Mike Fox (Kings School Chester B.C.), Nick Pettet (Pilkington Blades R.C.), Trevor Wild and Geoff Nuttall (Hollingworth Lake R.C.), Eric Bennett (Runcorn R.C.), Vincent Kehoe (Agecroft R.C.), Robert Hughes (Henry Meoles School R.C.), Neil Thomas (Liverpool Victoria R.C.), Kneale Barber (Northwich R.C.), Ian Fisher (Sefton R.C.), Stuart Potter (Merchant Taylors School B.C.), David Clark and Steven Bull (Ryde R.C.), Jim Morris (Brighton Cruising Club), Pat Glover (Shanklin and Sandown R.C.), J.C. Beechy-Newman (Greenbank Falmouth R.C.), Bill Colley (Putney Town R.C.), Harry Read (Poplar, Blackwall and District R.C.), John Eden (Guildford R.C.), Len Rey (Exeter R.C.), George Hooper (Thames Tradesmen R.C.), Mike Phillips (Thames Ditton Skiff and Punting Club), Mike Stephenson (St Ives R.C.), Richard Dawes (Folkestone R.C.), John Benjamin (Bradford-on-Avon R.C.), Stuart Moody (Poole R.C.), David Barnett (Worthing R.C.), John Filor (Bristol Ariel R.C.), Keith Whiteside (Eton Excelsior R.C.), John Harradine (Cambridge '99 R.C.), Nick Walmsley (Norwich Union R.C.), Ralph Bird (Truro R.C. and Newquay R.C.), Richard du Parq (Cygnet R.C.), Norman Murphy (Southampton R.C.), J.P. Morgan (Henley R.C.), Bryan Goult (Bideford A.A.C.), J.S. Bowden (Bideford A.R.C.), Stephen Walshaw (Eastbourne R.C.), R. Allen (Bristol and Severn R.C.), Robert Rivington (Falcon R.C.), Hugh Ashton (Wallingford R.C.), J.E. Biddle (Burway R.C.), John Partridge (Derwent R.C.), C.J. Fishburn (Leicester R.C.), George Lawson (Burton Leander R.C.), Kevin Bruton (Nottingham and Union R.C.), M.J. Theaker (Derby R.C.), Terry Robinson (Nottingham B.C.), W.P. Dutton (Loughborough B.C.), Chris Kenyon (Tees B.C.), M.G. Collins (Evesham R.C.), Bill Collins (Stratford-on-Avon R.C.), Robin Parkin

(Berwick-on-Tweed R.C.), Richard Coleman (Worcester R.C.), Wilf Mellor (York City R.C.), John Lambert (Tynemouth R.C.), Jim Nisbet (Tyne R.C.), Robin Scott (Cambois R.C.), John Bishop (Hexham R.C.), Terry Duffy (Midland Bank R.C.), Irene Foley (Alpha Womens R.C.), Julie Milne (London District Line R.C.), Geoff Pullen (Gravesend R.C.), John Burnett (Weybridge R.C.), J. Kerbel (Molesey R.C.), Mrs. L. Kaye (Stuart Ladies R.C.), David Biddulph (Kingston R.C.), Sharon Ayres (Rob Roy R.C.), J.P. Radgick (Twickenham R.C.), Elsie Stagg (Weybridge Ladies R.C.), Andy Muston (Cambridge University B.C.), Margaret Smire (Bedford Ladies R.C.), Eric Davies (St Neots R.C.), Stephen Casey (Peterborough City R.C.), Dennis Baker (City of Cambridge R.C.), Ian Birch (Bedford R.C.), Ralph Potter (Norwich R.C.), Colin McDougall (Leviathan R.C.), Graham Garner (Ancholme R.C.), Barry Hatton (Gainsborough R.C.), R. Warren (Pengwern B.C.), George Windsor (Ironbridge R.C.), Peter Finney (Bradford R.C.), Don Wood (Whitby Friendship R.C.), Jacka Stevens (Curlew R.C.), Nigel Smith (London R.C.), Raymond Mark (Talkin Tarn R.C.), Lyn Panon (Star R.C.) and Kevin Porter (Boston R.C.).

The following helped with regatta histories: Bill Colley (Hammersmith Borough Regatta), David Wilkin (Sunbury Regattas), Charles Dimont (Putney Town Regatta), John Burnett (Walton Regatta), Mrs. R.A. Hughes (Dartmouth Royal Regatta), R.S. Goddard (Henley Royal Regatta), John Allen (Reading Regatta), B. Hartland (Southampton Regatta), Margaret Marshall (Derby Regatta), David Clarke (Burton-on-Trent Regatta), Wally Barton (Bewdley Regatta), Eric Halladay (Durham City Regatta), Jim Nisbet (Tyne Regatta), Leonard Smith (Chertsey Regatta), Guy Wibberley (Kingston Regatta), Ian Codrington (Bedford Regatta).

The following helped with histories of their organisations: John Holroyd (Yorkshire and Humberside Rowing Council), Nick Champain (National Dock Labour Board), E.S. Earl (Fishmongers' Company) and Martin Spencer (Watermens' Company).

Finally, I should like to paraphrase a sentiment expressed in the Royal Chester Rowing Club centenary history and acknowledge those hundreds of oarsmen and women, unmentioned in club histories, who have maintained the good name of rowing, 'excited and upheld a spirit of emulation and encouraged an athletic and innocent sport'. Truly, without them there would be no history and I would have been denied the great pleasure of researching it.

Foreword

This is an attractive book; thoughtful and fluent. With easy insistence Neil Wigglesworth makes the point that it is not possible to insulate sport from the wider society. Rowing, he argues, is 'the finest barometer of social change provided by the sporting tradition' with its close association with educational ideologies, the class structure, amateurism and professionalism, patriotism and internationalism, elitism and populism, and urbanisation, commercialism and bureaucratisation.

Not the least of Wigglesworth's virtues is his balanced concern with continuity and change. He traces a long heritage of tension between 'aristocratic' and 'democratic' rowing cultures resulting in confrontation and change; but he also discerns the long-standing dichotomous aquatic traditions of 'prestige' and 'people' as continuous threads linking past and present and illuminating current concerns.

This is a book for those interested as much in the history of British society as in the history of British sport. Wigglesworth meshes the two in a most convincing manner.

J.A. Mangan
Editor of *The International Journal of the History of Sport* and of the Series: International Studies in the History of Sport

1

Introduction

> There is a wall of silence which divides us from the
> world of ordinary men and women before about
> 1820 which is difficult to penetrate.
>
> (Mary Prior, *Fisher Row – Fishermen, Bargemen
> and Canal Boatmen in Oxford, 1500–1900*)

The historian of rowing, like that of cricket, has some advantages
over historians of other sports in having access to copious club
minutes stretching back in some cases to the last years of the
eighteenth century and many illuminating illustrations of aquatic
events dating initially from the mid-eighteenth century and becoming positively commonplace from the time of the first university
Boat Race in 1829 (see Appendix 1.i). Documentary evidence of
rowing as a trade or occupation is not so easily traced, however;
besides, many historians of the sport have merely sought to record
the progress of rowing as boat racing among crews from the public
schools and Oxbridge colleges.

Thus it was that the earliest origins of the sport received scant
attention outside a dutiful paragraph or two on the Thames watermen as in the first attempt at an overall review by 'a rower of
thirty matches' entitled simply 'Aquatics'.[1] In this, the author, who
remains anonymous, laments the decline in aquatics, implying an
already substantial tradition and mentions its patronage 'some
years ago by almost every nobleman in the land' concluding that
'aquatics should be a pleasure to the amateur and bread to the
watermen'. There is substantial contemporary journalistic evidence of youngsters being encouraged by watermen to row but
such examples remain unrecorded in the early rowing literature,
an omission recently rectified to some extent by Osborne in his
pamphlet on boat racing.[2]

The very earliest use of the oar in trade or war was given negligible
regard until Woodgate's book of 1888,[3] which reversed the traditional 'Topsy theory' of spontaneous appearance and endeavoured

1

to trace back aquatic origins to the dug-out canoe. This approach was substantially refined and used most effectively by Desborough in his pamphlet of 1910[4] and Cleaver drew material from both for his history of 1957[5] which sought to be a comprehensive review of the sport in all its forms.

Although little time or space was generally expended on the occupational origins of the sport of rowing, we do find many allusions to them in a variety of publications: Brickwood in his training manual of 1876,[6] mentions the heavy clinker-built cutters commonly used by the Tyne watermen and remarks that several were specially built for use by the amateurs of the London Rowing Club for training purposes; Theodore Cook recalled[7] these old-fashioned boats, explaining that their varying beams required different lengths of oar, the longest being used in the middle of the boat and pulled, necessarily, by the strongest men, a tradition reflected today in the choice of the heaviest men for the central crew positions.

A universal result of using these heavy boats was the style of stroke employed by the watermen which was typified by other early commentators as 'oiling into the water with no attempt at a beginning' and consequently vilified as transgressing 'the primary rules of scientific oarsmanship'[8] so beloved of the gentlemen amateurs. The trade, and thus professional origins of the sport, were therefore belittled and in most cases simply omitted completely as with Jeffrey's book of 1897,[9] which states categorically that 'boats may be divided into broadly two classes, viz. boats built for speed and boats built for pleasure', failing to mention that both evolved from those built for work.

Nevertheless, it was in working boats that all the earliest practitioners, both professional and amateur, first pulled an oar, as in the case of Frederick Furnivall who learned his sculling in the 14ft sea dinghy of Billy Veers, a Staines fisherman, and who, many years later, fought the amateur authorities over the denial of competitive rights for the working man.[10]

The development of rowing as a sport passed through the traditional phase of noble patronage and was thereby popularised more quickly than would otherwise have been the case; however, this should not obscure the view of its previous history throughout the country. When the anonymous author of 'Aquatics' mentions patronage by almost every nobleman in the land, he refers to those aristocrats, frequently identified in the contemporary press, who promoted matches between well-known watermen in sculling or pair-oared boats as a diversion for society gatherings and as opportunities for gambling. Such events, usually called 'wagers' or 'matches', would often attract thousands of spectators on the River Thames and large crowds elsewhere but are rarely mentioned by the sport's historians who regarded them as 'parish regattas' or 'watermen's wrangles' which 'rarely afforded a true test of skills'.[11]

It must be remembered that, from the very first, the published material on rowing was produced by the public-school-educated gentleman amateur who deprecated any hint of commercialism and acted to repress it both on the water and in print, with the result that by the 1870s, there was a marked decline in professional rowing on the River Thames. Elsewhere, however, professional matches were still enormously popular, especially on the River Tyne where they 'signalled a general holiday with thousands attending' and the decline on the Thames was put down to 'dissensions among the watermen with the consequences that the lower orders have transferred their loyalty to the Boat Race'.[12]

This loyalty soon turned the Boat Race into the kind of commercial circus that its promoters wished, at all costs, to avoid[13] and its attendant vulgarities had even invaded Henley Regatta itself by the turn of the century.[14] Rather than seek to stamp out such developments, both the Henley and Boat Race organisations sought to manipulate the huge media coverage and turn it to their own commercial advantage, a strategy which has proved enormously successful and hugely profitable.[15, 16]

Despite subsequently vilifying the professional waterman, the new class of college amateurs often utilised them in coaching and training crews by placing them in pair oars and using them as models for each trainee in turn, thus ensuring a uniformity of stroke within the crew and 'in this way making more progress in one week than could be effected in one month's practice confined to the eight oar only'.[17] In 1857 Oxford University engaged Matt. Taylor, a well-known professional oarsman and boat-builder, 'not to instruct us in the art of rowing but to show us the proper way to send his boat along as quickly as possible',[18] an explanation made necessary since, by this time, questions had been asked about the suitability of watermen as coaches.

By 1876, the split between the professional and amateur was complete and Brickwood could say at last that 'the art of training has been rescued from the depths of empiricism in which the ignorant prejudices of illiterate professionals purposefully kept it',[19] a point taken up, rather unkindly, by Sherwood in 1900[20] who reprints a letter from the semi-literate Robert Coombes soliciting work from Brasenose College Boat Club: 'I have riting thouse fue lines ... etc'. Sherwood openly states the amateur position when he recounts how Oxford and Cambridge men largely controlled the boating world by keeping the 'quasi-amateur' at arm's length and admitted that 'we are doing this drastically and in doing it we have inflicted considerable hardships on local regattas and clubs, but our instinct is right – it is the instinct of self-preservation'.

Preservation from open competition was not strictly necessary since the top amateurs with their 'best' boats and scientific training could overcome most professional crews as did Woodgate's crew of 1864 which consistently beat Kelley's professional championship combination.[21] The preservation which amateurs really sought was from what they perceived to be a vulgar and meretricious culture which threatened their way of life, and the measures they took to achieve their ends resulted in a narrowly restricted entry into the aquatic world of regattas and clubs.

The growth of the many and varied rowing clubs and the development of the sport throughout the country is a vast topic which has escaped the attention of rowing historians who have concentrated largely upon the Metropolitan and Oxbridge scenes, leaving individual clubs to produce their own stories, many of which have now done so. Some authors have endeavoured to explain the rise and fall in club fortunes and many are the references to sewage and its effects upon rowing, particularly before the appointment of the Sanitary Commission in 1869 and yet these too refer to the favoured areas: the River Thames was accounted 'the largest navigable sewer in the world' in 1857[22] while the River Cam was in a similar state well into the 1870s.[23]

Sherwood's book on Oxford rowing introduces the determinant of technology when recalling the advent of the outrigger from Newcastle-upon-Tyne which depressed the fashion for college sculling completely since 'so few can afford to send to Newcastle for a boat and if anyone does get one, others do not care to contest against him'. Theodore Cook explained the decline in oarsmanship so apparent at the Henley Regatta of 1906 by remarking that fifty years earlier the rowers only gained membership of their clubs by winning races and implied that such membership had become socially, rather than athletically, determined.

The effects of engineering works upon rowing fortunes were discussed but only in relation to the tideway stretch of the River

Thames where embankments had increased river speed and brought about the demise of various regattas,[24] while the connection between personal prosperity and club progress was made only with regard to Tideway clubs which were, during the 1930s, 'full of members with Thames R.C. and London R.C. both putting out six to seven Eights every Saturday and Sunday during the winter'.[25] Further evidence of this prosperity in the south of England even during the Depression years was given by Byrne and Churchill[26] who quoted the 1934 list of Eton College boats numbering 'slightly under eight hundred, of which seven hundred and fifty were for the exclusive use of the boys', the present-day value of which would be around the million-pound mark.

As this proliferation of boats would suggest, much rowing at the college could be classed as 'boating' or recreational rowing, an element of the sport which had declined nationally following the First World War. During the late Victorian and Edwardian periods, there had been a boating boom of unprecedented proportions[27] on waters throughout the country, encouraged by cheaper transport and longer weekends, but evidence of this phenomenon is found predominantly in relation to the Thames Valley where the more prosperous inhabitants utilised their time and money in ever more extravagant pursuits. Day trips became weekend trips, which in turn evolved into week- and fortnight-long holiday tours commercially promoted by the boat hirers and proprietors of the many new riverside hotels.

As early as 1857 there appeared river guides which advised 'long rowing trips which are good for the body and soul, helping to sweeten the blood and tempers of men to no mean extent'[28] and much of the extant rowing literature comprises instructional tracts and river guides, primarily of the Thames Valley region (see Appendix 1.ii). Jerome's *Three Men in a Boat*, published in 1889, confirmed and extended the fashion for purely recreational rowing and by 1899 the activity had become so commonplace that Sydney Crossley could write the definitive work in which he describes boating as 'the most aristocratic and scientific of sports',[29] much confirmatory evidence of which can be found in Dodd's recent book on the same topic.[30]

In addition to 'aristocratic' and 'scientific', Crossley could reasonably have added 'aesthetic' since some mention of this element is rarely omitted from the literature; Oliver Wendell Holmes explained that it was in a boat 'that man finds the largest extension of his volitional and muscular existence',[31] which expresses, rather prosaically, the generally held view that a well-trained crew rowing in harmony

> is the most beautiful living machine that can be devised, the balanced power of bodies swinging together and blades gripping the water as every muscle helps drive the firm stroke through, an aesthetic satisfaction of perfect unison of strong bodies and flashing blades.[32]

Since the 1920s, eight further histories of the Boat Race, together with six of Henley Regatta, have been added to the literature, in addition to many volumes of a technical and instructional nature, while several of the older established clubs have produced their souvenir jubilee histories (see Appendix 1.ii).

As indicated earlier, only Cleaver and Osborne in recent years have endeavoured to cover the whole story of rowing and even their volumes are weighted towards boat racing and only then in the traditional locations of Oxbridge, Henley and Thames. Paradoxically, the only history which treats rowing in England as a genuine area for social inquiry is that written by Ueberhorst on the development of the sport in Germany,[33] which he introduced with a discussion of its English origins and determinants, concluding that they 'can only be understood on the basis of far reaching social change'.

Such change has continued into the present and is reflected today in the recent election of N. R. L. Thomas as the first provincial, non-establishment president of the Amateur Rowing Association. He has characterised the divided loyalties experienced within the sport by commenting that 'one of the oddities of the sport is in trying to deny the Henley and Boat Race images whilst also wanting to live in their shadow'.[34] The current loyalty felt towards the establishment traditions is typified by Topolski in his recent book on the Boat Race[35] where he conjures up the old-fashioned imagery of

> megaphones and coaching bicycles, sinking crews and frozen fingers, schoolboy caps and no reason to do it at all save for the fact that everyone expects us to and we've been doing it for so long that we don't know how to stop ... these are the things that make the boat race *the* Boat Race.

This loyalty has been amply represented in the literature of the last 150 years, a literature which for the most part has consistently denigrated those subjects of different loyalties, dismissing them as 'parish regattas', 'watermen's wrangles' or 'provincial entertainments' while typifying their protagonists as 'artisans' and 'pseudo-amateurs'.

The vast majority of rowing literature has been penned by Oxbridge graduates (see Appendix 1.ii) which helps to explain the narrowness of its perspective while press coverage of the sport, primarily in the *Illustrated London News* and *The Times*, suffers from the same constraint due to the nature of its market (see Appendix 1.i and iii). Unlike the literature of other sports, that of rowing has failed to use its material as a source of social inquiry and thus failed to illuminate those historical trends so well represented elsewhere.

The gaps in the rowing literature are so great that, in order to redress the balance of previous reporting, it has been necessary to undertake a comprehensive review designed to incorporate a wide diversity of material. This material has been obtained from previously untapped sources including the *British Rowing Almanack* from its inauguration to the present, contemporary reports from local newspapers around the country, club minute books and information from correspondence with personalities active in the sport today.[36]

The information gleaned from such sources will be used to illustrate the evolution of rowing activity within the sporting tradition by recourse to several major themes. For instance, in Chapter 2 (Occupational Origins) it will be necessary to discuss the cultural and geographical background of the various water trades and in so doing introduce the subjects of coastal rowing and women's rowing, elements conspicuously absent from existing literature; in Chapter 3 (Commercialism) the rural origins of rowing's commercial exploitation will be reviewed and the role played by the aristocracy and gentry in its development will be examined without losing sight of those played by various bodies throughout the country; in Chapter 4 (Professionalism) an attempt is made to link the growth of a class of paid oarsmen to gentlemen's involvement in the sport and to plot professional progress throughout the country as affected by various socio-economic factors.

In Chapter 5 (Recreationalism), particular attention is given to the geographical development of pleasure boating and the cultural diversity of its origins while dwelling upon its popularity among the middle classes as a retreat from professionalism and among women and working men as a release from social bondage; Chapter 6 (Amateurism) addresses the whole social ethic of amateurism in relation to rowing by tracing its effects upon the growth of clubs, regattas and administration and linking it to the demise of the professional; the two subsequent chapters deal with club development throughout the country from the earliest times to the present day as affected by geographical, cultural, social, economic, political and administrative factors; in the final chapter I endeavour to interpret the foregoing information so that the present situation may be seen in its appropriate historical context.

It is hoped that such an approach will redress the traditional imbalance of rowing histories in two major ways consistent with contemporary methods of research: first, to enquire 'from the inside through the relation between the sport and the participant'[37] and thus introduce some personal experiences to set against the institutional views so often expressed by the establishment; second, to enquire further in terms of 'geography and types of economic and social environment'[38] and thus bring into the rowing family those many thousands previously excluded or forgotten.

NOTES

1. Anon., *Aquatics* (Whittaker & Co., 1851), p. 48.
2. K. Osborne, *A History of Boat Racing in England* (ARA, 1975).
3. W. B. Woodgate, *Boating* (Longman Green & Co., 1888).
4. Lord Desborough, *The Story of the Oar* (Horace Cox, 1910).
5. H. Cleaver, *A History of Rowing* (Herbert Jenkins, 1957).
6. E. D. Brickwood, *Boat Racing* (Horace Cox, 1910).
7. T. A. Cook, *Rowing at Henley* (Oxford University Press, 1919).
8. R. P. P. Rowe and C. P. Pitman, *Rowing* (Longman Green, 1903), p. 31.
9. J. Jeffrey, *Rowing* (Dean & Co., 1897), p. 5.
10. *Frederick James Furnivall – A Record* (Frowde, 1911).
11. Anon., *The Aquatic Oracle, 1835–1851* (Marshall, 1852), p. 18.
12. E. D. Brickwood, *Boat Racing* (Horace Cox, 1876), p. 52.
13. Wadham and Peacock, *The Story of the Inter-university Boat Race* (Grant Richards, 1900).
14. T. A. Cook, *Henley Races 1903–1914* (Oxford University Press, 1920).
15. C. Dodd, *Henley Royal Regatta* (Stanley Paul, 1981).
16. C. Dodd, *The Oxford and Cambridge Boat Race* (Stanley Paul, 1983).
17. J. H. Walsh, *Manual of British Rural Sports* (Routledge, 1856), p. 484.
18. Drinkwater and Sanders, *The Boat Race* (Cassell & Co., 1929), p. 37.
19. W. E. Sherwood, *Oxford Rowing* (Henry Frowde, 1900), p. 22.
20. E. D. Brickwood, *Boat Racing* (Horace Cox, 1876), p. 52.
21. W. B. Woodgate, *Reminiscences of an Old Sportsman* (Eveleigh Nash, 1909).
22. Anon., *The Oarsman's Guide to the Thames and Other Rivers* (Searle, 1857), p. 101.
23. H. Armytage, *The Cam and Cambridge Rowing* (Kent & Co., 1899).
24. W. Winn, *The Boating Man's Vade Mecum* (Sonnenschein & Co., 1891).
25. V. Nickalls, *Oars, Wars and Horses* (Hurst & Blackett, 1932), p. 93.
26. Byrne & Churchill, *The Eton Book of the River* (Alden & Blackwell, 1957), p. 67.
27. N. D. Wigglesworth, *Victorian and Edwardian Boating* (Batsford, 1987).

28. Anon., *The Oarsman's Guide to the Thames and Other Rivers* (Searle, 1857), p. 9.
29. S. Crossley, *Pleasure and Leisure Boating* (Innes & Co., 1899), p. 10.
30. C. Dodd, *Boating* (Cambridge University Press, 1983).
31. O. W. Holmes, *Riding and Rowing* (Douglas, 1885), p. 19.
32. R. C. Lehmann, 'Are our Oarsmen Degenerate?' *New Review*, Vol. 7 (1892).
33. H. Ueberhorst, *A Hundred Years of the German Rowing Association* (Albrecht Philler Verlag, 1975), trans. Payne, p. 21.
34. *Guardian* (6 April 1985), 10.
35. D. Topolski, *The Boat Race – The Oxford Revival* (Willow Books, 1986), p. 11.
36. *British Rowing Almanack*: this publication has been produced annually since 1860 predating *Wisden* by four years and the only full set was made available to the author by the present editor, Keith Osborne. Much of its editorial comment reflects the establishment view at any given time and is thus invaluable for gauging the spirit and atmosphere of the age while its directory section on clubs provides information on the establishment and demise of clubs and regattas. On occasion, however, it is less than helpful as in the introduction to the 1865 edition which describes the contents as 'all those things which are fitted for such a work'.

    Local newspapers: it may be, as Macauley maintained, that newspapers provide unique historical information but they also provide, according to Samuel Johnson, 'principal amusements' and it is always as well to keep both evaluations in mind when assessing reports. As can be seen in Appendix 1.iii papers are produced for specific markets and their reports will tend to reflect these. In other, more extreme cases, they are simply unavailable for comment since they post-date the events under review, as in the case of Huntingdon Rowing Club which, despite any confirmatory evidence, claims an establishment date of 1856 while the *Huntingdon Gazette* only appears on the scene in 1885. In such circumstances corroborative information must be sought from regatta reports in neighbouring newspapers and in the minute books of other rowing clubs.

    Minute books: these also provide variable reading with some being full of 'much procedural whaffle' (Shrewsbury Boat Club, 1872) and some of 'unnecessary notes of an annoying nature' (Ancholme Rowing Club, 1919), while others exhibit unexplained gaps in their reporting, e.g. Poole Rowing Club during the years 1874–78. In a distressing number of cases, minute books have been lost (Shrewsbury Rowing Club), burnt (Gravesend Rowing Club) or destroyed by flood (York City Rowing Club) while in other cases they have been withheld as 'confidential' (Leander Club and Hereford Rowing Club). Elsewhere, there exists an embarrassment of riches, as with Curlew Rowing Club's 150 substantial volumes and Tynemouth Rowing Club's immaculate set of account books. We could wish that all clubs would follow the advice given in the 1962 *Rowing Almanack* that 'secretaries bear in mind that they are really not writing minutes but history' for many inaugural events remain unrecorded due to those concerned 'seldom thinking of a hundred years in the future' as the Thames Rowing Club archivist puts it. Despite these shortcomings, minutes do have the enormous advantage of speaking directly for those involved thereby avoiding the 'distortions' (C. L. R. James) and 'condescensions' (E. P. Thompson) of professional historians.
37. Cashman and McKernan (eds.), *Sport in History* (Queensland University Press, 1979), p. 227.
38. Walton and Walvin, *Leisure in Britain* (Manchester University Press, 1983), p. 4.

2

Occupational Origins

I never see a fisherman pulling his boat out to sea, a
lighterman plying his long sweeps or even a young
athlete with an oar on his shoulder but I am inclined
to salute him as the present exponent of a craft
which has moulded the fate of mankind.

(Lord Desborough, *The Story of the Oar*)

In tracing the occupation of rowing to its roots it is possible to come
to some firm conclusions about its geography and its use of equipment. The technology of carbon dating has established the pre-
historic past of a variety of boats found throughout Britain in recent
years, particularly those in Kentmere on the shores of Morecambe
Bay,[1] in the River Nene basin near the Wash[2] and several in the
River Mersey basin,[3] together with examples which are now on
show at the Harris Museum in Preston and the Castlefield Museum
in Manchester. All are of the single log construction and of similar
6ft lengths, although the River Humber basin has produced an
example 48ft long and 5ft wide,[4] and while many such craft will have
been propelled by paddles from the stern or by punting, one
example clearly shows signs of oar holes, indicating the use of two
rowing blades used either for pushing or pulling.[5]

Much rowing at that time would have been of the push variety
which enabled the oarsman to see where he was going and facilitated
manoeuvring in tasks such as spear fishing, evidence for which can
be seen on Egyptian tomb paintings from as early as the fourth
dynasty, 3766–3566 BC. Although rowing was primarily a craft-
based occupation, there is evidence to suggest that it became
recreative in early times since a funerary inscription of 1430 BC
to be found in the Scottish Museum in Edinburgh records that
Amenophis II 'besides being famous as a warrior was renowned for
his feats of oarsmanship'. It seems that the Egyptians used their
boats for occupational and recreational purposes and their larger
ships for trading and waging war and we can deduce from con-

temporary illustrations that these ships were pull-oared craft with single tiers of oars numbering from 20 to 44 on each side with a further deduction that they were responsible for carrying the knowledge of large-oared craft to Phoenicia and later to Greece.

As the Celts in Britain were progressing slowly in their basic canoes and coracles, the Greeks had refined the construction of large ships to a point hitherto unknown in marine architecture with their navies becoming formidable forces, using triremes with three banks of oars and professional oarsmen who were denigrated by Plato as a 'mixed and not very reputable crowd',[6] who were replaced in the Roman navies by convicts. As the Roman empire extended northwards into the Rhineland, the push-oar used widely north of the Alps to propel a variety of small boats was replaced by the more powerful pull-oar or 'Riemen' necessitated by the larger craft being used and the more dangerous and extensive waters being navigated. Documentary evidence of such craft can be found around Britain since there were 45 Roman harbours in the country, including those at Newcastle, York, Lincoln, London, Exeter, Gloucester, Chester, Warrington, Ribchester and at Lancaster, where an altar to Mars has been found which indicates the fourth-century presence of the Valentinian fleet of flat-bottomed craft propelled by oars and sail.[7]

A full three centuries before this, four such craft, each boasting 60 oarsmen, featured in the first written description of a boat race in Book Five of Virgil's *Aeneid*, while a medal of Constantine, dated AD 296 and presently on show in the Museum of London, portrays a four-oared coxed craft on the River Thames apparently being used as purely personal transport. The terminus for such traffic was at Westminster where there was a ford and later a bridge during the Roman occupation to which all important people were delivered by rowed barges, one of which was recently discovered in the Graveney marshes in Kent and is now displayed in the Greenwich Maritime Museum.

Saxon invasions hastened the end of the occupation and underlined the importance of fast and manoeuvrable ships such as those used by Hengist and Horsa in 429 which were 60ft long and used 30 oarsmen, an example of which was discovered at Sutton Hoo in Suffolk in 1939. One consequence of the importance given to such ships was the pride of oarsmanship which was regarded as a noble attribute and features in a reference made to the Northern Hero, Kolsen, in the Saxon Chronicle (MS A) to the effect that he 'excelled in shooting with the bow and used the oar with facility'.

Such skill and naval power were greatly admired by Alfred who established a large British navy; Edgar celebrated his coronation in 973 by organising a crew of eight Irish princes and rowing along the River Dee from his palace in West Chester to the church of St John and back. Florence of Worcester claims that Edgar circumnavigated Britain annually and that it was this show of naval power which accounted for his peaceful reign, a belief corroborated after his death by further Scandinavian invasions using 40-oared longships, one of which was employed by Olaf to pull down London Bridge in 1009. In 1013, King Swein of Denmark rowed his fleet up the Humber and Trent rivers as far as Gainsborough with no resistance and in 1066 Harold of Norway sailed and rowed up the Humber and Ouse rivers, taking York – only to suffer defeat later at Stamford Bridge.[8]

The Domesday Book of 1086 reports the substantial properties held by 'stirmen' or steersmen of the royal barges: Wulfeah in Bedfordshire, Edric and Thorkell in Evesham in Worcestershire, Hugolin in Berkshire and Stephen in Warwick and Southampton, men who often attained the high rank of Chamberlain in the royal household. Although such barges were used extensively by noblemen throughout the country, they were gradually forced off the waterways by the larger commercial craft which began trading on the major river systems of Thames, Severn and Humber, until the fashion for royal or state barges became merely a memory. The man usually credited with their revival was John Norman, Lord Mayor of London in 1453 who broke the tradition of horse-drawn processions by decking out one of his own trading barges and rowing from his riverside house down to London Bridge on the way to his inauguration at Guildhall.

Before long, other London guilds and companies secured the use of barges or had them specially built and from this time onwards these 16- or 20-oared craft with their luxurious state-rooms erected at the stern became a common sight on the London river. As the peaceful use of oared craft in trade and ceremony grew, their use as warships declined with the last oar-powered contest taking place at Lepanto in the Gulf of Corinth in 1571 when Venetian galleys defeated those of the Turks to ensure Christian hegemony over the Mediterranean and Adriatic trade routes. From this time onwards it was to be the sailed 'galleons' which dominated naval warfare.

In Britain at this time, the inland waterway trade was flourishing with extra navigation channels being cut throughout the country and being used by a bewildering variety of craft designed for their particular tasks and locations.[9] Watermen of all descriptions became commonplace and were merely one class of 'servingmen' or 'handicrafts men of any occupation' who were prohibited from 'unlawful' sports by a Proclamation of Elizabeth in 1559.[10]

The increasing prohibition from certain recreations and the incidence of punishment against those apprehended argues a much greater diversification of society and jealousy of ownership than was apparent before this time and can be partially explained by the new prosperity brought about by a higher level of commercial activity.[11] It had always been common for gentlemen to use their recreations as 'badges of social and physical superiority over the lower orders'[12] but, by the end of the seventeenth century, the emergent commercial middle class had joined them so that these two classes together 'participated in entirely separate areas of cultural activity from those of the lower classes'.[13]

The seventeenth and early eighteenth centuries saw an extension in commercial instruments leading to an increased volume of credit, and it was these commercial men, bankers and the like, who gradually supplanted the vested landed interests[14] while acquiescence on behalf of the lower orders was built into the system since there were few guns, no state education and limited politicisation with the rulers of the new Georgian Britain identified as 'corrupt, confident and competent'.[15] It was generally recognised that half the population lived below subsistence level with any diary of the period showing the depths to which many men and women had to stoop in order to supplement wages of a few shillings a week[16] and the situation was reflected in much contemporary writing, including that of James Thompson whose poem 'The Seasons', written in 1730, describes how the 'laborious crowds pull the heavy oars of society whilst the elite take the ruling helm'.

This combination of a monied 'elite' and a practically destitute 'crowd' led inevitably to a commercial exploitation of the latter by the former which began with occupational activities, typified in 'The Seasons', but soon extended to recreation in the form of sponsorship of various competitive activities including boat racing. London completely monopolised the trade and commerce of the whole nation 'drawing the riches and government of the three kingdoms to the southeast of the island'[17] and so the Thames watermen, who were responsible for carrying on much of this activity, became perhaps the most important subjects of occupational and recreational exploitation.

The very establishment of London was determined by easy water access and its growth depended upon the further exploitation of the river and so the local watermen became integral parts of Thames and London life from the earliest times. Putney ferry, mentioned as 'Putta's landing place' in Domesday Book, was important as the starting point of royal ferries to Fulham and Westminster, the latter used regularly by Edward I in 1290 and the ferryman would have been employed by the Crown in this capacity but also in others such as marking the royal swans between Henley, which marked the major up-river crossing place, and London Bridge; Swan Upping is still an annual ceremony regarded as a 'holiday' by the Freemen of the Company of Watermen who carry it out.[18] The waterman who was unattached to any royal or noble household would ferry passengers on his own account as at Gravesend where large numbers of them were given the right in 1381 to take fares to London on what became known as the 'long ferry', while the larger commercial barges were already a common sight on the river with a barge skipper featuring in Chaucer's *Canterbury Tales*.

As early as 1502 it became necessary to dredge the River Fleet in the City of London to maintain a substantial trade in 'fish and fewel' but to little effect since the river was nothing but an open sewer, as Jonson testifies a century later in his *Epigrammes* of 1616 when describing the boatmen of the Fleet disturbing with their oars the 'merd urinous loaded water'. So busy was the River Thames that Henry VIII found it necessary to regulate the activities of the watermen in a statute of 1514, citing their activities with 'river barges and wherrybote' as 'laudable custom and usage carried on tyme out of mynde'; his regulations were used as the basis for the formation of the Company of Watermen and Lightermen in 1555 which controlled all watermen between Gravesend and Teddington or 'Tide's End Town'.

The company motto echoing the spirit of the age was 'At the command of our Superiors' and the early membership rolls show a staggering 40,000 practitioners, 8,000 of whom were in household employment. Many of those registered have descendants still at work on the river today, such as the Phelps family which first registered in 1560 and which currently has four members on the books, all of whom work for rowing clubs. Much of the watermen's work was ferrying passengers to and from theatres on the south bank of the river and these were frequently closed during the summer months as precautions against disease. In 1593, the plague closed them for the whole year with the result that the watermen petitioned Lord Haywarde as the Lord High Admiral to give them financial aid since 'we poore watermen and oure wives and children have had much helpe and reliefe from suche people as come into the saide playhouses'.[19]

The boats used by the majority of self-employed watermen were described by Stow in his *London Survey* of 1598 as 'wherries', which were smaller versions of the large household or company barges and powered by six or eight oars, and 'skullers' rowed by one man only, with both being advertised by cries of 'oares, oares', often misinterpreted by visitors, as Stow relates, as pimping. There were certain social distinctions in the choice of boat to be used since the sculler was usually half the price of the wherry and, as Jonson says in *Every Man out of his Humour* (1598), some people would claim to have 'come in oares when they were but wafted over in a sculler'.

By 1632, John Taylor the waterman poet[20] could write in his 'Description of Thames and Isis' that 'there's many a seaman, navigator, waterman, fisherman and bargeman on this water themselves and families in number more than one hundred thousand are'; the numbers continued to grow to the extent that new regulations were introduced by the Watermen's Company in 1708. These new rules stipulated standards of behaviour which forbade the 'lewd and filthy jests' complained of in a contemporary pamphlet[21] and set down fees for certain journeys, such as those from London Bridge to Limehouse which was twopence in a sculler and from London Bridge to Windsor which was 14 shillings in a wherry.[22]

At the same time the apprenticeship system was overhauled so that no apprentice could take charge of a boat 'till he hath rowed two years with an able waterman', nor could he work at all on Sunday nor ply for work when drunk; after seven years of no pay, during which his master was contracted to maintain him, he would attain his freedom and become a full member of the company.

Part of the practical examination for journeyman and master status was a rowing race between certain points on the river for which particular times were prescribed and, under normal trading conditions, passengers would increase payment for faster trips with much sport being had between wherries or scullers on the same trip. The result of the new rules was that the system of water transport in London became extremely efficient and widely admired[23] and the trade became quite lucrative for those who could afford to buy their own boats at £12 or £15 since they could then expect to earn up to 13 shillings a week.[24]

The company also licensed lightermen, so called because they worked in medium-sized, shallow draught barges which were used to take cargoes from the larger ocean-going ships thus 'lightening' them. Their work would be to sail or, more likely, manhandle these barges or 'punts' up and down river at all states of the tide and wind using 30ft 'sweep oars', a skill still known today as 'driving under oars'.[25] These men always had plenty of work, a fact well attested by Steele in 1712 who described the river from Richmond to London Bridge as 'being loaded with the product of each shore'[26] and Defoe in 1726 who made the comment that the river was 'the channel for conveying an infinite quantity of provisions from remote counties to London'.[27]

Apart from the threat of disease, the watermen's trade was frequently disrupted by the weather: heavy rains and floods during the spring and autumn and ice on the river in winter. John Gay described how they 'cloathed all their tilts in blue when the rainy floods imperil',[28] using variously blue tarpaulins stretched over metal hoops to shelter their fares, but many still shunned boats and took to the carriages instead. The self-employed waterman was therefore frequently obliged to seek other work and often found it at the riverside taverns to which he would normally have delivered both the beer and the customers.

After the Fire of 1688, many watermen were enlisted as firemen while the more reputable of them were used as security guards for marine cargoes. During the many lulls in the summer trade they would hire out their craft for recreational use mostly to youngsters at Westminster School or to apprentices enjoying their free Sunday. William Hickey describes how, at eight years of age, he regularly absconded from the school and 'hired out a boat to cruise about Chelsea reach'.[29]

The trade was not without its dangers and there were countless capsizes, especially at London Bridge where the constrictions of piers, mills and waterworks created dangerously rapid water, amply justifying the contemporary saying that it was made for 'wise men to go over and fools to go under'. Up river, the water was regularly impounded by weirs through which ferries and cargoes had to pass periodically using 'flash' locks which were merely temporary gates in the wall of the weir itself, and on these occasions many accidents occurred, none worse than that at Goring in 1634 when 60 people lost their lives as the boatman steered too close to the arm of the weir.

Apart from natural disasters the waterman had to contend with his fares, some of whom were bent on self-destruction like the young woman 'far gone with child by a noble lord and by him refused assistance' who jumped from a sculler near Pickle Herring stairs,[30] others being of a murderous intent like the man who hailed a boat at Wapping New Stairs and during a dispute with the boatman 'threw him down, stamped on his body and killed him on the spot'.[31] Bearing in mind all these occupational hazards, it is perhaps not surprising that the watermen were always quick to supplement their incomes by indulging in relatively harmless 'wager' racing.

All such vicissitudes were avoided by the watermen in private service who lived comparatively ordered and sheltered lives, spending much time tied up at various 'stairs' or riverside piers waiting for their noble masters to return from business or club. They were paid the same rates as household staff which were about ten pounds a year and were dressed in household livery, which usually consisted of a braided jacket with a silvered badge strapped or stitched to the right arm, white canvas trousers and often a tricorne hat.[32] Their wages would be supplemented by extra gratuities for fast passages on regular routes such as Chelsea to Wapping or London Bridge to Greenwich and it seems likely that, when two or more craft set out together on the same route, there would be some wagering on the outcome.

The beauty of Greenwich according to Defoe[33] was 'owing to the lustre of its inhabitants, a collection of gentlemen of quality and fashion different from most if not all the villages in this part of England' and so there were many privately employed watermen here. Their presence was indicated by the existence of many inns, some of which – such as the Watermen's Arms and the Ferryhouse Inn – still remain. Further downstream at Gravesend there was a stronghold of their self-employed colleagues: the business here was always brisk, it being the terminus of the 'long ferry' up to London with passengers choosing to pay sixpence to travel with fifty others on large Tilt boats or one shilling for the much smaller wherries; the town's coat of arms reflected the marine trade featuring a Galleas or oar-assisted sailing boat.

Passing out of the Thames estuary and around the south coast, we find that Dover pilots and Folkestone fishermen were well established in modified rowing gigs of four and six oars which were used later in the eighteenth century as lifeboats,[34] while areas such as Southampton, long used to prosperity, had lost trade to London and suffered long periods of decay and decline in fortune. Although London had taken the trade of many such places it had encouraged the growth of others by stimulating the demand for their produce, with ports such as Bristol and Exeter more than doubling their turnover due to the almost insatiable requirements for wines and spirits.[35] Marine business necessitated the employment of dockers, watermen and lightermen while the ancient ferries were still worked by local fishermen looking for supplementary incomes, which no doubt explains the unreliability of the River Tamar ferry remarked upon by Defoe.

Further west again the fishermen also acted as pilots, bringing ships into the ports of Plymouth, Falmouth and Newquay. To do this, they used very light ship's gigs modified for speed, since the fastest crew naturally won the business. As competition became fiercer, the original 4-oared craft became 6-oared and finally 8-oared, the last of which were banned in the mid-eighteenth century, as they could easily outpace the exciseman's sailing cutter when out on smuggling trips. Many similar gigs, occasionally sponsored by local clergy as lifeboats, were built by the firm of Peters in St. Mawes. One of these, built in 1812, is still used today by Newquay Rowing Club. The basic design contributed a great deal towards that of the river gigs which were used in the first university Boat Race in 1829.

The Severn estuary was notoriously dangerous with its high tidal rise and fall and Defoe comments on the 'badness and danger' of the ancient Chepstow ferry whose ferryman features in the *Hundred Merry Tales* of 1526, complaining to the survivor of a fatal quarrel on the boat that he 'should'st have taryed and fought on lande for now thou hast caused me to lose an halfpenny fare'. There were various inland ports on the River Severn with Gloucester, Worcester, Bewdley and Bridgnorth being the main centres. Much in-fighting went on to secure cargoes until an Act of Parliament in 1430 settled the issue by stating that 'the River Severn is common to all the King's liege people to carry and re-carry all manners of merchandise as well in trows and boats as in flotes otherwise called drags'. From this time onwards, each port improved its navigation and access to win trade, a trend which continued throughout the country for the next three centuries as inland communication and trade depended largely upon river systems.

The years 1660–1720 experienced a doubling in length of navigable river to 1,200 miles, an extension greatly supplemented in the eighteenth century by a host of new canals, one of which linked the Severn and Trent rivers leaving Bewdley with a much reduced trade.[36] The watermen of the River Severn were arguably the most skilled of all, having to contend with the fast ebb and flow of the tides

1. A Cornish pilot gig (photographed in 1907), built to an eighteenth-century design which influenced the construction of the first university racing boats.

when manoeuvring the large barges on to the congested quays of ports like Bridgnorth, as well as handling the smaller craft for ferrying passengers and fishing. A craft used widely on the river for fishing was the coracle, which was designed to cope with the fiercest currents and was described by Caesar in *The Gallic Wars* as constructed with wickerwork covered with leather and propelled with paddles. They were produced in hundreds throughout the whole length of the Severn valley with their manufacture by the Rogers family in Coalbrookdale traceable back to 1658.[37]

Moving eastwards through Evesham whose ancient Hampton Ferry was the main River Avon crossing place, we reach the headwaters of the River Thames and pass down to Oxford which occupies the site of an old Roman ford. Its subsequent medieval ferry is still commemorated by the Ferry Inn at Sandford. Because of its important position on the river, Oxford was home to many types of watermen, some of whom supplied both 'Town and Gown' with all their requirements, and it is therefore not surprising that it was as early as 1583 that the first boatman was admitted to the freedom of the city, nor perhaps that there is a continuity of tradition among Oxford boating families stretching back at least four centuries.[38]

The river trade with London was, of course, extensive all along the valley, with Reading particularly 'driving a very good trade in the biggest barges'[39] and Marlow being the main point of passenger embarkation for the trip to Teddington and thence after a transfer to the City itself. Fishing was already undertaken by long-established families in traditional locations such as Windsor, Chertsey, Staines and Hampton Court.

Further east, and strategically placed on the River Nene at the site of Domesday's Gunworth Ferry, is Peterborough, linked to Wisbech since the navigational improvements of the seventeenth century by packet boat which plied the 21 miles for seven pence. In the following century, the adjacent river of the Great Ouse was substantially dredged and sluices were built, enabling cargoes to be brought for the first time up to St Neots and thus diminishing the importance of St Ives further downstream. St Ives had once enjoyed a great trade with Kings Lynn, a prosperity remembered today in the street name of Merryland which reflects the numbers of inns there which opened all night for the use of watermen.

In fact, the navigation history of the whole river from Bedford to Kings Lynn can be recorded by noting the names of inns with aquatic connotations such as the Jolly Waterman at Cambridge and the Boy and Oar at Bedford,[40] while it has been said of Bedford that the 'river has always been a mirror to the life of the town'.[41] Cambridge, like Oxford, lies at the easiest crossing point on its river with the original ferry at Chesterton leased out for 20-year periods for two marks per annum according to ancient custom and it had been firmly established on a major trade route since Roman times while the Tudor warehouse at Isleham bears witness to its flourishing sixteenth-century trade.

Cambridge Fair proved to be a great popular attraction, particularly in the eighteenth century when the London watermen brought their wherries from the capital on waggons 'to ply upon the River Cam and row people up and down from the fair to town'.[42] Ferry Path was one of the routes linking the colleges to the ferry point and was the traditional home for the boatmen employed to keep the Cam open for trade throughout the year, later becoming the location of the first boat-building firm which supplied working boats and racing boats to Town and Gown.[43]

As early as the thirteenth and fourteenth centuries, the water-ways around the Wash had been extensively recut and improved as far north as Lincoln on the River Witham; hundreds of miles of smaller rivers further north such as the River Ancholme were dredged, so that Hull became the trade centre for the whole north and north-east of the country, with towns like Brigg and Gainsborough owing their very existence to river connections. The Owston Ferry over the River Humber which provided the Bishop of Bayeux with 40 shillings a year in 1086 had become, according to Defoe, 'an ill favoured dangerous passage' which took four hours to complete using one of the old Humber Keel boats based on the Scandinavian 'kogge' design, pulled along with long sweep oars and carrying livestock as well as people.

Improvements on the River Ouse were authorised by Cromwell in 1657 and the rivers Aire and Calder were made navigable to Leeds and Wakefield in 1690, while Bradford or Broadford enjoyed prosperity based on the wool, paper and corn trades carried on by barges from wharves at Shipley built around 1700. York had been served for centuries by two ferries, one of which was worked by the Hill family whose boatyard on Manor Shore produced many of the wherries and state barges used by tradesmen and guildmen through-out the seventeenth and eighteenth centuries, later producing boats for racing, a tradition of continuity paralleled by the Brown family in Durham.

On the coast, the Whitby fisheries prospered in medieval times and the London coal trade and the later whaling industry created a thriving port during the eighteenth century employing some 3,000 men in a variety of water-based trades. But, as prosperity declined during the nineteenth century, some joined lifeboat crews and earned one pound an outing which was a useful sum for men earning less than three pounds a week. The local church-based lifeboat committees around the country believed that rowing was the most important factor for getting the boats off beaches in bad weather and therefore solid rowing craft and experienced oarsmen were vital for successful rescue.

The tenfold increase in trade out of Newcastle during the eighteenth century created dangerous congestion at the mouth of the River Tyne and the loss of the *Adventure* in 1789 produced enough local concern for the first craft officially designated 'life-boat', to be constructed and launched later in the same year at South

Shields. The National Lifeboat Committee established in 1824 took the traditional view about the superiority of oar-powered craft and the last pulling lifeboat was withdrawn, appropriately enough, at the South Shields station as late as 1968.[44]

Further up the coast at Berwick-on-Tweed, the fishermen worked in teams from locally built, high-sided, clinker Cobles designed to be pulled along by three oarsmen using single sweeps or by two scullers. They were quite unlike the lighter, flat-bottomed craft used by their colleagues in the western fisheries of Furness and Fylde, which could be sculled by one man while his partner trawled the nets.

There were extensive river and sea fisheries throughout the north-western region of England with many of them coinciding with local ferry sites as at Penwortham on the River Ribble, Hollin on the River Irwell, Rock Ferry on the River Mersey and at Ecclestone on the River Dee where the ferry had been the property of the Grosvenor family as Serjeants of the Dee since Domesday times. The ferries themselves were often over treacherous stretches of water, as at Rock Ferry where the boatman pulling across the River

2. An example of the old-style (but still used) Northumberland Coble, rowed by Grace Darling in her rescue and by local fishermen in 'water sports'.

Mersey would certainly have his work cut out as any present-day commuter would testify. The nature of north-western water made the boatman skilful, but the nature of their work made their employers wealthy since the rights of both fisheries and ferries lay with the local lords. Both fishermen and boatmen needed to supplement their incomes when opportunities presented themselves.

The office of boatman was often a public position and we find in parish registers such as those at Didsbury in Cheshire that there were parish boatmen who lived in boathouses adjacent to the ferry.[45] It seems likely that the position was of some importance in the community, which is perhaps not surprising when much inconvenience and expense might be saved by a short but potentially perilous journey across the river.

The boathouse itself might have doubled as an inn and so it is still possible to identify old ferry sites by recourse to the names of inns such as the Boathouse Inn in Preston and Salford both of which became centres for professional racing oarsmen during the nineteenth century. The fortunes of trade in the north-west were determined by the degree of silting experienced. The ports of Lancaster, Chester and Preston were virtually forced out of business by heavy silting which allowed Liverpool to become, as Defoe said, 'the Bristol of this part of England', while adverse river conditions played no small part in depressing all water-based activities, including those of river sports and regattas.

With so much rowing activity around the country, it is hardly surprising that a sporting element entered into the aquatic scene very early on, although this is not always possible to document, for, as Mary Prior says in her account of Oxford watermen, 'a wall of silence divides us from the world of ordinary men and women before about 1820 which is difficult to penetrate'.[46] However, Gravesend Borough Records which date from 1571 do mention boat racing in 1698, 1699 and 1700, promoted by aldermen such as Sir John Marsham. Their origin was probably in the custom of local watermen 'goozing' or waiting in the river channel to assist incoming boats, with the fastest crew gaining the commission.

This was regulated into annual races for 1-, 2-, 4- and 6-oared boats, the winners of which would be heroes for the day, particularly the individual sculling champion who would be presented with a prize boat and paraded around the town accompanied by his supporters and the local band. All winners would be presented with colourfully painted 'back boards' for their wherries which would be used as support for their passengers while advertising the boatman's excellence. Many such boards can be seen displayed today at Watermen's Hall in the City of London. There is evidence of fishermen's boat racing and aquatic sports at Chester in 1733 where they were held in the newly cut river channel close to the centre of town. This allowed the traditional River Dee estuary sports to gain a greater audience with the public notice advertising the event mentioning, among many others, a special race for fisherwomen.

On the River Yare in Norwich during the 1780s there were individual sculling contests which became commonplace at the turn of the century[47] and we are told that boat racing in Falmouth started in the eighteenth century with local oystermen racing their 'dredgers' for wagers.[48] Similar activity among the Sussex boatmen, who used whaler type boats to worry the French in the 1790s, led to the establishment of the Brighton Cruising Club later in the following century and Newquay Rowing Club was promoted after many years of local pilots racing their gigs up to ten miles out to sea in search of work.

Retrospective reports in the local paper indicate a flourishing fishermen's regatta at Poulton-le-Sands (Morecambe) in 1804,[49] whose advertising poster for 1844 mentions the 'Grace Darling Prize to be rowed for by women', an indication of the wide publicity gained for Grace Darling's effort in rowing out to the *Forfarshire* shipwreck off the Bamburgh coast in September 1838 and rescuing several survivors. One entry for this prize was the famous crew of fisherwomen from Saltash in Devon led by Ann Glanville who worked the River Tamar ferry, a crew which became so successful at local regattas that it travelled all over the country beating men's crews at Portsmouth, Newcastle and Fleetwood where, in 1849, its members were presented to Queen Victoria.

The *Illustrated London News* mentions a River Thames regatta in 1843, at which the last 'two races were rowed by women all of them no less than four generations on the river and all of them winners'.[50] Some publicans used the prospect of women racing as a commercial attraction as at Lambeth in 1833 when 'the wives and daughters of fishermen contested against each other and never did we see a rowing match so well attended' but the report refuses to detail the racing as it 'would be a gross insult to the understanding of our readers'.[51]

There were races for fishermen and women in the late eighteenth century in places as far apart as Lake Windermere,[52] on the River Severn where they raced in coracles,[53] and at Sheringham in Norfolk

3. The prize boat at Greenwich Regatta in 1846. Awarded to the winner of the most senior sculling race of the day, it was worth many months' wages – hence the jubilations.

25

where they used 'pair-oared crab boats'.[54] By 1876 Brickwood in his book *Boat Racing* could say that 'sea rowing has improved in the last ten years with salt water crews holding their own with some of the best Thames professionals', citing crews from Margate, Ramsgate, Hastings and Worthing.

If the bucolic racing of fishermen and ferrymen represents one aquatic tradition then another is represented by the 'ridottos' and 'regattas' of the nobility during the eighteenth century. The names themselves derive from the Venetian dialect of Italian and can be loosely translated as 'gatherings' and 'boat races',[55] both of which occurred on the Grand Canal in Venice as early as 1274,[56] with long processions of household barges being followed by races in a variety of small boats using 'pull oars' and gondolas using 'push oars'.

The normal procedure would be for competitors to attend mass in the Basilica della Salute and receive the 'benediction of the gondoliers' before racing. The whole affair was staged as part of a religious ceremony used to propitiate the patron saint of fishermen. Certainly by the eighteenth century, when the English nobility on the Grand Tour would have been aware of it, the Venetian Regatta had become a huge, week-long event of processions, races and masked balls, and hence it is not surprising that the fashion for such happenings should have transferred to England, along with many other Italian and continental customs.[57]

Canaletto, the artist most associated with the portrayal of river scenes, was extensively patronised by the Duke of Northumberland and the Duke of Richmond who commissioned him to paint a view of the Thames from his house in Chelsea, practically next door to the famous Ranelagh Pleasure Gardens,[58] which staged a Venetian 'regatta' in June 1775. The broadsheet advertising the event and the tickets distributed for it, designed by two Venetians called Cipriani and Bartolozzi, indicate more of a fashionable 'society' occasion than any serious sporting event, the former containing a song of welcome cautioning the lords and ladies to 'suspend your fantastical round and bless your sweet stars that none of you drown'd'. While none of the lords or ladies did drown, at least seven others did so at various points along the river shore where refreshment booths and gaming tables had been set up to accommodate the 200,000 spectators who had come to bet on the only race of the evening but who congregated during the day to watch the huge gathering of decorated barges preparing to make the procession up river to Ranelagh.

People in the eighteenth century liked to have a good precedent for such events in classical times or else be able to justify them on moral grounds and the regatta at Ranelagh qualified on both counts. A contemporary pamphlet entitled a 'Circumstantial Account of the Ensuing Regatta' justified the event by citing precedents in Greek and Roman times together with the British royal patronage of 'entertainments of this kind on the water' while also mentioning the advantage given to the navy by encouraging watermen in the execution of their skills.

Although generally regarded as the first occasion on which the word 'regatta' was appended to such events, Ranelagh in 1775 merely followed in an English tradition of water entertainments which dates back to John Norman in 1454. It continued through Elizabethan times, with water masques and jousts, to royal processions such as that mentioned by Pepys when Charles II arrived at the City of London from Hampton Court 'with one thousand barges and boats, I know for we could not see the water for them'.[59] The tradition was carried into the eighteenth century in the form of water pageants such as that organised for George I in 1717 and featuring Handel's *Water Music*.

In 1732 the Italian influence began to appear when Vauxhall Gardens promoted the first ever 'ridotto al fresco'[60] in which boat-loads of people in fancy dress processed up and down the river partaking of refreshment and listening to the water-borne orchestra. Some hundreds of 'elite society' were present, accompanied, for some of the time at least, by Prince Frederick who arrived from Kew in his own barge and stayed until four o'clock in the morning.[61] William Hickey mentions a similar event held by the Earl of Lincoln, but on this occasion actually termed a 'regatta', in July 1768 in which the boats were rowed to Hampton Court where 'an elegant collation was prepared in tents, thence back to Weybridge by river where a magnificent dinner awaited with fireworks and superb illuminations, concluding with a ball'.[62]

There is no mention of boat racing as a component part of such events until Ranelagh in 1775 and then there was one race only between 12 pairs of watermen for whom a prize fund had been raised by gentlemen of the Savoir Vivre, Almack, Whites and Guthrie clubs whose entertainment must have been somewhat spoiled by the wind and rain which would have made the racing unsatisfactory.[63] The race started between six and seven in the evening and only 1,300 tickets were issued to club members who were admitted to viewing positions on the numerous company barges tied up on either bank of the river. This provision created a floating street, up which the contestants rowed with the winner being awarded 10 guineas, and second and third places receiving 7 and 5 guineas respectively, each of which was equivalent to several months' wages.

The fashion of regattas as mere processions and society entertainments spread to Oxford and Cambridge universities where such events became traditional at 'Commemoration' and 'Commencement'. Further afield there were regular aquatic processions and festivals on Lake Windermere[64] and the first such event on the River Tees occurred at Stockton in May 1788.[65] River pageants became fashionable at town shows as at Shrewsbury in 1794[66] and ceremonial processions were established on the River Tyne at Newcastle, where on Ascension Day the Mayor, Master and Brethren of Trinity House together 'surveyed the boundaries of the Tyne' in a train of brightly painted and decorated barges.[67]

Strutt mentions that this type of water pageantry was of essential service to the London watermen in giving them regular employment on the barges themselves while also 'giving occasion for the introduction of many pleasure boats which in modern times have greatly increased',[68] but in fact the fashion for such displays was already waning and many households and guilds were beginning to dispense with their barges altogether.[69]

The promotion of boat racing as part of the overall entertainment sprang from the seventeenth-century custom of idle watermen organising races among themselves and opening a 'book' for the general public of which many gentlemen, no doubt, took advantage. Pepys mentions such an occasion in 1661 when

> being through the bridge and finding the Thames full of boats and galleys, found on inquiry that there was a wager to be run this morning, but upon the start the wager boats fell foul of one another till at last one of them gives over, pretending foul play and so all our sport is lost.[70]

Such results were far from uncommon and we might surmise that gentlemen backers would soon come to resent the blatant fixing of such matches which were, after all, only means of supplementing the boatman's income at times of slack trade. Thus it was that the gentlemen themselves began to organise boat racing among the watermen, as in 1722 when members of the West End clubs promoted a match close to Ranelagh Gardens[71] and in 1723 when the governor of the Tower of London gave a boat and oars to be rowed for by eight watermen of the Tower Liberties between Wapping and Whitehall.[72] Even the Prince of Wales gave a silver cup worth 25 guineas to be rowed for between Putney and Whitehall by seven pair-oared boats to mark the 12th birthday of his son.[73]

Such boat-race promotion had become commonplace by the end of the century with commercial theatres like Astleys donating a prize wherry for a watermen's race each year, the winners of which would be 'carried in procession to the Royal Amphitheatre, Westminster Bridge, at which place a capital routine of entertainments will be presented'.[74] The nobility who lived on the Thames shores would regularly sponsor boat races 'for the encouragement of the watermen' as at Twickenham where Sir John Fleming Leicester presented the winners with silver tankards before a 'great concourse of the nobility amongst them the Duchess of Gloucester and the Duke of Queensbury in a skiff'.[75]

It seems that this fashion for promotion and sponsorship derived from the immediate popular success of Doggett's 'Coat and Badge Race', first organised in 1715 by Thomas Doggett, a prominent Irish comedy actor who had recently been bought out of his part ownership in the Drury Lane Theatre. As a regular user, along with most of the theatre-going public, of Strand and Temple ferry stations, he would have been familiar with the watermen's habit of 'wrangling' and wager racing but his is the first name to be associated with organising such a competition. His motivation in choosing the watermen for his patronage is partially explained by his regular use of their services, travelling each day from Blackfriars to the theatre and also perhaps by his fellow feeling for them, having at one time shared, as an old travelling player, the estimation of many of their public as rogues and vagabonds.

Of course, as seen above, the fortunes of the theatres directly affected those of the watermen and so, as a proprietor, Doggett would share with them the misfortunes of closure for health reasons or in periods of royal mourning, as in 1714 when theatres closed for six weeks out of respect for Queen Anne. However, by this time, Doggett, often known as 'quarrelsome Doggett' from his stage persona,[76] had sued his partners at Drury Lane and received several thousand pounds in settlement which, together with his savings from many successful years on the London stage, encouraged him to retire.

Much of his success had stemmed from his popularity with the Prince of Wales who patronised all his productions and even commanded repeat performances of some roles. One of these in 1713 was that of Sailor Ben in *Love for Love* for which Doggett had prepared by living for a while among the watermen of Wapping. It is not surprising, then, that he should choose to commemorate the accession of his patron by sponsoring a race for watermen, the first of which took place on Monday, 1 August 1715, a day when church bells rang, bonfires flared and vast crowds turned out on to the streets to mark the anniversary of the King's accession.[77]

The race was for six newly qualified watermen rowing against the tide between the Old Swan Stairs at London Bridge and the White Swan Inn near Chelsea Bridge, using their normal working boats weighing a ton. For many years thereafter, large crowds would follow them upstream, barracking those they had bet against, and pelting unpopular competitors from the bridges. The winner, having rowed hard for some two hours, received a resplendent coat, together with a silver arm badge and, more importantly, the likelihood of preferment.

So successful was the first race that Doggett proclaimed that it should be 'continued annually on the same day for ever'[78] and he is quoted in 1722 by the Clerk to the Watermen's Company as 'making his way through 'friars intending to take water at Temple stairs in order to witness my Coat and Badge race and later repair to the White Swan to drink a cool tankard and shake the hand of the winner'.[79] This was the last time he was able to be present as he died soon afterwards, having left adequate provision in his will for the continuation of his race. The organisation of it passed, through a connection of his executor, to the Fishmongers' Company who dutifully perform the task to this day and in their Hall it is possible to study the Race Book, which contains the names of every winner from 1715 to the present without a break, a continuity of tradition unmatched by any other sport.

The race remained a prominent part of river life for many years after Doggett's death and the theatrical connection was maintained by Charles Dibdin who wrote a ballad opera entitled *The Watermen*, which featured the Coat and Badge Race. This received its first performance on 8 August 1774 and contained the song 'Hero and Leander' which became extremely popular due to the frequent public renditions of it by the watermen themselves. The future of the race can be traced through the columns of *The Times* and by the turn of the century it had become a rather ceremonial affair for which the Fishmongers' Company met at their Hall and entertained 'in a very sumptuous manner the Earl St. Vincent, several Lords of the Admiralty and other distinguished characters', with the winner being appointed to the post of Admiralty Waterman.[80]

This ceremonialisation was just one way in which boat racing was used by others for their particular ends during a transition period when it was transformed from rural pastime to regulated sport. The diversity of occupational origin led naturally to a variety of rowing development throughout the country, where geography and culture determined much of the progress. Since the overwhelming concentration of nobility resided in London, it is not surprising that it was on the Thames that boat racing was first nobly patronised, nor that it was to some extent ceremonialised. The next step in its transition was taken when it became commercialised, a subject covered in the following chapter.

NOTES

1. 'Boats of Kentmere', *Cumbria Magazine*, Dec. 1978, p.8.
2. P. Waszack, 'The Development of Leisure and Cultural Facilities in Peterborough' (BA thesis, Huddersfield Polytechnic, 1976).
3. M.E. Wynne, 'The Role of the River Mersey in the Bronze Age' (MA thesis, Liverpool University, 1959).
4. F. Henthorne, *A History of Ancholme Rowing Club 1868–1976* (Humberside County Council, 1980).
5. T. Kirkland, *A Guide to Southport and North Meoles* (Rivington, 1826).
6. Plato, *Laws IV 707a*.
7. *Roman Shipping and Trade in Britain and the Rhine Provinces* (Council for British Archaeology, Research Report 24, 1978).
8. Note that the Humber keel-boat of today is modelled on the design of ships such as those used by Swein and Olaf. See H. Fletcher, *A Life on the Humber* (Faber & Faber, 1975).
9. A great number of craft are displayed at Exeter Maritime Museum, e.g. State Barge, Pilot Gig, Northumberland Coble, Thames Wherry, Severn Coracle, Exe Salmon boat, and Medway Doble.
10. *Proclamation of Elizabeth* 1559 (British Library shelf mark G6463 (406)).
11. J.A. Sharpe, *Crime in Early Modern England 1550–1750* (Longman, 1984).
12. M. Vale, *The Gentleman's Recreations 1580–1630* (Brewer, 1977), p.2.
13. J. Stevenson, *English Urban History 1500–1780* (Oxford University Press, 1982).
14. S. Checkland, *British Public Policy 1776–1939* (Cambridge University Press, 1983).
15. J. Cannon, *Aristocratic Century* (Cambridge, 1985).
16. I.M. Davis, *The Harlot and the Statesman* (Kensal Press, 1987).
17. *The Political Works of Andrew Fletcher Esq.* (London, 1732).
18. H. Harris, *Under Oars* (Stepney Books, 1978).
19. H. Humpherous, *A History of the Watermen's Company* (Microfilm, 1981).
20. John Taylor, 1580–1654, born in Gloucester and apprenticed to a Westminster waterman; pressed into the navy, as many watermen were, on seven occasions; ended his life as a publican in Oxford.
21. Anon., *A Kind Caution to Watermen* (1708), which claimed that the watermen treated each other with all the 'opprobrious language that their wit can invent'.
22. These charges compared very favourably with carriage fares of the time such as that from Haymarket to Red Lion Square, a short distance, for 1s. 6d.
23. C. de Saussure, *A Foreign View of England in the Reigns of George I and George II*.

'You never have disputes with watermen for you can go to no part of London or the nearby country but the rate is fixed by authority, everything is regulated and printed.'

24. R. Campbell, *The London Tradesmen* (Gardner, 1747). The trade of waterman is placed under 'sundry trades that could not be ranged under any general head'.
25. H. Harris, *Under Oars* (Stepney Books, 1978).
26. *Spectator* (11 Aug. 1712).
27. D. Defoe, *A Tour through the Whole Island of Great Britain* (1726).
28. J. Gay, 'Trivia', in a compilation edited by Walsh (Fyfield, 1979).
29. *Memoirs of William Hickey*, Vol. 1, 1749–1775 (Hurst & Blackett, 1923).
30. Reported in the *Ipswich Journal* (24 Jan. 1784), 4d.
31. *Parker's General Advertiser and Morning Intelligencer* (4 Sept. 1784), 3c.
32. Varieties of dress can be seen particularly well in *Greenwich Hospital* by Canaletto (1753) kept at Greenwich Maritime Museum.
33. D. Defoe, *A Tour through the Whole Island of Great Britain* (1726).
34. R. Kipling, *Rescue by Sail and Oar* (Tops'l Books, 1982).
35. R. Davis, *The Rise of the English Shipping Industry* (Macmillan, 1962).
36. A. Burton, *The Changing River* (Gollancz, 1982).
37. 'Coracle making, Severn Reflections', *Manchester Guardian* 8 Sept. 1958 (8 a–c): 'every farmer butting the river had a coracle and many were used for poaching'.
38. M. Prior, *Fisher Row – Fishermen, Bargemen and Canal Boatmen in Oxford 1500–1900* (Oxford University Press, 1982).
39. D. Defoe, *A Tour through the Whole Island of Great Britain* (1726).
40. D. Summers, *The Great Ouse* (David & Charles, 1973).
41. *Bedfordshire Magazine* (Summer 1983), editorial.
42. D. Defoe, *A Tour through the Whole Island of Great Britain* (1726).
43. M. Heron, *Ferry Path – the Story of a Cambridge River Street* (Cockayne Press, 1974).
44. R. Kipling, *Rescue by Sail and Oar* (Tops'l Books, 1982). The actual boat is in the Exeter Maritime Museum.
45. F. Moss, *Sketches, Reminiscences, and Legends of Didsbury* (Deansgate Press, 1890) quoted the Didsbury Parish accounts for 1673 which incorporate payments for 'Chedle bote'.
46. M. Prior, *Fisher Row – Fishermen, Bargemen and Canal Boatmen in Oxford 1500–1900* (Oxford University Press, 1982).
47. *Norfolk News* (26 April 1803 and 12 July 1804), 2b.
48. Greenbank Falmouth Rowing Club, preamble to minute book 1.
49. '50 years ago', *Lancaster Guardian* (5 Aug. 1854), 11a.
50. *Illustrated London News* (19 Aug. 1843).
51. *The Times* (4 Sept. 1833), 6c.
52. D. Matthews, *Lake Festivals on Windermere* (Windermere Nautical Trust 1982).
53. '50 years ago', *Eddowes Shrewsbury Journal* (10 Sept. 1849).
54. *Norfolk News* (6 Aug. 1783), 4a.
55. G. Boerio, *Dizionario del dialetto Veneziano* (Cecchini, Venice, 1856).
56. G. Bellavitis, *Itinerari per Venezia* (L'Espresso, Roma, 1980).
57. C. Hibbert, *The Grand Tour* (Methuen, 1987).
58. W.G. Constable, *Canaletto* (Clarendon, 1976).
59. *Pepys' Diary* (23 Aug. 1662) at which point he also mentions that he 'offered 8 shillings for a boat to attend me for the afternoon, but they would not'.
60. Public Notice advertising the re-opening of the gardens after refurbishment, 7 June 1732.
61. W. Wroth, *London Pleasure Gardens of the Eighteenth Century* (Macmillan, 1896).
62. *Memoirs of William Hickey*, Vol. 1, 1749–1775 (Hurst & Blackett, 1923).
63. J. Hampden, *An Eighteenth Century Journal 1774–1776* (Macmillan, 1940).
64. D. Matthews, *Lake Festivals on Windermere* (Windermere Nautical Trust 1982).

65. Cleveland County Library, local collection, ref. SST. 797. 1.

66. *Salopian Journal* (25 June 1794), 3b.

67. S. Middlebrook, *Newcastle on Tyne, Its Growth and Achievement* (Kemsley, 1950).

68. J. Strutt, *The Sports and Pastimes of the People of England* (White, 1801).

69. For example the Fishmongers' Company built their last barge in 1773 and it was broken up in 1850; their Hall contains a scale model of it.

70. *Pepys' Diary* (18 Mary 1661).

71. *Daily Courant* (23 June 1722), 2c.

72. *Daily Courant* (15 Nov. 1723), 2d.

73. *The Times* (25 May 1748), 6a.

3

Commercialism

The boat races brought together, as they always do,
an enormous mass of visitors from all the neighbouring towns.

(*Rochdale Observer*, 15 Oct. 1864 on the
'Aquatics' at Hollingworth Lake)

Most recreational activities, based either upon honest trade or mere
playfulness, had been the subjects of some commercial exploitation
before the eighteenth century, usually at neighbourhood level.
Where the locality included access to water, the activities inevitably
involved some form of aquatic performance, normally of a light-
hearted nature. This encouraged the participation of watermen of
all descriptions seeking to supplement their wages with gambling
and prize funds. The tradition goes back many years and there is
evidence in the Royal Library of water quintain and jousts in
the fourteenth century while John Stow in his *Survey of London*
describes water quintain played in the sixteenth century close by
London Bridge to take advantage of the pull through the arches:
'upon the bridge wharves and houses by the river side stand great
numbers to see and laugh thereat'.

Similarly, he mentions jousts on the river for which contestants
were rowed about in wherries. The object was to knock your
opponent overboard and this was normally achieved as 'for the most
part one or both were overthrown and well ducked'. Such events,
particularly in the summer season, would attract large crowds which
in turn encouraged the attendance of all the myriad street-sellers of
the locality and turn the scene into a rural panorama reminiscent of
the old-established holy-day feasts that took place in villages up and
down the country.

The transition from country to town had its effects on recreational
activities as rural pursuits were carried into urban settings and
modified by mass use and commercialisation. Rowing, like football, evolved in this way.[1] During the nineteenth century, some

activities, including rowing, remained as rural remnants but changed their form to meet the increasingly commercial demands made upon them.[2] As we have seen the River Dee estuary sports moved when practical into the centre of Chester in 1733, motivated no doubt by the commercial pressures exerted by city centre sponsors such as the Red House Inn. Further north, on Lake Windermere, the Lake Sports were part 'noble display' and part commercial attraction which resulted in the attendance of huge crowds at the lakeside fair and entertainments.[3]

Aquatics became a recognisable sport with Doggett's Coat and Badge Race in 1715 and the racing professional waterman attracted, both before and after this time, considerable public interest and thereby the involvement of certain commercial parties like the proprietors of Vauxhall Pleasure Gardens, Astley's Theatre and public houses such as the Red Barn at Battersea. From the time of Ranelagh Regatta in 1775, it became common for theatre and garden proprietors to sponsor rowing events and then promote them as part of the evening's entertainment as with Astley who regularly brought on stage the winner and his prize wherry 'at the conclusion of a new divertissement prepared expressly upon the occasion of the race'.[4]

Out in the countryside, the promotion remained low-key but was nevertheless designed to help the local tradesmen and publicans who would expect to make considerable sums at events like Snatchem's Sports at Sunderland Point near Lancaster, promoted by the Golden Ball public house, or the Poulton Sports a few miles around the coast where wheelbarrow races, sack races and wrestling were as prominent as the rowing events.[5] Similar events, staged as rural 'fayres' and sports, were more common on the coast than inland and were often promoted by local shopkeepers who provided prizes in cash or kind for the contestants, as at Torbay Regatta and Sports in 1814,[6] while the inland town and city events were more regularly sponsored by innkeepers, such as the match between six watermen for 24 sovereigns donated by the landlord of the Nine Elms Tavern of Battersea in 1823.[7]

The same year Edmund Kean joined a theatrical tradition donating a prize wherry named *Othello* for competition among seven pairs of watermen in commemoration of Garrick's last performance in June 1776; this profited not only the watermen but also a new Theatrical Fund and at the same time drew 'an immense crowd which lined the banks of the river, barges and bridges'.[8] Innkeepers rang the changes as often as possible to attract extra custom and keep the interest of regular customers, and Mr Pay of the Ship Tavern at Lambeth staged in 1830 a 'Novel Rowing Match' by awarding various cuts of meat as prizes and calling the sculling contestants 'cabbages', 'beans', 'carrots' and so on. So successful was this ploy that the match 'attracted many more thousands on the river than if the premiums amounted to one hundred pounds',[9] a situation which would seem to indicate the preference of simple rural values over hard-nosed commercialism.

This did not last for long and from 1835 onwards there was an enormous increase in river sports, explained by a commentator in 1860 as the result of bigger prize funds, to the effect that 'there is hardly a spot on the River Thames from Twickenham to Gravesend that cannot boast a regatta'.[10] Many of these 'happy British festivals', as the *Illustrated London News* described them, were attended by 'all classes from the fascinating belle of the drawing room to the hardy wife of the weather beaten fisherman, from the votary of fashion to the toil worn mechanic'.[11]

The enormous influence exerted by publicans during the Victorian and Edwardian periods is partially explained by the variety of functions that the public house fulfilled since, apart from food and drink, it could provide 'light and heat, cooking facilities, furniture, newspapers and sociability' and was often therefore the very centre of local society.[12] It was only to be expected that it should serve as the venue for many recreational activities and that the publican should act as the promoter of sporting events throughout the country.

It is not feasible to mention all individual promotions in aquatics but reference to some will provide the flavour and extent of the activity: unspecified local publicans promoted boat races from Stockton-on-Tees to Cargoe Fleet on the River Tees during the 1840s[13] while others did so in Norwich;[14] Mr Riley, the proprietor of Pomona Gardens in Manchester, regularly sponsored boat racing to attract the crowds to his establishment,[15] and John Crook of the Boathouse Inn on the River Ribble in Preston sponsored racing among the local clubs, some of which boated from his boathouse and for whose members he applied for a spirits licence in 1865;[16] Blyth publicans together backed the 'Great Coble Race' between a miner and a professional oarsman which thousands went to watch[17] and at almost the same time Henry Newall was developing rowing on Hollingworth Lake near Rochdale to attract custom to his newly opened Lake Hotel.[18] During the 1870s, the Alhambra Music Hall in Barrow-in-Furness promoted sculling matches to boost trade and

Mr Turvey of the Bankfield Hotel, also in Barrow, sponsored sculling between women contestants to do the same.[19]

During one week only in Newcastle-on-Tyne, the local press indicated that 25 public houses were sponsoring some form of sporting activity, some of which was rowing.[20] In Lancaster, the promotion of the local aquatic sports had passed from the Golden Ball Inn on the north shore to the Royal Blue Anchor on the southern quayside and the newly designated 'Quayside Sports' were extremely popular throughout the 1880s and 1890s.[21] Naturally enough, the close proximity of drink had some unfortunate results, such as those experienced at the water sports promoted by the Rosherville Gardens at Gravesend in 1850 when the winning crews repaired to the Town Arms where they lit the traditional victory fireworks, which burned down a goodly part of the adjacent neighbourhood.[22]

Despite the potential hazards of staging such events, it was not long before local authorities began to see the commercial advantages and, as we have seen, the local Gravesend Council had sponsored boat racing as early as 1698 to support the industry of its watermen; it was, however, many years later in 1846 that the first Town Regatta was officially organised by the municipality.[23] The spread of the railways during the nineteenth century meant that more people were travelling more widely around the country, particularly to coastal resorts. As Walvin remarks, in 1800 only the upper classes were able to visit the seaside while, by 1900, millions had come to regard 'an annual visit to the sea as a fact of urban life'[24] with the result that there was considerable competition among resorts for tourist business.

For example, Southport had served Liverpool as a dormitory for many years and as early as 1834 there had been annual boat races sponsored by Peter Hesketh Fleetwood, the local landowner, but with the coming of the railway the local chamber of commerce decided to provide an attraction for the growing number of visitors. In 1843, therefore, a two-day regatta was promoted with the result that the 'lodging houses were so full that many had to sleep on sofas'.[25] By 1848 the Liverpool, Crosby and Southport railway line had been completed and the rail company gave regular financial support to the annual gala week sports, and by 1864 the Pier Company of Southport was backing a yearly regatta held from the pier itself which 'provided amusement for those whose visits are so welcome to the town and so necessary for its continued welfare'.[26]

The middle years of the century saw similar developments

throughout the north-west area of the country, an area which was particularly well served by early rail links, and even by 1840 both Lancaster and Chester were welcoming outsiders to their traditional water sports which were described along with other similar events as merely 'excuses for riots and drunkenness',[27] having been organised by the local publicans. Fleetwood had held such events from its inception in 1834 but the coming of the railway and the opening of the new North Euston Hotel in 1841 was celebrated with a special regatta on 9 August, which was promoted to attract as many visitors to the new resort as possible.[28]

Encouraged by its success, Preston Council included a Guild Regatta in its commemoration festivities in 1842.[29] Lytham on the Lancashire coast and Hollingworth Lake, known as the 'weavers' seaport', soon followed suit with their very own aquatic attractions, with the result that by the 1850s the commercialisation of rowing in the area was well established and led directly to professionalism and a strictly non-commercial reaction which produced some of the earliest amateur clubs in the country.

Over the Pennines in York, similar events were being developed, beginning with a 'Grand Regatta on the Ouse' in 1843, sponsored by the city's Mayor and Sheriff in order to promote the excellence of the York stream 'unaffected by tide, never inconveniently crowded with boats and vessels and exceedingly convenient for any aquatic performance'.[30] The regatta marked the resurgence of economic fortunes in the city following a long period of decline which bottomed out in the early 1830s and was turned around by its new and strategic position on the Great North of England Railway and its further development as a national rail centre.[31]

By 1865 the regatta had grown to giant proportions and was designated the 'Grand Yorkshire Regatta' perhaps to demonstrate that rail connections now brought day-trippers from all over the county. The North Eastern Railway in particular laid on special excursion trains to bring visitors from far afield into the regatta enclosure which was only a matter of yards from the station.[32]

The 1840s were good times for regatta development generally since the railway system began to extend across the country in earnest: the Newcastle and Carlisle line not only brought spectators into the obvious centre of Newcastle for boat racing but also promoted the growth of the previously isolated township of Brampton, due entirely to its proximity to Talkin Tarn and its aquatic entertainments. Ever since the first train connection, the traditional sports at the tarn had attracted special excursion trains from Carlisle and Newcastle, requiring 'streets of tents on the shore to accommodate tradesmen, visitors and competitors'.[33] They continued to attract increasingly large numbers of spectators, so that by 1899 the local paper could congratulate the sports' organisers on transforming Brampton into a 'summer resort'.[34]

Remaining in the north of England, it is possible to see that wherever there was suitable water, the potential for aquatic entertainment was fully realised. In areas with particularly good water this is understandable and the Berwick-on-Tweed authorities thought it worth while playing to their strength by incorporating the annual flower show into the regatta so that the combined attraction 'should afford a greater inducement for visitors to come into town'.[35] Whitby, especially desirous of promoting itself as a resort, had staged water sports from the 1830s[36] which had become by the 1870s a veritable three-day carnival and the 'principal event of the Whitby season', resulting in the town's being overrun by rail excursionists from Newcastle, Middlesbrough, Peterborough, Grantham, Newark and Manchester.[37]

However, even where the water was positively unsuitable, local councils persisted in staging events as in Goole and Leeds: the former hosted a regatta on the meandering River Ouse promoted by the Lancashire and Yorkshire Railway which attracted 'hundreds of spectators brought by boat, rail and road until the town presented quite a busy appearance'[38] while the latter utilised the reedy, shallow lake in Roundhay Park to present races which nevertheless enticed 20,000 visitors at sixpence a head.[39]

On the River Severn in Worcester, which was already served by the Birmingham and Gloucester rail link in the 1840s, the regatta was backed by the Royal Worcester Porcelain Company[40] and by 1890 it could be said to add 'to the prosperity of the city as much as the carnival in Venice or the battle of the flowers on the Riviera'.[41] Perhaps encouraged by the happy experience of Worcester, first Shrewsbury introduced a regatta as an 'interesting novelty for the recreation of the townsfolk'[42] and later Ironbridge extended its traditional fête to include water sports and boat races which brought 'numbers from a great distance, courtesy of arrangements made by the Great Western Railway who ran cheap trains from Worcester, Dudley, Wolverhampton and other places'.[43]

Evesham, like Berwick-on-Tweed, brought together its horticultural fête and regatta from 1863 onwards to attract visitors more successfully from Birmingham and other nearby industrial towns which it continued to do for many years,[44] facilitated by convenient rail connections. Although close by, Stratford-on-Avon, lacking an early rail link, had to wait until 1874 to establish its regatta to take advantage of the newly opened East and West Junction Railway.[45] Even venues which boasted only rather inadequate facilities for boating were encouraged by their centrality on the rail network to provide regattas, so that Lincoln from the early 1850s onwards provided a regatta which was generally considered to be a 'popular holiday attraction'.[46]

Towns which enjoyed excellent water facilities together with extensive rail connections naturally attracted the greatest number of visitors. Bedford, for instance, was required eventually to spread its regatta over two days due to overwhelming support from spectators and competitors alike.[47] The era of the professional champion and personality saw some local authorities acting as sporting entrepreneurs, as in the case of Kings Lynn whose council regularly provided substantial purses to entice well-known scullers to perform on the nearby Eau Brink Cut and also promoted the annual regatta there which 'occasioned a general holiday with Lynn inhabitants streaming in shoals to the scene of the action reinforced by others from Cambridge, London and even Manchester and Newcastle by special trains'.[48]

Similar special trains, laid on by the Isle of Wight and Newport Junction Railway, brought holiday excursionists to the Ryde Town Regatta which was jointly sponsored by the railway companies and the Pier Company,[49] while the London and Brighton Railway Company transported both the competitors' boats and the day-trippers to the enclosures of the Worthing Town Regatta; the local Pier Company, as co-sponsors, profited hugely 'with three thousand seven hundred persons passing through the turnstiles'.[50]

The regattas of those days tended to be held on Tuesdays or Wednesdays in order to utilise the half-day holiday and because the promoters were often the shopkeepers themselves but, naturally, many local shops remained open to entice custom from the hordes of day-trippers and in most cases extra facilities were provided for the holiday-makers. In Nottingham, for example, the local river steam-boat company and the proprietors of Colwick Hall Gardens combined with the regatta authorities to produce an all-inclusive package deal costing a mere one shilling which made available one more diversion in a city which, by 1898, had become a 'thriving centre of popular entertainment'.[51]

So popular did Nottingham Regatta become that the organisers had to relocate it on the Trent Bridge Embankment, to ensure

4. Worthing Pier on Regatta Day, 15 August 1892.

sufficient room for the 10,000 or so people who regularly attended, and in addition they extended the enclosure, the entry to which was already at a premium.[52] For some smaller towns, the regatta festivities assumed major importance, as in Hereford where they were considered 'a means of making better known the many attractions of the city as a residential neighbourhood and especially drawing attention to the beauty of the River Wye and its boating and fishing facilities'[53] and Burton-on-Trent where the regatta was run 'entirely as a town matter'.[54]

During the 1930s, many towns lost their annual regattas due to background economic circumstances beyond their control when subscribers to prize funds simply could not be found. Some others, like Derby, managed to retain the event after much exhortation in the local press, which made the point that the town had so few functions of which it could be proud that it was vital to keep the regatta at least.[55]

Later still, following the Second World War, the economic difficulties suffered by many locally organised regattas were somewhat alleviated by the Chancellor of the Exchequer who 'looked into the question of regattas with a view to clearing them from entertainment duty'[56] and subsequently managed to do so.

It is, then, possible to trace the commercialisation of rowing as boat racing to the rural tradition of water sports originating in medieval times, and yet the overt manipulation of the activity for the purposes of mass entertainment, promotion and profit only became evident during the eighteenth century. From this era, it is possible to monitor its development through its utilisation for various purposes by publicans, garden proprietors, theatrical impresarios, town councils, chambers of commerce, and rail and pier companies.

These individuals and agencies became increasingly aware of the commercial benefits of providing novel yet convenient entertainments to an ever-expanding market of urban dwellers and were quite prepared to exploit rowing as simply one of many such amusements. The communal and institutional exploitation of rowing as exemplified above was pre-dated by the purely personal approach of a class of gentlemen who pursued the promotion of aquatics, using as their subjects local watermen such as those noted in the Aquatic Register of 10 August 1765, who had 'served their country all the last war'.

These particular gentlemen had generously subscribed a substantial prize fund for the competition of their neighbourhood watermen who then provided their sponsors with 'the greatest

wager ever rowed'. Gentlemen were generally interested in promoting the welfare of the contestants but only as a subsidiary
consideration to the excitement and profit they hoped to derive
from the situation, and this form of patronage was particularly
common between the years 1715 and 1835, a period coinciding with
the high point of gambling in England. Such wagering was commonplace among the gentry and even among their children at the larger
public schools where there was 'much gambling, contracting of
debts and drinking, some of it official'.[57]

It was for fear of encouraging more of the same that pupils of Eton
College and Westminster School were prohibited from taking part
in boat racing in any capacity. Nevertheless, the Eton Boating
Book, which gives contemporary information about activity at the
College, provides evidence that as early as 1793 judging by the
number of boats involved, the practice of rowing was 'of some
standing' with regular 'matches' taking place between local watermen and backed by the pupils, in addition to the more acceptable
ceremonial processions, as on 4 June.[58]

As with William Hickey, for example, it was quite usual in the
eighteenth century for a young gentleman to take out boats for
purely recreational purposes but not, at that time, for competition
since it was seen to be a manual and somewhat demeaning activity,
too well associated with plebeian watermen and their disreputable
wranglings. However, later in the century, after decades of patronage and sponsorship of the same watermen, we find the gentlemen
taking to the oars themselves, very often using watermen as professional steersmen and competing for the purposes of gambling and
not for sport alone.

At the turn of the century, for the first time, the newspapers begin
to report a mixture of racing activities with some featuring gentlemen only and others watermen only, but both as excuses for betting,
as with the Guards officer in 1801 who drew 'a gig from Brighton to
Lewes in four hours'[59] or the 'noble boatman, stripped and at the oars'
at an event sponsored by Cumberland Gardens the following year.[60]

The gentlemen would pick their champions for certain events and
prepare them in the best possible way for the forthcoming wager as
did 'Major W.' who bought a brand-new light cutter called *Eclipse*
for his crew of picked Gravesend watermen to row in an 80-mile race
against some London watermen sponsored by Mr Durand in which
the boats set off 'furnished with sandwiches of cold fowl, brandy and
water', to little effect for the Londoners who were distanced and
picked up by Durand's yacht.[61] Some idea of the racing conditions at

the time is provided by a report of a similar race sponsored by the Duke of Manchester in 1804 which relates how 'one man was nearly knocked overboard and drowned while another was struck with a boat hook and remained senseless for some time'.[62]

As far as gentlemen were concerned, whether competing themselves or merely watching, not the least of the entertainment was the dinner which followed the recreations, normally held during the morning at traditional venues like the Star and Garter at Richmond, the Ship at Greenwich or the Falcon at Gravesend where the prizes would be awarded and the debts settled.[63] There is less evidence for gentlemen's participation in rowing or 'aquatics', as it was generally known, during the war years ending in 1815, but a resurgence is noticeable thereafter with events such as that featuring six pairs of Hussar officers rowing a match on the River Thames,[64] 'Gentlemen's Races' on the River Yare in Norwich[65] and races against time from Oxford to London.[66]

This post-war trend culminated in a 'Grand Amateur Rowing Match' in which six pairs of gentlemen raced for a wager worth 200 sovereigns and in doing so attracted a huge crowd of 'well dressed spectators, mainly women'.[67] This event encouraged the staging of the first 'away' match by an Oxford University crew against some London amateur gentlemen for a purse of 200 sovereigns and described by the *Sporting Magazine* of July 1828 as rowed from Westminster Bridge to Putney Bridge 'with the Londoners labouring under every disadvantage but steered by the waterman John Mitchell of Strand Lane, winning easily'.

It seems that to row for a money prize did not automatically disqualify a contestant from amateur status, at least during the first half of the nineteenth century when the question of pecuniary advantage appeared less than vital. The prize of 200 sovereigns for example became commonplace, with another Oxford v. London match taking place at Henley in 1831 for that amount.[68] Even as late as 1861 the winner of the English Amateur Sculling Championship, otherwise known as the Wingfield Sculls, took all the entrance fees of £5 per entry.[69]

The emphasis continued to be laid on financial inducements as gentlemen amateurs participated in further extraordinary aquatic feats in the pursuit of what was called, in later times and different circumstances, 'the accursed greed for gold'. For example, two gentlemen rowed from London Bridge to Gravesend, thence to Richmond Bridge and back to Westminster within fifteen hours for a substantial purse[70] and a Mr Robinson rowed from London Bridge to Erith and back, some 40 miles, in less than five hours, winning in the process £500 with nearly 'two thousand pounds being won and lost on the match'.[71] More unusual, considering the deepening of social divisions, were the matches in which gentlemen and watermen rowed together for a prize, such as George Lander who rowed with Williams in a match for £100 in a timed race from Oxford to Waterloo Bridge, winning the wager in 18 hrs 42 mins.[72]

The greatest match was probably that between the Grenadier Guards and the Royal Artillery in six-oared cutters which took place from Greenwich Palace to Woolwich Arsenal in 1839 for a purse of £1,000 with the Lords Fitzclarence, Scarborough, Gunston and Waterford all wagering huge sums on the outcome and, as the report indicates, 'immense sums changing pockets on the occasion in sporting circles'.[73]

The *Aquatic Oracle or Record of Rowing* from 1835 to 1851, drawn up by an amateur,[74] notes some 3,000 such matches for gentlemen mostly on the River Thames in London and Henley which indicates their promotion at a rate of over three a week for the years under review. Bell's *Life* magazine for 9 January 1859 lists what the correspondent calls 'Principal Rowing Matches', by which he means those involving gentlemen amateurs, noting 33 in Putney, 6 in Barnes, 4 on the River Irwell in Salford, 2 at Henley and 1 apiece at Lancaster, Oxford and Talkin Tarn, all of which occurred during 1858.

Considering the climate of the age and the constitution of the university boat clubs, whose members were almost exclusively drawn from Eton College and Westminster School, it was inevitable that the two should organise a rowing match, the first intimation of which was a scribbled note of a challenge by the Cambridge captain immediately followed up by a letter from Stephen Davis, the Cambridge University boatman and boatbuilder, to his counterpart at Oxford fixing a time in Whitsuntide week for the Varsity Match.[75]

The venue for the match was to be Henley-on-Thames since neither the River Cam nor the River Isis were wide enough or straight enough for an effective race and the tidal London river was considered to be too choppy to provide fair racing conditions. Henley, on the other hand, offered a one mile straight course which was sufficiently wide at all points to allow a clean contest with no blade clashes or fouling, added to which the town council decided to promote the match, realising its commercial attractiveness for the locality. The council lost no time in bringing together a host of noble practitioners of aquatics from the schools and universities, together with those from the Guards' regiments and the newly formed London clubs, presenting them all with a preliminary wager race between local watermen for which the municipality had provided a tempting prize.

At 7.15 p.m. on Wednesday, 10 June, following the watermen's race, the varsity boats were launched before a crowd estimated at 25,000 among which 'were to be seen the very flower of the kingdom, for such surely may be called the fine high spirited young men of the universities and of Eton and Westminster'; the same report continues with a denial of the rumour that the match was being rowed for a very large cash prize, saying that it 'was by no means a gambling match but a trial of strength and skill'.[76] The match had been widely advertised as one to be rowed for 500 guineas but this was strenuously denied by some crew members and may have been a further ploy on behalf of the town council to attract greater public interest.

It does seem, however, that since the watermen's race was promoted entirely as a gambling match for the entertainment of the assembled gentry, it would have been highly unusual if heavy betting on the university race had not also taken place. Indeed, some intimation of the less than desirable concomitants of the match must have reached the notice of university authorities since a projected match in 1831 was prohibited at the express instructions of the Vice-Chancellor of Cambridge University. These instructions derived, according to the boat club members, from the Vice-Chancellor's confusion concerning the 'town's rowing and its rowing and his anxiety to check any debauching in the latter class was the means of preventing the healthy exercise of the former'.[77]

Nevertheless, in 1836, another match was contested on the London river from Westminster to Putney and this time even *The Times* confirmed, in its edition of 20 June, that 'the match is to be rowed for four hundred pounds' and in 1839 the present series of races was begun. It seems that once again, at least for a certain social class of oarsman, the winning of money was not sufficient cause for exclusion from amateur rankings.

The match of 1840 commanded great public attention and substantial coverage in *The Times*, whose report notes that there was 'no spot on the river banks from one terminus of the race to the other that had not an occupant'. The same report continues to mention that both crews were using 'cutters' especially built for the occasion and had a 'vast deal of practice and though considered as amateurs were equal if not superior to any rowers on the river' and concludes with the usual note applauding 'these sorts of amusements'. Nor could the correspondent forbear to deprecate similar provincial events as entertainments, 'got up merely by publicans to pillage the unwary and to enrich themselves'.[78]

The Times' report of the following year's match concluded in like vein by commenting that the 'match has assumed a different and ten fold more attractive form in consequence of the patronage bestowed upon it by the aristocracy of the country'[79] and, for the first time in 1842, the event was designated a 'race' rather than a 'match', thus leaving behind for good the connotations of financial impropriety. The commercial aspects of the event, however, remained and grew into enormous proportions with crowds thronging the banks even on practice days, making Putney Bridge impassable and presenting the sellers of light- and dark-blue memorabilia with an almost insatiable demand which also necessitated the constant and total use of the river steamers whose attention often caused havoc with training sessions and, occasionally, with the race itself.[80]

Most newspapers and journals followed the progress of the crews for weeks before the race and certainly by 1868 it was being hailed as the 'greatest aquatic contest of the world before the prestige of which the slowly departing glories of the professional championships and even the gala splendours of Henley must fade away'.[81] Moreover, *The Times*' correspondent weighed in with a leading article extolling the race as 'alive with that instinct which urges every Englishman to be as good as his neighbour and which keeps the whole nation on a par with other nations'.[82] So comprehensive did the press coverage become that it has been cited as marking the beginning of modern sporting journalism since never before had athletic contests been written about so extensively and, as the first mass spectator sport, rowing became hard news rather than merely feature material.[83]

This mass popularity was heavily deprecated by some who lamented the decline of the event from 'true sport for its own sake' to be commercialised by 'gamblers and newspapers with cabmen, butcher boys and omnibus drivers sporting university colours in all directions, flaunting them in all sorts of indescribable company'.[84] The cost of participation in the race to the university clubs was considerable as the *Golden Penny* magazine of 26 March 1898 bore witness in its detailed accounting of the necessary expenditure, viz. the cost of trials on home waters, £120; a new boat and oars, £65; boat carriage to Putney, £15; rent of house at Putney with servants, £90; housekeeping bills, £150; champagne and liqueurs, £25; horse for the coach, £25; trip to Brighton to prevent staleness due to over-training, £15; steam launch on race day, £45; watermen on race day, £20 and finally the cost of the umpire's launch and the race dinner which was shared, producing a grand total for each club of £600.

Thus, by the turn of the century the race had assumed the proportions of a business enterprise with many thousands of pounds being spent directly or indirectly on its production and presentation. By 1927, the Cinematograph Company had arranged to record it on film and in the same year Barnes Council collected a small fortune from the 16,700 customers it had charged for a view of the finishing line handily located adjacent to its property.[85] The British Broadcasting Corporation first televised the event as early as 1938 and in recent years it has become one of the largest of all outside broadcasts while attracting the generous commercial sponsorship of Ladbrokes, the bookmaking firm, and of Beefeater Gin.

Since the departure of the fixture from Henley after 1829, there had been several races on the one-mile straight between various crews including gentlemen and watermen, and their success, together with that of other events around the country, encouraged the town council and the larger boating clubs to promote the idea of an annual regatta in the town. The idea of such an event was by no means original and there were several precedents around the country: Durham hosted a regatta in 1815 which became a regular event in 1834; the Yare Amateur Championships, sponsored by the Norwich firm of Colmans, for the Carrow Cup was instituted in 1816; the Ryde Royal Regatta had featured galley races for amateurs since 1829 and in 1834 there began regular regattas at Newcastle and Tewkesbury, all of which proved to be considerable popular and commercial successes.

The Trinity College Boat Book of September 1838 recounts a long discussion about the possibility of establishing a prestigious amateur rowing event now 'that rowing had taken its proper place amongst national pastimes', concluding that Henley was the best location for such an event presumably because it had a long straight course and was convenient for Oxford and London, added to which it was known that the council, as in 1829, was keen to host the event. Hence, at a public meeting in Henley Town Hall on 26 March 1839, it was proposed and carried that 'the establishment of an annual regatta would not only be productive of the most beneficial results to the town of Henley but also be a source of amusement and gratification to the neighbourhood and the public in general'; the first regatta was duly held on Friday, 14 June of that year.

The first stewards of the regatta, men such as Fuller-Maitland and Williams-Freeman, were ex-'varsity' men who extended the regatta's challenge only to crews from Oxford, Cambridge and London universities, the schools of Eton and Westminster, guards officers or well-established gentlemen's clubs and they required most particularly that all eight-oared boats were to be steered by amateurs and specifically not by professional watermen. From the very first occasion, the event attracted much public attention and commercial interest, with booths springing up along the banks and across the bridge, thus hampering the progress of many who attended merely to watch the racing.

By 1860 the town council had been obliged to buy land near the bridge in order to prevent the construction of a grandstand which would have obscured from general view the finishing post and so have seriously affected the popularity of the regatta and the trade that came from it. During the early 1870s, the Prince of Wales began to attend the regatta during Ascot week and the fashionably inclined followed suit with their complaints of unpunctual transport remedied by official letters from regatta stewards to the Great Western Railway demanding better service on the London–Henley line.[86]

This new surge of interest brought in its wake further commercialisation in the form of 'hawkers, stall holders and other objectionable characters' all of whom were eventually banned from the banksides.[87] Nevertheless, the regatta committee had begun to realise that, properly managed, the commercial element of the event could be made to produce a profit for the organisers and not merely an entertainment for the spectators, and the new constitution of March 1881 established a trend of acquisition and development that has extended to the present day. The Lion Meadow, being adjacent to the finishing line, was developed as a paying enclosure, local brewery land was acquired and rented out to provide annual income, the small grandstand was re-sited and enlarged, programmes were improved and repriced and for the first time the press was encouraged to attend.

In 1880 another riverside meadow was bought for regatta use and in the following year an entrance charge was levied on access to the course through a local farm while further land purchase meant that all the land on the Berkshire side of the course was in the hands of the stewards by 1918. Reviewing the 1902 season, the Rowing Almanack noted that the development of the regatta into practically a business concern was facilitated by the excellence and frequency of the rail service from London and that the whole proceedings were 'good for Henley folk in filling their coffers', a situation which prevails today due to the continuing exploitation by the regatta authorities of every conceivable commercial potential.

The watermen who had plied the traditional aquatic trades for centuries began to be aware that there were some financial advantages in supplying their services and skills to the new classes of leisured ladies and gentlemen which emerged during the eighteenth century. Renting boats to schoolboys at Eton and Westminster had assumed commercially viable proportions in the last quarter of the century and this practice had become so common during the 1780s that *The Times* issued a warning explaining that 'Westminster School has lost several pupils in cockle shells and the thousands of pounds made by the principal fellows who let them out have been marked with the watery grave of many a fine boy'.[88]

Similar problems occurred at Eton where the local boatmen had taken to renting out boats to college pupils in the 1790s in the days of Tolladay who was followed at generation intervals by Searle, Salter and Parkins until in 1909 the boathouse was taken over by the college itself and became the Eton Boathouse Company which continues to subsidise rowing at the school. Further afield, Jim Ward of Nottingham let out his boats to schoolchildren and was roundly criticised for doing so when one of them drowned,[89] and several fatalities had occurred on the River Ribble at Preston, when John Crooks let his boats out on regular Sunday boating sessions.

Throughout the country, the local boatmen had curtailed their normal tasks of ferrying and fishing to cater for the growing demand for recreational and racing craft both of which many men rented out and built, men like John Cross in Cambridge who had left the employ of the river conservators to make the new-style racing craft for college clubs as early as 1817. Salter's of Oxford and Searle's of Putney and Eton would send off finished craft all over the country using, in Searle's case, 'their own machine or boat carriage since the canal people declined to take them and the railway was not considered safe for long boats'.[90]

Many firms, however, were not in such a big way of business and simply provided boats for the immediate locality such as Sam Chetham in Bedford, Hobbs in Henley, Jennings in Liverpool, Barnsdall in Gravesend, Jordan in Hereford and a host of others, all of whom made a decent living throughout the nineteenth century from a combination of building and hiring a variety of boats for clubs and public alike.[91] Many clubs owed their very existence to boat

5. The Swan Hotel at Thames Ditton, 1898, typical of many riverside hotels that boosted trade by offering boats for hire. The Swan gained greatly by being so close to Surbiton and convenient rail connections.

51

hirers who allowed members to use craft at reduced rates such as Cambridge Town Rowing Club which started from Fosters boathouse, Gateshead RC at Jewitts, Eton Excelsior RC at Goodmans, Pengwern RC at Ellis's, Nottingham RC at Radfords and Bristol RC at the boat hirers at the Pilgrim public house on Bristol quayside.

Public houses close to water utilised this facility to increase business and many became known primarily because of their aquatic connections, with some actually promoting rowing matches and entertainments. The majority, however, simply rented out a few boats as a sideline such as the Doves at Hammersmith, the Half Moon at St Neots and the Angel at Gainsborough. Some boat-hiring inns were the centres of professional rowing, having been taken over by retired professional watermen such as Harry Steer at the Bridge Inn at Derby, John Crooks at the Pleasure Boat Inn at Preston and Harry Lang at the Fountain Inn at Salford.

Certain areas of the country more than others lent themselves to the occupation and recreation of boating and there the local councils used the availability of boat-hiring facilities as an inducement for visitors to come to the locality. As early as 1837, Shrewsbury was suggesting the 'hiring out of boats by the day at moderate charges to take pic-nics and excursions up the river to the picturesque and woody banks at Shelton'[92] and some time later the House of Industry boathouse thanked the public for their 'liberal support for several seasons in hiring boats for fishing, pleasure and racing'.[93] The boating station at Bath was established in the early 1850s and there the pleasures of boating were mixed with the civilities of cream teas while in Ryde the watermen had virtually abandoned their normal fishing tasks during the summer preferring to sell 'trips around the bay' to tourists.[94] The development of rail connections up the Thames valley and the fashion for boating created enormous demands for boat hire in the area and many hotels advertised themselves as pre-eminently suitable for the aquatic trade, as with the New Thames Hotel which was built in 1887 specifically to meet the growing demands of the popular river resort of Maidenhead and which prided itself on providing 'every convenience with boats, canoes and steam launches for hire at very competitive rates'.[95]

Volume VII of the *Railway Magazine* for 1900 reflects the contemporary fashion in describing the inaugural trip of a combined rail and river excursion from Paddington, which included a water-borne lunch and Henley dinner all for the price of one guinea. It was soon so well subscribed that from July it ran every single day throughout the rest of the summer season.

The popularity of boating was certainly not confined to the Thames valley and at coastal resorts particularly there was enormous business to be done in providing tourists with aquatic diversions which, in turn, employed hosts of watermen. In Morecambe, for instance, there were 99 licensed boat hirers and carriers in 1886 using 180 boats[96] and in Folkestone there were 88 boatmen hiring out 106 at two shillings apiece per hour.[97]

Even out-of-the-way places contrived to follow the fashion with Gills of St Neots in Cambridgeshire boasting of 120 visitors in 1904, each paying £5 for one week of boating,[98] and Huntingdon's official guide for 1922 promotes the river as 'the great attraction being picturesque and unvulgarised where Childs and Hall rent out all manner of craft'. In some places which were less than appropriate for boating, it was often the case that facilities were made available artificially: in one of the first municipal parks laid out in Birkenhead in 1844, there was a boating lake provided at the then enormous cost of over £2,000;[99] and the canalised pool at Brayford in Lincoln was utilised by three boat-hiring firms who supplied craft for the holiday crowds which were often three deep on the quaysides waiting to use the 'new whiffs and novelty canoes'.[100]

Titus Salt took advantage of the dammed mill stream to erect a public boathouse for the use of his employees in Bradford while Marshall Stevens, the first General Manager of the Manchester Ship Canal Company, formed the Trafford Park Estates Company to purchase the park and develop it by laying aside land for a golf course and letting the lake out for boating where it was possible 'to hire a boat for tuppence or thruppence an hour, either family boats or racing skiffs'.[101] During the 1880s, Southport actually built a boating lake adjacent to the sea so that visitors could enjoy non-tidal boating throughout the day and Fleetwood followed suit in 1924, while many local authorities included such facilities in their postwar plans like Hull council which had Ferens Lake dug in the city's new East Park.

After the First World War, during which much recreational activity had naturally been depressed, the business of boat hiring began to boom again and, for a few years at least, those firms that had survived the war enjoyed great prosperity. For some rowing clubs, this became a serious matter since their boatmen refused to continue hiring out to them at preferential terms when already oversubscribed with public demand at market rates and this situation encouraged many clubs to relocate;[102] others which were unable to do so either amalgamated with neighbouring clubs or simply went out of business altogether. During the late 1920s and 1930s fewer people took part in boating as other counter-attractions became available and its commercial influence declined commensurately.

However, the twin attractions of the Boat Race and Henley Regatta continue to promote an image of aquatic activity which is sufficiently commercial to entice wide patronage and profitable sponsorship, a success which is strenuously sought for other rowing activities by the Amateur Rowing Association.

The original protagonists of boat racing, the watermen themselves, had gradually found their activities exploited by various agencies and ultimately usurped completely by the burgeoning middle class. This take-over was occasioned by the rise of an amateur ethic in reaction to the growth of an overtly professional class of oarsman produced by the rise in commercial promotion of the sport which began during the 1830s. Although the era of professionalism lasted a mere fifty years before its closure by the strict application of amateur prohibitions, it represents a vital stage in the development of rowing, and it features as the subject of the following chapter.

NOTES

1. A. Metcalfe, 'Sport in Nineteenth Century England' (Unpublished paper, presented at 2nd symposium on history of sport, Banff, Alberta, 31 May 1971).
2. A. Metcalfe, 'Sport in Nineteenth Century England – An Interpretation' (Ph.D. University of Wisconsin, 1968).
3. Public Notice for Regatta on Keswick Lake, 1783.
4. *The Times* (4 June 1798), 4f.
5. E. Kenerley, *The Old Fishing Community of Poulton-le-Sands* (Lancaster Museum Monograph, 1982), p. 25.
6. Correspondence with Len Rey, Exeter Rowing Club (2 Sept. 1985).
7. *The Times* (25 Sept. 1823), 5c.
8. *The Times* (12 June 1823), 5d.
9. *The Times* (17 Aug. 1830), 3f.
10. W. Lennox, *Pictures of Sporting Life and Character* (Hurst & Blackett 1860), p. 72.
11. *Illustrated London News* (19 Aug. 1843), p. 22.
12. B. Harrison, *Drink and the Victorians* (Faber, 1971), p. 47.
13. *Boating* (Middlesbrough County Library, ref. 797.i).
14. *Norfolk News* (19 Aug. 1845), 7a.
15. J. Walsh, *Manual of British Rural Sports* (Routledge, 1856), p. 487.
16. *Preston Guardian* (22 July 1865), 5d.
17. *Newcastle Daily Chronicle* (2 Feb. 1863), 5c.
18. *Rochdale Observer* (6 April 1861), 2b.
19. *Barrow Herald* (22 June 1878), 2f.
20. *Newcastle Daily Chronicle* (23 Jan. 1885), 6a.
21. Minute book, *Quayside Aquatic Sports*, 'Review of 1885'.
22. *Gravesend Reporter* (19 Sept. 1830), 3c.

23. *Gravesend Chronology* for 1846 (Gravesend Library Service, 1980).
24. J. Walvin, *Beside the Seaside* (Allen Lane, 1978), p. 11. It may be appropriate at this point to indicate the close correlation between rail extension and regatta development. Early rail systems in the *north-west* explain the introduction in the 1840s of several regattas: Lancaster, Fleetwood, Preston, Southport, Manchester, Liverpool, Chester. Similarly in the *north-east*: Tynemouth, Ebchester, Durham, Stockton, Newcastle with both areas showing greater concentrations than elsewhere. The early *Thames Valley* line encouraged the events at Henley, Reading and Oxford and the *Birmingham and Gloucester* line assured the regattas at Tewkesbury, Worcester and Gloucester of substantial support. The *London and Birmingham* and *Great North of England* lines gave the events at Derby, Nottingham and York an accessibility which encouraged the attendance of competitors from every direction. The arrival of the rail connection inspired the promotion of boat racing in Exeter, Ipswich, Dover, Worthing and Talkin Tarn (Carlisle). *During the 1850s* rail spur lines and extensions were responsible for much regatta development. The *Lancaster–Carlisle* link brought Talkin Tarn regatta into the north-west circuit and many Manchester crews began competing there; a *spur to Littleborough* encouraged huge crowds at Hollingworth Lake regattas; *Berwick* regatta was inaugurated and received crews from north-eastern clubs; extensions to existing lines through *Bedford, Lincoln, Burton and Huntingdon* made the establishment of events a possibility by providing convenient boat transport for the first time; Kings Lynn and the Eau Brink Cut was established as a favourite venue for professional racing; suburban lines like that to *Kingston* encouraged the formation of club and regatta alike. New lines to outlying places such as *Whitby and Norwich* encouraged and facilitated the enlargement of existing events in quite spectacular fashion. Finally, the extension of the south-west line from *Exeter to Dartmouth and Plymouth* in 1859 allowed a much wider range of crews to attend Dartmouth and Teignmouth Regattas. *During the 1860s* even the smaller towns were being connected to the existing rail system, one effect of which was to bring them into the ambit of neighbouring regatta circuits; thus racing activities were established at St. Ives and St. Neots for the first time despite their proximity to other clubs. In the west a similar evolution occurred at Evesham, Bridgnorth and Stourport, while suburban extensions brought Walton, Staines and Molesey regattas on to the scene. The spur line into Bournemouth accounted for the new regatta there in 1865. The 1870s saw the completion of the rail network in all but the smallest details and the last places to be directly affected with regard to regatta development were Stratford-on-Avon in 1874 and the Isle of Wight in 1875.
25. *Liverpool Mercury* (22 Sept. 1843), 8d.
26. *Southport Visitor* (7 Sept. 1844), 6b.
27. Lancaster Rowing Club, minutes (20 Aug. 1842).
28. J. Sutton, 'Early Fleetwood' (M.Litt. Lancaster University, 1968).
29. C.L. Hardwick, *A History of the Borough of Preston* (Worthington, 1855).
30. *York Gazette* (14 Oct. 1843), 3a.
31. C.H. Feinstein, *York 1531–1981* (British Association, 1981).
32. *Yorkshire Gazette* (30 Sept. 1865), 3d.
33. *East Cumberland News* (20 Sept. 1843), quoted in *A History of Talkin Tarn Rowing Club* (TTARC, 1984).
34. *East Cumberland News* (27 Dec. 1899), 2e.
35. *Berwick Advertiser* (27 Aug. 1869), 4a.
36. J.P. Davidson, *Social Life in Whitby in the Nineteenth Century* (Waingate printers, Whitby, 1972).
37. *Whitby Times* (24 Aug. 1906), 2b.
38. *Goole Times* (18 July 1868), 5f.
39. *Leeds Mercury* (10 July 1874), 5c.
40. R.J. Davis, *Boating in Worcester in the Nineteenth Century* (Russell, Worcester, 1981), p. 5.

41. *Worcester Herald* (8 March 1890), 3c.
42. *Eddowes Shrewsbury Journal* (20 Aug. 1856), 4b.
43. *Shrewsbury Journal* (24 Aug. 1864), 5a.
44. *Evesham Journal* (19 June 1886), 8f.
45. W. Collins, *A Short History of Stratford on Avon Boat Club* (Boydon, S-o-A, 1974), p. 12.
46. *Lincoln Journal* (27 July 1869), 6f.
47. *Bedfordshire Times* (27 July 1876), 9a.
48. *Lynn Advertiser* (3 June 1865), 2b.
49. *Isle of Wight Observer* (25 Aug. 1877), 1b, c.
50. *South Coast Mercury* (20 Aug. 1892), 3a.
51. R. Church, *Economic and Social Change in a Midland Town: Victorian Nottingham 1815–1900* (Cass & Co, 1966), p. 103.
52. Nottingham City Regatta, minutes: secretary's report for 1909.
53. Hereford Regatta, minutes: note to subscribers, June 1909.
54. *Burton Daily Mail* (4 May 1920), 4a.
55. *Derby Daily Express* (16 July 1930), 10a.
56. *Manchester Guardian* (26 April 1946), 12c.
57. J. Chandos, *Boys Together – English Public Schools 1800–1864* (Hutchinson, 1984), p. 112.
58. Byrne and Churchill, *The Eton Book of the River* (Alden Blackwell, 1952), p. 23.
59. *The Times* (3 Dec. 1801), 3b.
60. *The Times* (31 May 1802), 3d.
61. *The Times* (1 Feb. 1804), 3b.
62. *The Times* (27 June 1804), 3f.
63. W. Lennox, *Pictures of Sporting Life and Character* (Hurst, Blackett, 1860).
64. *The Times* (23 July 1818), 4d.
65. *The Times* (19 June 1824), 4b.
66. *The Times* (4 Aug. 1824), 4c.
67. *The Times* (23 Aug. 1826), 4a.
68. *Bell's Life* (26 June 1831), 6a.
69. Wingfield Sculls, minute book: Rules for 1831.
70. *The Times* (30 Sept. 1829), 4c.
71. *The Times* (12 Nov. 1835), 4d.
72. *Bell's Life* (28 Sept. 1837), 4f.
73. *The Times* (15 July 1839), 4b.
74. *The Aquatic Oracle* (Simpkin & Marshall, 1852).
75. Cambridge University Boat Club, minutes (23 March 1829).
76. *Jackson's Oxford Journal* (11 June 1829).
77. Cambridge University Boat Club, minutes (17 Nov. 1831).
78. *The Times* (16 April 1840), 7e.
79. *The Times* (15 April 1841), 7a.
80. *The Times* (16 April 1859), 5c.
81. *Baily's Monthly Magazine of Sports and Pastimes* (April 1868).
82. *The Times* (6 April 1868), 5d.
83. B. Hayley, *The Healthy Body and Victorian Culture* (Harvard, 1978) p. 127.
84. C. Dickens, *The Dictionary of the Thames* (Macmillan, 1887), p. 86.
85. *The Times* (5 April 1927), 10a.
86. Henley Regatta, minutes (17 June 1880).
87. Henley Regatta, minutes (21 Dec. 1880).
88. *The Times* (17 June 1788), 4b.
89. Nautilus Crew, minutes (17 June 1855).
90. Letter in Nautilus Crew minutes (3 April 1858).
91. Boat builders and hirers established during the nineteenth century: Addy (Salford), Bowers (Putney), Biffens (Hammersmith), Barnsdall (Gravesend), Bells (Poulton

le Fylde), Browns (Durham), Cross (Cambridge), Coates (Chelsea), Chetham (Bedford), Crook (Preston), Childs (Huntingdon), Cooper (Ironbridge), Dowthwaites (Lancaster), Doo (St Ives), Ellis (Shrewsbury), Gross (Calstock), Gill (St Neots), Green (Chester), Hobbs (Henley), Jewitt (Gateshead), Jordan (Hereford), Jennings (Liverpool), Keightley (Boston), Leggott (Goole), Leggott (Ancholme), Leemings (Lancaster), Skevington (Gains-borough), Steers (Derby), Stott (Hollingworth Lake), Tolladay (Eton), Woodhouse (Maidenhead), Ward (Nottingham), Wards (Lincoln).

92. H.R. Pidgeon, *Memorial of Shrewsbury* (Eddowes, Salop, 1837), p. 15.
93. *Eddowes Shrewsbury Journal* (29 Sept. 1848), 7c.
94. Ryde Rowing Club, minutes (4 July 1878).
95. C. Dickens, *The Dictionary of the Thames*, advertising section (Macmillan, 1887).
96. *Lancaster and Morecambe District Directory* (Cook, Derby, 1899), p. 35.
97. *Parsons Directory of Folkestone* (Folkestone Herald, 1910), p. 7.
98. *Huntingdon and the Great Ouse, St. Neots and St. Ives* (Homeland Hand Books, 1905), p. 15.
99. Birkenhead Improvement Commission, minutes (23 Aug. 1844).
100. *Lincoln Gazette* (26 April 1867), 8c.
101. *Trafford Park 1896–1939* (Manchester Polytechnic, 1979), p. 26.
102. Midland Bank Rowing Club, minutes (20 April 1920).

4

Professionalism

Two men wi nae claes on pulling for bare life on lang
planks o' wood.

(Tyneside landlady, 1850)

The idea of receiving money for winning sporting contests dates at
least from the sixth century when Solon decreed that any Athenian
gaining victory at the Olympic Games should receive 500 drachmae.
Despite the truncated nature of the professional era in English
rowing, a professional attitude at least had been imbued in
the indigenous watermen from the seventeenth century onwards
through the involvement and patronage of the nobility and gentry.
In addition we have seen that both aristocracy and royalty had their
own barges and staffs of boatmen who were laid off work, unlike
other household staff, on those occasions when not required.

These occasions were quite frequent and often determined by river
conditions, such as the great winter freeze-ups or spring floods
which caused employers to take to the roads while the constantly
rising number of bridges made increasing numbers of watermen
redundant. Under these conditions it was usually desirable for watermen to derive some income from a variety of self-employment and
even at times of river icing they were ingenious enough to turn an
honest penny by using their 'tilts' as sledges.

Further supplementary income was gained in the form of boats,
silverware or cash as prizes provided by a host of commercial
entrepreneurs in a variety of boat-race promotions. Such activities
were certainly not restricted to the London area and rural contests
like those at Aldeburgh in Suffolk described in Thomas Crabbe's
poem of 1763, 'The Boat Race', were common throughout the
country and had been institutionalised in the Doggett's 'Coat and
Badge' race of 1715.

So it was that by the beginning of the nineteenth century,
the threefold influence of the rural sports tradition, gentlemen's
patronage and commercial exploitation had produced a class of

Wonders on the Deep; OR, *The most Exact Description of the Frozen* R I V E R *of* T H A M E S :

Also to what was Remarkably Observed thereon in the last great Frost, which began about the middle of *December*, 1683, and ended on the *8th* of *February* following. Together with a brief Chronicle of all the Memorable (strong) Frosts, for above 600 Years. And what happened in them to the Northern Kingdoms.

6. A seventeenth-century view of the frozen River Thames, showing resourceful watermen using their 'tilts' as sledges (*bottom right*).

59

watermen who were able and willing to derive financial benefit from any number of occupational and competitive aquatic activities. During the 1830s there was a plethora of wager matches sponsored by the gentlemen of newly formed boat clubs and featuring prominent local watermen, often picked for their racing prowess as shown in their own parochial events.

Sometimes these were between several contenders, such as that where we find the first mention of Robert Coombes who won a purse donated as 'an encouragement for industry and civility of conduct'[1] and at other times they were races against the clock similar to the 'Herculean Task' undertaken by John Williams who was backed to row from Richmond to Gravesend and back in twelve hours and did so for a purse of 500 sovereigns.[2] These events proved enormously successful as entertainments for the 'aquatic fancy' and their success led to the inauguration of the first professional sculling championship in 1831 when John Williams of Waterloo Bridge challenged Charles Campbell of Westminster for the sculling championship of the Thames.[3] This event later became known as the Championship of England and later still as the Championship of the World and its English winners were awarded the ceremonial distinction of being taken into royal service as oarsmen of the Royal Barge.

Gentlemen oarsmen also contended for prize funds in wager matches both separately and together with chosen watermen as partners and the distinction between professional and amateur was perceived to be one purely of class and not pecuniary benefit. However, as time wore on the classically educated gentlemen of the new boat clubs began to place a premium on rowing for the love of it while the watermen were forced by economic necessity to extend their pursuit of prize money. For the working man the concept of pure pleasure was difficult to comprehend in the face of the rigours and uncertainties associated with work and he followed in a long tradition of pragmatism which saw the lower social classes utilising their leisure more imaginatively and constructively than those above them.[4] Thus, when not officially at work, the waterman would always endeavour to earn extra income in whatever ways were open to him.

The new gentlemen's clubs sponsored racing among watermen and fostered the growth of a professional racing class throughout the country as at Warrington Regatta in May 1828 where a prize boat was offered to local watermen, at Dartmouth Regatta where the Regatta Club promoted professional four-oared races in 1834 and at Tewkesbury where the local boat club offered a 'handsome sum of money to be rowed for by Tewkesbury fishermen' in 1836,[5] while Leander Club in London was nurturing the talents of future champions like Robert Coombes and John Phelps in regular pair-oared matches.[6] Gentlemen also took to patronising the Doggett's Coat and Badge Race in increasing numbers, supplanting to a great extent its traditional working-class support, and we find for the first time substantial reports of the race which mention the hoards of supporters from the Guards Club and the variety of craft which followed the race up river, many filled with 'elegantly attired females'.[7]

At the same time, the commercial sponsorship continued and was sufficiently attractive to entice oarsmen from around the country on to the River Thames. At Wandsworth Regatta, 1833 for example, silver cups were presented by the White House Tavern in a contest between ten four-oared boats, one of which hailed from Newcastle-on-Tyne and was crewed by the Clasper family.[8] Such events were taken so seriously that injury and even death would result from over-exertion in the pursuit of a much-needed prize.[9]

The first gentlemen's boat clubs were those formed by the schools of Eton and Westminster in the late eighteenth century which followed many years of recreational rowing and were named not after the schools but the boats themselves. Thus we find mention of the Monarch Boat Club at Eton in 1793 and the Isis Club at Westminster a few years later although exact dating is impossible since the Westminster boat ledger only begins in 1813. Rowing at Westminster was disparaged by a succession of headmasters due to the drownings of pupils using the boats of local watermen. These were called in school slang 'funnies' – and the early 'Funny Club' derived its name from the term. It was a boating club of ex-Westminster pupils, probably formed towards the very end of the century, using watermen as coxes and coaches.

This habit of employing professional watermen became commonplace and almost certainly derives from the edict of 1788 laid down by the Westminster School headmaster to the effect that pupils should use rented boats only when accompanied by a waterman.[10] The ad hoc arrangements at the schools became organised into school boat clubs in 1813 at Westminster and 1816 at Eton College but past pupils had already formed the Funny Club and most likely the Guards Club for officers. We may suppose that they also had a hand in the establishment of the Star and Arrow clubs, names which probably derived from the Star dining room in Covent Garden, so called after the men of rank who ate there, which opened in 1774,[11] and the Robin Hood coffee house in St James Square, opened in 1789, whose sign featured a bow and arrow.[12]

College records would also suggest the influence of old Etonians on the formation of the earliest Oxford college boat club at Trinity in 1820 and of Westminsters on that of the earliest Cambridge club at Emmanuel in 1824. Meanwhile the London clubs, consisting of a few friends rowing regularly in jointly owned boats, operated from established boathouses of local watermen such as Searle of Lambeth from where the Star, Arrow and Funny clubs boated and which was frequented by Westminster scholars whose boat-club ledgers mention other 'clubs' such as the Fly in 1813, Defiance and Temple in 1817 and Eagle in 1824.

Generally regarded as the oldest established rowing club still in existence, the Leander Club claims 1818 for its beginning but, as its own published history relates, 'in all probability there never was an inaugural act and, if there was, no record of it remains' with the accepted date being established by cross-referencing various contemporary aquatic reports and deciding upon the earliest likely year of formation. Initially, the club boated from Searle's boathouse. Its coat of arms shows a star and arrow and so it seems reasonable to conclude that members of the Star and Arrow clubs occasionally rowed together in a boat called *Leander* and being competitively successful gradually coalesced into a club of that name. The name Leander could well have derived from the song 'Hero and Leander', popular among the river boatmen, the refrain of which would have been well known to anyone regularly out and about on the river, and would also have commended itself to the aquatic gentlemen of the day through its classical allusions.

The first rowing clubs or boat crews were hardly truly amateur since they made extensive use of watermen who served as trainers, coxes and often as stroke oars; at Eton College, for instance, it was not until 1828 that college boats appeared without watermen at stroke position or until 1837 without them as coxswains. For many years after this, it was common throughout the country for amateur clubs to procure the services of professional trainers in the preparation of crews for regattas. The new clubs continued to foster the professional side of the sport with ever larger funds, like that for the Grand Scullers Match promoted by the Red House Club at Battersea for 400 guineas; there was 'an assemblage of aquatic fancy equalled but never surpassed with two thousand spectators and two hundred boats present'.[13]

Only the day before, there had been a match in which the Guards

Club, coxed by a waterman, had rowed for a prize of 500 guineas from Vauxhall to Kew in a race followed by 'a vast number of four, six, eight and ten oared boats among them "Leander", "Corsair", "Emerald" etc., with many thousands of pounds changing hands'.[14] When viewing the situation in aquatics at this time, it is tempting to echo the Whig economist's definition of the working class as 'beasts of burden produced by nature for the purpose of being useful to the non-productive and consuming classes',[15] since they were used by the upper-class sportsmen for entertainment and profit, particularly when recruited to row alongside them in such matches as that between Captain Ross and Squire Osbaldstone for 300 guineas.[16]

All the early clubs were established as small subscription clubs for the purposes of wager racing and they used whatever means were available to them in order to win such matches. These included the employment of notorious professionals who were adept at devious steering and fouling manoeuvres such as Noulton of Lambeth and Parish of Westminster, both of whom were regularly used by the leading clubs. Leander Club particularly employed their services and its members were not even averse to making adjustments to their equipment to secure an advantage, as they did in a match for £1,000 against the Guards Club when they fixed 'a steel rudder of very light construction' which enabled them to win a 10 mile race in 1 hr 3 mins.[17]

Not surprisingly, Leander became well known as a winning club with a professional attitude to racing and so it was something of a shock for everyone that they lost to Cambridge University in 1837 and the *Morning Post* probably reflected contemporary sentiment in bemoaning the defeat of 'Leander the beautiful, Leander the brilliant which has stood above the foremost for years against every club on the river'.[18] The club put defeat down to the fact that, most uncharacteristically, they had agreed with Cambridge that the respective professional steersmen (Noulton and Parish) should refrain from fouling and the following year they challenged the university crew to a 'no-holds-barred' contest in which the same coxswains were given their heads. Leander won comprehensively by consistently forcing their opponents on to the river banks and moored barges throughout the match.

The Times' report of the race is instructive of the contemporary 'amateur' attitude towards the sport, giving nine column inches to a description of rowing as 'a sport which now ranks only inferior to the turf' and containing reference to the thousands of spectators on foot and horse, concluding without a hint of remonstrance that 'the science of fouling was developed in all its sense and the manoeuvring between the coxswains was splendid'.[19]

Until this time, the university clubs had themselves employed professional steersmen but following the Leander victory under less than satisfactory circumstances, the 1839 Varsity Boat Race was steered by amateurs for the first time 'in order to make the affair as even as possible; the attendance on the shore was the most extraordinary we ever witnessed on any occasion'.[20] However, the clubs continued to use professional coaches with Oxford using John Noulton and Cambridge, Robert Coombes. They also persevered with trial matches against professional crews who were paid for the purpose.[21]

Clubs outside London and not directly influenced by university precedent continued using watermen as coxswains during the 1830s and early 1840s, clubs such as the Gloucester Water Witch, Tewkesbury Sabrina, Norwich Rovers, Chester Cestria, Lancaster Red Rose and the Liverpool Crusader all of which promoted their own boat races. These races were between friends, usually for prizes consisting of engraved silver tankards or medallions, but during the 1840s, when the trend against the use of professionals finally reached the provinces, these races were gradually phased out to be replaced by inter-club races crewed entirely by amateurs.

Even when it was fashionable to despise the professional in his pursuit of prize money, there remained among the amateur ranks a residual professional attitude which was in no way thought to detract from amateur status: Lancaster Rowing Club accounts for 1845 show income of £20 derived from prize money while the volume on *Aquatics* penned by an amateur can boldly recommend, 'once having got the lead give your antagonist as much back water as you can as he follows in your wake',[22] and as the anti-professional fervour reached fever pitch in the 1860s and 1870s, many amateur clubs continued to follow financial inducements.

Nottingham Rowing Club came to an agreement with the neighbouring professional Trent Club to the effect that Trent might use Nottingham's facilities only on payment of half their race winnings.[23] Further up the river at Burton-on-Trent, the amateurs managed to prevail upon the local professional club to alter its name to avoid confusing potential gentlemen subscribers, thus increasing the amateur club's income,[24] and even well-known amateurs trained with professionals, as W.B. Woodgate did with Hoare in 1866. On these occasions not only did Woodgate pay Hoare, he also used their races for wagering. Although some objections were raised against his subsequent entry for the Diamond Sculls at Henley Regatta, they were overturned on the evidence of his membership of a bona fide amateur club.

Woodgate himself cites a similar case when racing in a pair-oared boat against a professional crew on a Kingston Regatta course, promising them £5 if they won and remarking 'that they never saw the way we went – I record these spins as records of what amateurs could do in my day'.[25] Amateurs continued to row with professionals for prize money as at Newcastle in May 1869 when Mr Taylor and Wallace rowed against Mr Gulston and Renforth in a 'novel match on the Tyne'.[26] They also took prize money themselves in so-called 'amateur' events like those at Bourne Regatta where the four-oared races had prizes of £6 each[27] with similar prizes being offered at Bradford-on-Avon Regatta in 1883.[28]

Even trophy presentations were not exempt from financial assessment since their value was sometimes questioned as in the case of a winning Evesham crew at the Bewdley Regatta of 1881 which contained a silversmith who revalued the prize trophy at well below the advertised figure and successfully sued the organising committee for the difference.[29] Such deviations from the amateur code were usually regarded as unimportant considerations for gentlemen whose very membership of an amateur club was deemed to excuse them.

For the professional watermen, it was a relatively short step from helping the gentleman amateur in his boating aspirations in wager matches to performing on their own in professional races at regattas often promoted by amateur clubs in conjunction with town or city authorities. Many Doggett Coat and Badge winners, like Searle and Phelps, set up boathouses during the eighteenth century which catered for the gentry but later became home to professionals where, for a time at least, the two classes co-existed amicably, and similar arrangements were to be found at boathouses attached to public houses such as the Red House at Battersea. The earliest professional personality was Jack Broughton who won the Coat and Badge in 1730 but later left the river altogether, setting up Broughton's Boxing Rooms and introducing a form of rules into the sport that earned him the title of 'Father of British Boxing'. For nearly 50 years, boxing was carried on in rowing clubs as off-season training along with 'pedestrianism'.

Before the eighteenth century, the gentry and watermen remained strictly apart as 'master' and 'man' but during this century they came together as joint participants in aquatics, a trend which strengthened in the first third of the nineteenth century, being typified by joint gentlemen/watermen crews, something which would have been quite unthinkable a century before. Subsequently, the novel growth of separate boat clubs for gentlemen and the denigration of professional practices led to a split between the classes which lasted until the 1950s.

This rift between gentlemen and professionals grew strongly from the late 1830s onwards and its most obvious manifestation was the introduction of a welter of different racing classifications evident in the programmes of Thames regattas of the time and spreading to the provinces in following years. So, for the first time, we see events at regattas like Chester in 1838 and Warrington in 1841, restricted to 'watermen', 'artisans', 'tradesmen's sons', 'apprentices' and so on with the purpose of shielding the 'gentleman amateur' from the heat of open contest.

The negative influence of ostracism combined with the positive effect of substantial prize funds produced a class of professional boat racers that determined the progress of rowing as a sport for fifty years between the 1830s and 1880s, during which time many professional clubs were established and many reputations made. It is not surprising that the first of these clubs sprang up in the larger conurbations of Salford and Newcastle during the 1840s, often referred to as the 'hungry forties', from the premises of boat hirers and publicans for the purposes of securing decent equipment and training facilities so that crews could successfully contest the money races at the many regional regattas.

The new breed of professionals lived and breathed boat racing and because they had access to good training waters, expert coaching and excellent equipment, much of which they made and constantly improved themselves, the leading crews and scullers often won considerable sums of money every season but none relied entirely upon race winnings for a livelihood, most being self-employed as boat-builders, hirers or publicans. The River Irwell in Salford was the centre for professional rowing in the north-west and produced many scullers and oarsmen who rowed throughout the country, men such as Dick and Mark Addy, Jack Parkinson, Harry Lang, Robert Dawes and Steve Butler, all of whom began rowing from boathouses attached to public houses on the river.

Mr Addy had taken over the Mary Ann boathouse near Victoria Bridge the year that Mark was born, in 1838, so that both he and his brother grew up among boats and boat-racing men; further down the river were Harry Lang's Fountain Inn and Steve Butler's Boat-house Inn, both of which attracted the general public for pleasure boating and some for racing, and the concentration of like-minded enthusiasts produced the first professional clubs – Shakespeare and Clarence – which raced at the early regional regattas at Lancaster, Chester and Liverpool, not without some success.

Initial success encouraged the boating men of the rivers Irwell and Medlock to establish their own regatta: in 1842 they inaugurated the Manchester and Salford Regatta Club whose boathouse was situated on the Manchester bank near the confluence of the two rivers and housed the 16 four-oared craft owned by the predominantly working-class membership. In a similar fashion, the tradition of professional racing on the River Tyne sprang from sculling races between working men, often colliers, shipwrights or foundrymen. These took place off the quayside in the town centre and were promoted by local public houses such as the Queen's Head, actually situated on the quay itself.

It was in these races that Harry Clasper first found prominence as a regular winner while still working as a 'keel-man' on the coal barges. The popular success of the events themselves led to the inaugural Tyne Regatta in 1834 by which time Harry, at the age of 23 years, was well known as a sculler and crew oarsman, having competed on the River Thames against the London professionals many times. By 1850 he was internationally famous and happily ensconced as owner of the very Queen's Head that first sponsored his career.

The aquatic activity following the first Tyne Regatta encouraged the formation of a local club, the Northern Rowing Club, and for many years the membership of all classes co-existed happily until the 1860s when amateur fervour split its ranks and produced an equivalent but purely amateur institution. The proliferation of regattas during the 1850s throughout the country promoted the establishment of further professional clubs in urban areas where the popularity of boat racing had produced regattas: the early racing in the 1830s on the River Derwent in Derby between crews from local firms such as Tardews Foundry had led to 'one-boat' crews such as the Arrow and Ariel, and in Nottingham the Trent Club was established to contend against them.

On the tideway in London and immediately upstream, the clubs were exclusively amateur, but further downstream past Greenwich we find the Argonaut Club in Blackwall catering for professionals along with those of the Phoenix and Nautilus on the River Lea. On the coast, the tradition of rowing for money had always been strong with Ann Glanville's crew of fisherwomen being but one of many trade-based crews racing for prize money at fishermen's regattas, but no established professional clubs are discernible other than the Isca Club in Exeter, mentioned in the preamble to Exeter Rowing Club minutes, and the Vulcan Club similarly noted in Bideford Rowing Club's reports and both placed in the 1830s.

There appear to have been no organised clubs on the south coast despite the rowing activity there. However, on the Yorkshire and Northumberland coasts we find clubs at Whitby, Scarborough, Staithes, Runswick, Bridlington and Hartlepool, which often contended with each other for substantial sums of money without ever leaving the area for competition elsewhere.

As we have seen, the earliest documented accounts of racing for money date from 1698 at Gravesend, closely followed by the Coat and Badge Race in 1715. The annual Greenwich Regatta, which involved racing for money, began in 1776[30] and so the London watermen were entirely used to professional competition, unlike those taking part in other areas who were often not trade professionals at all but, like Clasper, merely artisans who found they had a talent for racing boats. People such as this began racing in Derby on a regular professional basis off the central Derby Quay in the early 1830s and so too those who took part in the first Tyne Regatta, although the local newspaper report of the event maintained that 'the sons of the North are alike, pre-eminent for prowess, game and skill accustomed to aquatic exercise'[31] with fishermen competing in coble boats, salmon boats and even lifeboats.

Professional sculling on the River Thames had reached a stage of sophistication unparalleled elsewhere, due entirely to the influence and development of the Coat and Badge Race, and produced a professional championship as early as 1831, which was contested for many years by London men only, while Thames scullers like Harry Kelley would venture out of town to take on, and beat, provincial talent such as Buttle of Norwich, defeated by Kelley on the River Yare.[32] The prize money on the London river was usually higher than elsewhere and, in the early days, travelling extensively with a boat was prohibitively expensive and inconvenient, so London crews only contested 'away' matches when the purses were large enough to make it worth while, as with the Great Contest between Clyde and Thames rowers for £100 a side on the River Mersey in 1839, which the Londoners won before a pier head crammed with 'one moving mass of people' by dint of pulling longer strokes.[33]

The *Aquatic Oracle* of 1852 cites few matches outside London but does mention London crews at matches in Liverpool in 1840, Portsmouth in 1848 and Wakefield in 1850 while omitting the match in 1841 between Thames watermen and a Norwich crew on the River Yare which the Londoners won, due, it would seem, to a superior boat which was 'the most perfect specimen of a four oar ever seen in Norwich'.[34] At a weight of only 120 lb it must have underweighed the opposition craft by a huge amount. This underlines another advantage enjoyed by Thames-based oarsmen in the early years of national competition, since they received the benefit of many years' experience of building boats specifically designed for speed, whereas provincial crews continued to use craft basically designed for their original trade function.

This advantage was not to last as the Tyne boat-builders began to produce a new and much lighter style of craft during the 1840s. The first York Regatta held in 1843 only excited local interest with some Manchester and Newcastle scullers attending to contest the small cash prizes of £1 and £2[35] and the dominance of the south was consolidated for a while by the establishment in 1844 of the Thames National Regatta promoted by the local aquatic gentry for the encouragement of racing among professionals and patronised by the Queen, the French Emperor, the Belgian King and the Duke of Cambridge.[36]

This event showed how close the competition had become between the Newcastle men in the form of Clasper's crew and the London crew of Robert Coombes since the latter only won by a mere boat's length with the Geordie crew rowing a stroke 'peculiar to themselves', but one which was to revolutionise the sport in years to come as the best suited to the new smooth-skinned 'fine' boats being experimented with by the Tyneside builders. So keen did the gentlemen amateurs remain to encourage the professional side of the sport that a few days after the National Regatta a subscription was raised to promote a four-oared race for professional oarsmen at Henley Regatta in boats to be steered by gentlemen to avoid any unseemly fouling.[37]

This race remained a regular feature of the regatta until the middle 1850s when the stewards and fashionable public deemed it unsuitable. Later the same year, Coombes and Clasper raced off for the Championship of Tyne and Thames with Coombes winning and yet with Clasper's conduct being 'worthy of the highest commendation'. Not only had he skilfully produced a 'beautiful and well designed skiff which would do credit to any professional boat builder but throughout the race manfully contending for the prize'.[38]

While this level of racing was now current on the main rivers of the country there remained the races between working men, mechanics and fishermen that we find at Chester, Lancaster, Worcester and all the traditional venues for aquatic sport. We find professional four-oared racing in the south-west, particularly at Dartmouth Regatta and Teignmouth Regatta throughout the 1840s, but only between local crews, since the local rail network remained unconnected to the national system until 1859.

In the north of England where the system had been well developed from the earliest times there were regular excursion trains to take spectators to the great professional matches – such as that between Clasper and the River Clyde professional Carroll on the River Mersey in October 1845 and the 'Great Rowing Match on the Tyne' in 1846. This is particularly interesting for the special trains that were run from Newcastle and Redheugh stations 'on each side of the river to proceed alongside the boats in order to afford a public view of the contest throughout the race',[39] a facility afforded by buses at international regattas today and considered a real innovation.

This particular race between Newell, the Londoner, aged 36 and 10st 4lb, and Clasper, aged 35 and only 9st 3lb, created un-precedented interest with the crowds of spectators estimated at any-where between 50,000 and 100,000 strong; thousands of pedestrians abandoned the task of following the race and could not afford sixpence for the special train. *The Times*' report concluded that 'such a sight was perhaps never witnessed before in any part of the kingdom' and following Clasper's defeat 'the race terminated with-out a solitary cheer, the banks of coaly Tyne were dumb, enormous sums of money will have been won and lost'.[40]

Nevertheless, Clasper carried on experimenting and developing his boats and also spent great efforts on improving his oars which he shortened and deepened in order to maximise the area in contact with the water and so increase their propulsive power, and yet the Londoners continued to win in their lighter boats while using the old style watermen's 'fishtail' blades.[41]

The Royal Thames National Regatta suffered an early decline due to the difficulty in finding people willing to share the trouble and responsibility of organising what had become a leviathan event but it did have its success in attracting provincial crews to the River Thames in the early years. In 1849 it was staged with a 'view to encouraging emulation amongst all classes and, as an inducement to enter, the four oared races should be open to all crews and place money paid as "expenses"'. This relaxation of the stringent classification regulations indicates the unease which was felt on the River Thames that events elsewhere in the country were stealing a march on the southerners and that control of the sport was passing out of southern hands and into those of provincial and professional oarsmen and organisers.

Indeed, it did seem that the professionally organised matches between the well-known rowing personalities were taking over the sport, at least as far as popular support was concerned, and as rail transport spread and cheap excursion fares became more available such matches proliferated and events initially promoted by gentlemen's clubs were in danger of becoming top-heavy with professional entries. One of the motivating factors behind the establishment of the Thames National Regatta, and one disguised by publicly expressed sentiments of altruism, was the desire to syphon off the professional element from existing regattas and so establish a separate tradition which was clearly distinguishable from the gentlemanly activities.

This failed to materialise and the story of the following thirty years was one of marginalisation of the professional oarsman, at first by restricting his activity in regattas to ever more narrowly defined racing categories, and later by excluding him altogether. Thus, the relaxation of entry qualifications in 1849 must have caused much soul-searching and is indicative of the divided loyalties of many amateurs who felt that a strong professional tradition was possibly beneficial to the sport as a whole while at the same time wishing to keep it entirely separate from their own.

Even in the 1850s, most professional oarsmen were landsmen of various trades who raced for extra income and relatively few could expect to make a living out of the sport alone as did Coombes and Clasper. Typical of the majority of crews were those of the Lady of the Lake and Nautilus which rowed for £20 at Nottingham in 1852, and which comprised a builder, brewer, butcher, plumber and sundry other tradesmen who nevertheless produced 'one of the best contested races ever witnessed on this or any other river'.[42] Similar contests among landsmen's crews took place around the country during the 1850s usually following upon a tradition of ad hoc wager racing as at Stockton-on-Tees where annual regattas were held from Clarence Staithes to Newport and at Derby, which by 1860, due to its centrality and excellent rail connections, had become a centre for professional racing on a course extending from Fox's Wharf in the town centre out to Darley Grove in the immediate countryside.

The early regattas attracted top professional crews from New-castle, London and Manchester for prizes of £60 or so and the local crews of non-watermen stood little chance against them with the local press expressing the hope that 'in future some more stringent rules will be enforced to prevent crack crews from farming provincial prizes'.[43] It is not surprising that the last professional entry was accepted in 1863. The Great Northern Regatta which became known more simply as the Tyne Regatta had lapsed in 1846 due to the difficulty of raising prize money, but was re-established in 1851 by a few enthusiasts 'who adopted the several prizes with careful discrimination to the interests of all classes, gentlemen amateurs, landsmen and watermen'.[44]

This event, together with the Manchester and Salford Regatta, became the top fixture designed for a mixed entry which ranged from the purely amateur to 'crack' professional, with the ailing Thames National as the only event which concentrated upon profes-sional watermen. The presence of the Trent crew in Nottingham encouraged the attendance of other professionals from around the country at the August Bank Holiday regatta in 1858 with the sculling prize being one of Clasper's own boats valued at £30 and the four-oared event also worth £30 in cash and attracting entries from Gateshead with Matthew Taylor's crew, Newcastle with Clasper's crew, and Harry Ault's Shakespeare crew from Manchester. Ault's crew defeated Trent in a close final. So close was the result, that the Shakespeare crew offered the local crew an open challenge for the future:

> If the Nottingham Trent crew think that they would have any chance for the final heat at Derby, the Manchester crew will row them for fifty pounds and row at Nottingham without expenses or will stake fifty pounds against thirty pounds if they will row at Manchester.[45]

In this way, the network of professional contests grew, with each area producing crews and scullers who could contend for the prizes at regattas while side-betting considerable amounts of money on the results, encouraging a level of fixing and fouling which became unacceptable to many regatta committees who organised and promoted the racing.

Whatever the misgivings felt by such committees, it was still the case that amateurs continued to sponsor professional rowing by incorporating events in their regattas as at York, where the example of professional sculling between the Tyne champions Clasper, Chambers and Cooper was expected to give 'a stimulus to aquatic sports that will not only be lasting but will produce some first rate oarsmen'.[46] Highly respected figures on the amateur side of the sport like A.A. Casamajor, the London Rowing Club Wingfield and Diamond Sculls champion, supported the professionals by acting as umpires at matches such as that between Matthew Taylor of Gateshead and John Carroll of Glasgow in 1859.[47]

The professional scullers tended to attract greater attention than the crews, since their very individuality gave the media and public a greater chance of identification. Betting was simplified by recourse to past performances and present form would be followed by hoards of spectators on training sessions. Matches would be arranged almost in the form of elimination contests on the way to a national title and the professional traditions of rowing in English-speaking countries abroad meant that home-grown talent was soon contending against North American and Australian champions.

Robert Chambers, the natural successor to Harry Clasper, met Thomas Green of Australia on the River Tyne on 16 June 1863 for a match worth thousands of pounds in gambling money and the Championship of the Tyne. Commenting on the occasion, a free sheet of the day spelt out the changes in the sport when it boasted of 'half the world travelling o'er to lay wor Tyneside law, the tother half now may try an still we'll keep the craw, aw says aw'll lay me brass on Bob an work the winnin seam'.

Following Chambers' victory, there was a series of contests to find the national champion with the final elimination race between three contestants taking place at the Eau Brink Cut near Kings Lynn. At this match Harry Kelley beat Robert Chambers and Robert Cooper, thus re-asserting the prowess of the Thames, and went on to defeat Hamill of Canada for the Championship of the World in 1865, the first time that it was thus designated.

The affection in which many of the local champions were held can be gauged by the testimonial raised for Robert Cooper in January 1866 to compensate him for losing at the Kings Lynn match the previous year at which £100 was presented along with a golden salver engraved: 'with respect and sympathy for his disappointment'. Similar testimonials were not uncommon and would often be vital in supporting a losing oarsman who would have staked everything on victory and gained absolutely nothing for a creditable performance or genuine endeavour.

Most scullers would have financial backers, in Cooper's case this was Henry Barlow of the Cumberland Arms close by the quayside in Newcastle; they would cover training and living expenses in return for a substantial percentage of any winnings and, of course, the opportunity to make large sums through betting and match making apart from attracting, in the case of publicans, extra clientele anxious to rub shoulders with a national personality.

Oarsmen like Henry Clasper who had been successful enough through racing and boat-building to live comfortably were few and far between, while many could only supplement a meagre occupational income. This point was raised at Cooper's testimonial by a gentleman from Tyne Rowing Club, who, in denigrating those who talked of working class improvidence, cited the common Newcastle family situation of ten members living on 18s per week and commented 'as improvident in one week as many men would spend on one meal'.[48]

The top crews and scullers endeavoured to race as many times as possible in order to maximise their income. We find Mark Addy, for example, the 'Salford Hero', so-called from his life-saving exploits, rowing in the Shakespeare crew throughout the Midlands and North while sculling and winning against Thames champions in London for purses of £100 and £200. While still only 18 years of age in 1866 he beat May on the Putney championship course for £60; in 1867 he beat the ageing Coombes for £100; and in 1869 he beat William Sadler, the current Thames champion, for £200.

The *Rowing Almanack* of 1870 commented that the race ended in a 'practical walkover for the countryman with Sadler not having the slightest chance with him'. The Shakespeare crew would contest big money matches at Newcastle, Nottingham, Derby and so on but individual crew members would form their own combinations to race at the more local and parochial events. Yet even then it is noticeable that such crews would only compete where there were cash prizes available and avoid events which presented cups and trophies, however elaborate and expensive.

At the Aquatic and Athletic Festival at Hollingworth Lake near Rochdale in 1871, a magnificent trophy worth 30 guineas was on offer to the winning crew in the watermen's four-oared race and the organising committee was embarrassed to find it had no entry at all for the event. After much deliberation it offered cash prizes of £10 and £5 and immediately received six entries, with Addy's crew winning.[49]

The following year, he repeated this success but added the sculling title for good measure. Such regular weekly income during the racing season made the sport remarkably attractive for someone as talented as Mark who could take part in crew and sculling events with equal facility. It did, however, often encourage over-ambitious racing programmes as in 1870 when he entered the same festival, winning both events but losing both at the inaugural Bury Regatta only a few days later.

It is interesting to note that the stewards at Bury had restricted the racing categories more narrowly than was usual by denying the travelling professionals entry into the 'open' classification, one which would normally be regarded as a bonus after their designated professional' race had been contested. The stewards' move was designed to encourage a wider entry in that division than would normally be expected and serves as an example of the efforts made to restrict the activities of professional oarsmen to their own class alone.

Many such local events took place during the 1860s: at Stratford-on-Avon, where there were races between tradesmen rowers; at Ironbridge, where professional crews from Bewdley and Shrewsbury competed; in Leeds on the River Aire where there were Great Handicap Skiff Races 'open to all' with stakes of £20;[50] at Barrow on the Walney Channel, between local professional scullers such as Turvey who was the proprietor of the Bankfield Hotel and Strong, a local ferryman already successful on rivers Tyne and Thames; and at Lancaster, where 'immense concourses' of people assembled on the quay to witness local matches for £5 and £10.[51]

We find mention of other such parochial events at Sunderland, Huntingdon, Hastings, Cleethorpes, Deal and Dover. Indeed, the *Rowing Almanack* records around 250 similar matches for each year during the period 1865–69. Moreover, it is noticeable that the same publication includes for the first time the classification 'professional' in its racing categories for 1869, viz. A (Amateur), L (Landsman), P (Professional), V (Various), W (Waterman), W. App (Waterman's apprentice) and T (Tradesman).

Following the establishment of professional clubs and the tradition of rowing for money at practically all the existing regattas, including those of nominally amateur status, professional rowing and sculling enjoyed perhaps its most successful decade during the

1870s and it is instructive to note that it is also this period that witnessed a huge growth in the number of amateur clubs. Despite this, the club situation remained complicated for many years with the status of existing members being defined and re-defined as cultural mores changed throughout the late Victorian and Edwardian periods, fluctuations which encouraged the establishment of hosts of new clubs designed to meet new membership criteria and creating a massive fragmentation in the sport.

Such changes had already occurred on the River Thames with the new gentlemen's clubs at Putney formed during the 1840s and the establishment of the National Regatta for watermen in 1844, while areas such as Manchester and Newcastle still allowed a mingling of classes in clubs like the Northern Club on the River Tyne, which was established simply to cater for the local love of aquatics and without any particular membership qualification required. The club's annual regatta always seemed to be a great success embracing, as it continued to do, amateur and professional racing, drawing thousands of spectators down to the 'haughs' by Scotswood suspension bridge every year. It was financed by a combination of popular sponsorship raised around the local public houses and by individual patronage solicited from local gentry and businessmen.

However, even the Northern suffered from cultural fragmentation with some of the original gentlemen members becoming disenchanted with the overt professionalism and splitting off to form Tyne Amateur Rowing Club in 1852, with others leaving to form Tynemouth Rowing Club in 1867. On the other hand some of the club's 'crack' crews decided that the level of professional training was not high enough and left to form the ultra-professional Albion Club, also in 1867. The result was that the Tyneside scene became a cosmopolitan mixture of extremes soon to be supplemented by smaller firm and trade clubs such as Ryton, Blaydon, Walker and Armstrong which filled the gaps left by the specialist clubs.

Such separations became common in all the rowing venues around the country, encouraged by local economic and social conditions, and were positively approved and strengthened by the gentlemen's clubs and associations, culminating in the Amateur Rowing Association of 1882, which gradually squeezed out the professionals and tradesmen from participation in its regattas, with the result that alternative associations grew up to champion rowing for the working man.

Meanwhile, the spread and popularity of the professional sport seemed to know no bounds with the Leeds Regatta in 1874 attracting 'some of the best known men in the country' to its reedy and shallow lake venue,[52] and the Redcar and Staithes clubs competing on the North Sea for a prize of £200 in May 1873 while, on the River Thames, the local Sunbury watermen were 'stimulated by the success of events in the surrounding areas to inaugurate a regatta on Monday next',[53] an act calculated to upset the predominantly gentrified inhabitants and one which had long-term consequences for rowing in the area.

In 1877 the professional sculling championship had become such a media event that the owners of the *Newcastle Daily Chronicle* sponsored it as the 'Championship of England' and published full-page maps of the rowing course from the High Level Bridge to the Scotswood Suspension Bridge for the benefit of its readers. In later years, the *Sportsman* magazine took over the sponsorship, giving it a more national appeal, although it continued to be held, more often than not, on the Tyne even when a Thames champion was competing. Such a champion was Elliott who rowed Boyd, the northern champion from Blyth, in 1880 on the Scotswood course only to lose by a 'distance' to the local man whose prowess was rather chauvinistically described as a product of 'Tyneside's spirit of boat rowing which is inbred with the people'.[54]

The international aspect of the sculling championship and, indeed, of rowing generally had made headline news back in 1871 when the English champion, James Renforth, from Newcastle had taken his crew across to Canada to row for the unofficial world crew championship and had died in the race itself. The consequent outpourings of woe in the press must have brought news of the sport to practically every home. The *Newcastle Chronicle* spent 28 column inches on the disaster: 'Poor Renforth is dead, at first there was general astonishment in the city which has now settled down to the stupor of genuine sorrow'.[55] It followed this up with a further 24 inches on reporting his funeral which had been rescheduled for a Sunday so that working men could attend: 'The Champion Oarsman of the World was buried at Gateshead in the presence of one hundred and fifty thousand persons' and continued to explain how the coffin and hearse had special glass panels fitted, so 'great was the desire to take part in or witness the solemn occasion'.[56]

By 1880 the international sculling championship was attracting oarsmen from around the world and in November of that year an American company promoted an international regatta on the River Thames, which attracted a strong worldwide entry, viz.

7. Edward Hanlan of Toronto beating Elias Laycock of Sydney on 19 February 1881 for the World Sculling Championship. Notice the press launch and the umpires – one for each sculler – in the bows of the racing eights.

Hanlan (Toronto), Trickett (Sydney), Laycock (Sydney), Ross (New Brunswick), Elliott and Hawden (Newcastle), Nicholson (Stockton-on-Tees), Langan, Blackman and Clasper Jnr (Wandsworth), Anderson (Hammersmith), Feeley (Barrow-in-Furness), Hosmer (Boston, Maine), Riley (Saratoga, NY), Smith (Halifax, NS) and Gibson (Putney). As *The Times*' report implies, such events were, if not exactly common, then certainly not unusual, since the 'usual steamers will leave London Bridge to follow the proceedings'.[57]

English scullers were rarely successful, with Boyd being the last home-grown champion for many years, succeeded first by Hanlan of Canada and then by Beech of Australia who, during 1886, managed to amass winnings of £3,334,[58] indicating that the sport could easily support a high level of activity and involvement by those willing and able to commit themselves to the necessary rigours of training and travelling. The incentives became even greater when the purse for the World Championship alone reached £1,000 in 1889. Such prizes produced a super class of full-time racing professionals of a type quite alien to the British tradition of the oarsman who would race primarily as a sideline to his water trade or as a diversion from his landsman's occupation.

It was not until 1913 that Ernest Barry, a Doggett's winner in 1905, regained the Championship for England by adopting the lifestyle of his nearest foreign competitors, which included accepting £2,000 of sponsorship from the *Daily Mail* in the form of travelling expenses.

In the years before Barry's success, the rowing establishment had grown ever more apprehensive at the failure of the professional side of the sport to produce a champion, and a few of the larger London clubs promoted a new National Regatta in 1891, the object of which was to 'encourage professional rowing so that it should ultimately produce a man capable of winning back the sculling championship of the world'.[59] Not only does this seem rather perverse when the very same people and clubs had done all in their power, over the previous decade at least, to marginalise and extinguish the professional altogether but the manner in which they chose to do it was bound to lead to failure. They insisted that there should be no amalgamation of north and south country crews, no use of light racing boats of the type used in internationals and no use of lightweight coxswains, all of which served to keep racing standards down.

By the end of the century, the professional scene had been

reduced to a relatively few individual sculling matches for the English Championship, often retained by the same man for years at a time, and the remnants of professional events at amateur regattas. Most amateur regattas had dispensed with the professionals but some, such as Durham, Southampton, Tyne, Ironbridge and Gravesend, retained single events the prizes for which were a few pounds or in the form of vouchers redeemable at local shops. As the 'out and out' professional was marginalised by the new amateur establishment, many working men who had been accustomed to scull and form crews for pecuniary advantage joined the newly created trade-association rowing clubs and continued racing for prizes such as dessert services, sets of crockery, silver spoons and even sacks of oranges or potatoes.[60] Sculling handicaps, such as the Gateshead Christmas Handicap, were established to provide racing opportunities for the talented working man and some local clubs like Blyth, North Seaton and Cambois in the north-east continued to run club races for cash prizes.

The professionalisation of rowing had the effect of producing a racing elite amongst the watermen of England which in turn produced personalities whose popularity often remained after their racing careers were over. This enabled many to secure employment in coaching and training amateur club oarsmen; for example, as mentioned before, Noulton coached Oxford University Boat Club, Leander Club and Norwich crews due to his skill in steering and stroking a boat. Jack Walter of Gravesend won the local sculling match in 1828 and the family connection with the local regatta and club has been maintained by Harry Walter who won in 1874, 'Wag' Walter in 1897, and is represented today by Jim Walter, a lighterman, who coaches the Gravesend Amateur club. Harry Kelley, the professional sculling champion from the 1850s, was still busy coaching F.L. Playford for the amateur championship in 1879 and Tommy Randall prospered so well that he was able to present Oxford University Boat Club with a ceremonial chair constructed from a famous club boat and, through his aquatic connections, became father-in-law to Lord Stonier.

During the 1860s, club minutes tell the story of professional employment throughout the country with Harry Clasper's son John being taken on as coach and boatman to Derwent RC in Derby in 1864 and 1865, and James Renforth employed by Tynemouth RC being paid three guineas for two weeks' work in 1869, while Charlie Hartwell from the Thames was engaged as trainer by Bedford RC the same year, and Spence, a Glasgow professional, moved to

Berwick-on-Tweed RC. Many Oxbridge clubs re-engaged their local professionals in 1870, when the rule against watermen was rescinded on account of the difficulty experienced by the smaller colleges in finding suitable amateur coaches.

The 1870s saw Derwent RC employing Biffen from Hammersmith, paying him £15 10s for a month of coaching,[61] and another of Clasper's sons was engaged by them the following year. The Pengwern Club of Shrewsbury appointed Tom Hoare, the Thames National champion, as club professional in 1876; James Renforth's brother Stephen was employed by Stratford-on-Avon during 1880; Robert Coombe's grandson was taken on by Worcester RC as trainer in 1898 on the basis of 'two pounds ten shillings a week and ten shillings for every win';[62] in Hull, the rowing club used the Middlesbrough professional Jack Charney, as a 'trainer in scientific oarsmanship'.[63]

Once employed, the rule of these trainers was law, and Bideford RC minutes express the sentiments of all club committees when they warn 'all rowers that failure to obey the orders of the trainer will result in expulsion from the club'.[64] Many such 'ogres' became staunch friends of the clubs, like Jimmy Green of the Thames family of boatmen who was trainer and boatman to the Royal Chester Club for fifty years beginning in 1885.[65] Ernest Barry became so well known that he coached abroad for years and was, perhaps, the first in a tradition of thorough-going scientific coaches which finds its expression today in the extensive organisation of national rowing squads throughout the world.

Nowhere was the cult of personality fostered more than in the north-east of England, which boasted the preponderance of professionals, and we have seen how highly regarded were the local champions such as James Renforth, Robert Cooper, Robert Chambers and above all Harry Clasper whose 'patient industry, indomitable perseverance and laudable ambition represented the true elements of Northern character'.[66] Being regarded by their own people as heroes, such men found doors open to them at many levels in society, with Renforth in particular ending his short life in eminent social positions including one in the Central Masonic Lodge in Newcastle, due, one may suppose, to the sponsorship of his financial backers.

The local tradition of boat racing prompted popular songs about the sport and its characters – songs about Renforth's life and death appeared at the local music halls only a matter of days after his death.[67] The fervour with which boat racing was followed in the region led inevitably to a keenness of competition and level of games-manship which sometimes bordered on cheating, as 'books' were opened on each sculler in every heat and event. The better known scullers were seeded to reach finals under a handicapping system. Even today, stories of the lengths to which some competitors would go to ensure themselves an advantage are recalled, since the continuity of tradition has been retained through the Christmas Handicap which, although now defunct, still remains vivid in the memories of many in the north-east.

Hexham Boat Club has members who recall Jack Hopper, who worked in the local wool warehouse and who was sponsored by a Newcastle firm of bookmakers to enter the Handicap in 1922 under the name of Smith; he was heavily backed as an unseeded contestant, eventually repaying this interest handsomely by reaching the semi-final stages; a fine performance in an enormous field which contained fifty or so widely experienced scullers. Jack would recall to boat-club members[68] how competitors would indulge in a variety of tricks to de-stabilise opponents, including forcing nails into boat keels to alter smooth running, using razor blades in boat seams to open up leaks and inserting toothpicks under oar leathers to unbalance the blades in the water. Such 'tricks' must have been current in the region for many years since the Agecroft RC minute books recall a Manchester sculler hiding his sculling boat under haycocks and sleeping with his blades for fear of foul play.[69]

Hexham Boat Club had a tradition in the Christmas Handicap since another member, Jack Dodd, had won the event in 1905 from a field of 109 entries before a crowd reputedly 100,000 strong with most of Hexham having taken the 25-mile train journey to cheer on their man. The tale of Billy the Bull Whalloper is still told, explaining how he returned very drunk to Hexham after the race and was badly crushed against the town walls by a horse-drawn cart only to wake the next morning in hospital minus one leg shouting 'Dodd's won the Handicap'.

Men like Dodd and Hopper were among the last examples of a class of oarsman who straddled the amateur and professional codes belonging to bona fide amateur clubs but continuing to race for money. This tradition lasted longest in the north-east where the distinction between classes of oarsmen had always meant less than elsewhere, apart perhaps from the south-west which shared a similar sense of place, identity and isolation. Many of the professionals failed to consolidate their positions in the amateur clubs and, having no trade to fall back upon, suffered the fate of many ex-sportsmen in becoming seasonally unemployed in a range of unskilled occupations. Some managed to retain a connection with rowing as boathouse caretakers, cleaners and handymen, while others joined the growing ranks of vagrants, like Bristol Ariel Rowing Club's trainer of the 1890s, John Hobbs, who was last seen 'dressed in a seedy top hat and frock coat peddling Oxo cubes outside the main gate at Woolwich Arsenal',[70] in itself a poignant indication of the fluctuating fortunes of two professional sports.

No discussion of professional rowing would be complete without mention of the technical advances in boat and equipment construction which made racing such a dynamic activity involving not only competition but craftsmanship, industry and business sponsorship. The first boats specifically designed for speed were those built in Cornwall for the pilots who plied for trade by racing out to incoming ships. The craft they used were modified fishing cobles or 'gigs' which had been lengthened and narrowed by boat-builders on the rivers Fall and Tamar, particularly at yards such as those of Peters at St Mawes and Goss at Calstock. These yards had been building similar craft during the eighteenth century and produced even 'finer', that is narrower, craft, called 'flash boats' for local river gig racing, one of which, from Plymouth, was bought by Exeter College, Oxford in 1824 for college 'bump' racing.

This style of boat provided the initial racing design from which those of today have gradually evolved. Other early college boats were built by London builders such as Searle or by local boatyards like Cross in Cambridge and Davis & King in Oxford, who soon adapted their designs to the new influence, producing boats like that used by Oxford University in the first university Boat Race, which shows the unmistakable racing-gig style of high bow, low gunwales and stern, together with the greatest beam towards the bow.

There were no outriggers and the oarsmen would use the very long fishermen's sweep oars, which hardly varied in width from handle to blade and whose use would be facilitated by placing the oarsmen in alternately off-set positions so that each would retain the same space for his arm work and be pulling roughly the same poundage as the others. The seats or thwarts were static and, thus, all the work of propulsion lay in the strength of groin, back and arm muscles, together with the extent to which the crew could maintain an exaggerated forward and backward 'swing' from the waist in order to 'catch' the greatest arc of water with their blade tips. The idea of using outriggers to extend the fulcrum of the oar outwards and increase the blade poundage had been well understood for centuries

8. The original Oxford University boat of 1829 alongside its 1939 equivalent.

and utilised in the early days of Doggett's Coat and Badge Race, when extra baulks of wood were attached to the gunwales of competing wherries.

It was not until 1828 that the first relatively sophisticated wooden outriggers were fitted to a crew boat by Anthony Brown of Ouseburn-on-Tyne at a time when boat racing was becoming popular on the river. In the early boat, the oars were attached to a single thole pin on the gunwale or on the 'rigger, with a rope grommet which allowed the oar to come alongside the boat without dropping overboard'. This idea was utilised by one of the first lifeboat inspectors in the 1830s to invent a swivel rowlock a full century before they were generally adopted for racing boats, which used fixed wooden or metal 'gates', the open tops of which would be secured with leather thongs.

The first boat fitted with iron outriggers was the *Eagle* made by Frank Emmet of Dent's Hole-on-Tyne and for many years various regattas placed these craft in separate racing categories, classifying them as 'gigs' as opposed to the inrigged 'cutters'. Many clubs continued to use the old-fashioned, heavier craft until after 1846 when the outrigger was first used in crew racing on the River Thames, by which time their efficiency had been proved beyond doubt by northern crews at Thames National Regattas.

In addition to the outrigger, the north could lay claim to improvements in the oar since Harry Clasper spent much time and effort in producing what became known as 'Clasper sculls'. These replaced the old-style 'fish-tail' blades with new models shorter in the loom and wider in the blade, which were acclaimed as 'the best and finest model yet introduced for balance and width'.[71] Despite such innovations, northern crews were still at a disadvantage on the River Thames since their boats were substantially heavier than the southern equivalents.

The tradition of fast and light boats had passed from the south-west of England to Oxford and Cambridge and was taken up by London builders, who were already skilled in building racing craft but never travelled north, and it was only the defeat by Coombes's lighter boat at the National Regatta of 1844 that determined Clasper to experiment with new construction methods designed to produce a lighter craft still, with which to overcome the southerners.

All the original boats had been 'clinker'-built, i.e. with overlapping planks in the coastal manner in order to withstand rough seas and stony beaches, but such construction presented a larger than necessary surface area to the water and also set up a turbulence which positively retarded boat speed. Clasper, realising this, began building with adjacent planking while at the same time placing the keel inside the boat skin rather than outside, thus producing a totally smooth-skinned 'carvel'-built craft.

This new-style craft, the beam of which he had managed to reduce from the normal 3½ft down to 2ft by increasing the overall length while retaining stability by fitting substantial iron outriggers, revenged the previous year's defeat and beat Coombes's crew convincingly on the Thames in 1845. The new technique was used by Matthew Taylor of Gateshead in the construction of a smooth-skinned eight-oared boat for use by Royal Chester Rowing Club at the Henley Regatta of 1854, the success of which set the fashion for such boats nationally. London Rowing Club ordered one immediately and Taylor himself was taken on as trainer and boat-builder first by Oxford University and later by Eton College.

The outrigged boat of any description was only adopted slowly by the local, provincial clubs but when it was, the oarsmen took to it with a passion and most would echo the sentiments of a youthful member of the Nottingham Nautilus club in 1855 when, after his first outrigged outing, he fancied himself 'as safe and comfortable as in my other boat with less work to do for the same speed – it requires a faster stroke but will go well with practice'.[72] Clasper produced many such boats for club use throughout his life, selling them quite dearly at £12 each as late as 1868.[73]

Initially, the riggers were made of solid iron but in 1891, following technological improvements brought about by cycle manufacture, they became tubular with a consequent reduction in weight from 8lb to 3lb each and for this reason much of the internal wooden cross-bracing used in the boat hull was replaced with new tubular steel bracing. The introduction of outriggers into racing boats meant that there was no longer the necessity for crew positions to be offset as of old, since the rigger itself compensated for the variations in individual placements, with the result that boats became longer in order to accommodate 'in-line' rowing, in which so much individual 'state room' was required for the body swing and arm pull.

The next innovation was the sliding seat, the principle of which like that of the rigger had been well understood for many years, being used by professional Tyneside scullers from the earliest days of racing and consisting of allowing the whole body to move forwards on the fixed seat some three or four inches when catching the water at the beginning of the stroke, and backwards at the finish of the stroke. This manoeuvre effectively lengthened the stroke in the water by some eight inches or so and, assuming the oarsman had sufficient strength, he could send his boat along at a faster pace than his opponent while pulling fewer strokes and thus conserve his energy more efficiently over longer courses.

The first time that such a sliding principle was used in crew rowing was by the John O'Gaunt crew from Lancaster in the Stewards Cup at Henley Regatta in 1870. *Bell's Life* describes the experiment in not wholly complimentary terms, likening the crew's motion to 'a piston and a pair of scissors',[74] but by then Robert Chambers and other Tynesiders had perfected a working model sliding seat for use in sculling boats and used it as early as 1865 in the championship match with Kelley. The sliding-seat arrangements had been designed and manufactured by Adam Deas, a Gateshead sculler, and first introduced into crew boats in November 1871 in a four-oared race between the Tyne crews of Thomas Winship and Robert Chambers.

They were adopted by London Rowing Club and used by their crews at Henley in 1872 in the Stewards and Grand Challenge events, both of which they won. Thereafter 'as if by some pre-

THE WINNING "STROKE."

PUBLICAN. "'Ooray! Glad you've won, Sir."
DIZZY. " Thanks. I knew those SLIDING SEATS would upset 'em !"

9. Contemporary politics comment from *Punch*, 27 August 1869.

concerted movement, sliding seats became popular – in fact, all the rage'[75] – and so widely recognised, that the new sliding seats featured in contemporary political cartoons.

The first such seats used bone runners sliding on brass strips that needed so much oiling that trousers were ruined; they were soon replaced by glass and then polished gas piping, with wheels being introduced in 1885. These were designed to run along vulcanite grooves, a greatly modified version of which still exists today. The new seats found acceptance everywhere and certainly nowhere sooner than at Berwick Rowing Club which ordered a set of four from James Purves and Sons at a cost of £9 14s 2d as early as 1872, practically as soon as it was possible to buy them on the open market.[76]

Elsewhere, the demand for them depended upon the state of the local competition and the balance of advantage to be gained by fitting them. Most crews eventually decided that they did improve boat speed and they were fitted as a matter of course to all new boats by the turn of the century, by which time the brass lockable, swivel rowlock had also superseded the old-style fixed thole pins, although the university crews refrained from using them until the 1950s.

Many rowing traditionalists found the new equipment destructive of good style in that it encouraged a speed of action which detracted from the rhythm and smoothness necessary for efficient boat propulsion and yet experiment after experiment had proved that boats fitted with the new 'sliders' did go faster than those without, even when used by less efficient oarsmen. It is no doubt true that many amateurs denigrated all the innovations as products of professional experience. The arguments in favour of old-style 'amateur' rowing using fixed seats which demanded a hard 'catch' at the water using shoulders and body swing, against those advocating the new easy 'professional' style, which merely required a fast entry into the water followed by strong leg extension, rumbled on into the 1930s and were given free rein in a series of letters to *The Times* in 1933 which served to confirm the editor's opinion that rowing theory was always calculated to produce a 'controversy of almost theological fanaticism'.[77]

Such arguments are still common today in rowing circles and will undoubtedly continue for as long as boat racing exists but few realise that they, like many other current concerns, have their origins in a rowing tradition of which little is heard now. This tradition originated in aquatic rural sports and was developed primarily through noble patronage and commercial sponsorship so that professional tradesmen gradually evolved into professional competitors. By this time the tradition had produced folk heroes, a national network of boat-builders, worldwide international championships and a popular interest capable of selling hundreds of thousands of newspapers and bringing whole cities to a standstill.

That such enthusiasm could be engendered by an activity described by a Tyneside landlady as 'two men wi nae claes on pulling for bare life on lang planks o' wood'[78] may be difficult to credit but its effects were quite sufficient to produce a positive reaction from the gentlemen amateur. Gradually at first, but later with greater urgency, this class of oarsman began to distance itself from professionalism by concentrating on recreational boating and withdrawing into strictly amateur clubs. The tradition of boating for pleasure is old and, during the nineteenth century, led naturally to the establishment of clubs whose purpose was to encourage rowing for its own sake. The following chapter, therefore, deals with the development of recreational rowing as a prelude to a discussion of the amateur clubs.

NOTES

1. *The Times* (8 Sept. 1830), 3a.
2. *The Times* (14 Aug. 1932), 3c.
3. *The Times* (9 Sept. 1831), 2d.
4. For a full discussion of this phenomenon see D. Dunkerley, *Occupations and Society* (Routledge & Kegan Paul, 1975).
5. *Tewkesbury Yearly Register and Magazine* (21 Sept. 1835), 7a.
6. *The Times* (11 Aug. 1838), 5c.
7. *The Times* (2 Aug. 1840), 6b.
8. *The Times* (24 June 1833), 5c.
9. *The Times* (7 Aug. 1840), 6b.
10. *The Times* (21 Oct. 1788), 2b.
11. J. Timbs, *Clubs and Club Life in London* (Chatto & Windus, 1872), p. 67.
12. B. Lillywhite, *London Coffee House* (George Allen & Unwin, 1963), p. 50.
13. *The Times* (7 July 1829), 3c.
14. *The Times* (6 July 1829), 6a.
15. C. Edwards, *Blackwoods Edinburgh Review*, Vol. xxcii (1830), 561–2.
16. *The Times* (16 June 1830), 5a.
17. *Bell's Life* (4 July 1829), 4.
18. *Morning Post* (10 June 1837), 2b.
19. *The Times* (14 June 1838), 3c.
20. *The Times* (4 April 1839), 3d.
21. *The Times* (28 March 1849), 8a.
22. *Aquatics* by 'An Amateur' (Whittaker & Co., 1851), p. 28.
23. Nottingham Rowing Club, minutes (2 March 1836).
24. Burton Rowing Club, minutes (8 March 1865).
25. W.B. Woodgate, *Reminiscences of an Old Sportsman* (Eveleigh Nash, 1909), p. 87.

26. *British Rowing Almanack* (1870), Review of 1869.
27. Poole Rowing Club, minutes (21 Aug. 1873).
28. Bradford-On-Avon Rowing Club, minutes (21 Aug. 1883).
29. H.R. Smith, *Dark Blue and White – A History of Evesham Rowing Club* (Evesham Journal Press, 1948), p.31.
30. *Kent Mercury* (17 Aug. 1839), 5d.
31. Derwent Rowing Club, minutes, introduction to Book I.
32. *Norfolk News* (18 July 1839), 5d.
33. *The Times* (1 Nov. 1839), 5c.
34. *The Times* (26 Aug. 1841), 3d.
35. *Yorkshire Gazette* (14 Oct. 1843), 6a.
36. Royal Thames National Regatta, programme (23 June 1844).
37. *The Times* (27 June 1844), 7a.
38. *Illustrated London News* (28 Dec. 1844), 21.
39. Public Notice for the Newcastle and Carlisle Railway Co. (22 June 1846).
40. *The Times* (24 June 1846), 5a.
41. *The Times* (12 Aug. 1847), 3b.
42. *The Times* (7 May 1852), 5f.
43. *Derby Mercury* (29 July 1862), 6b.
44. *Northern Examiner* (25 Aug. 1854), 7c.
45. *Bell's Life* (3 July 1859), 11.
46. *Yorkshire Gazette* (30 Sept. 1865), 8a.
47. *Newcastle Courant* (22 April 1859), 5f.
48. *Newcastle Chronicle* (10 Jan. 1866), 7d.
49. *Rochdale Observer* (26 Aug. 1871), 4c.
50. Leeds Regatta Club programme (14 July 1868).
51. *Lancaster Guardian* (17 Oct. 1868), 5b.
52. *Leeds Mercury* (10 July 1874), 2f.
53. *Surrey Comet* (16 Sept. 1876), 7d.
54. *Newcastle Daily Journal* (10 Feb. 1880), 4a.
55. *Newcastle Chronicle* (24 Aug. 1871), 3a–c.
56. *Newcastle Chronicle* (11 Sept. 1871), 3a–c.
57. *The Times* (6 Nov. 1880), 6b.
58. Information from John Partridge, FRICS President of Derwent Rowing Club, based upon contemporary house prices. Further evidence of professional income follows with a career breakdown for three major contestants:
    Robert Coombes The London Champion, rarely ventured far from the River Thames unless it was very much worth his while. The London prize money was generally greater than elsewhere and 'away' matches were unpredictable on unfamiliar waters. *1835* 5 matches in London (£25); *1836* 1 match in London (£25); *1837* 2 matches in London (£20); *1838* 4 matches in London (£30); *1839* 5 matches in London (£30); *1840* 1 match in Liverpool and 1 in Le Havre (£200); *1841* 1 match in Greenock (£50); *1842* 1 match in Newcastle (£150), 1 in London (£50); *1843* 1 match in Le Havre (£10); *1844* 4 matches in London, Newcastle and Henley (£280); *1845* 4 matches in London (£200); *1846* 1 match in London (£100); *1847* 3 matches in London (£280); *1848* 1 match in London (£100); *1849* 1 match in London (£100); *1850* 1 match in London (£100); *1851* 1 match in London (£200); *1852* No winnings; *1853* 1 match in London (£100); *1854* and *1855* No winnings. *A career total in 20 years of £2,080.*
    Harry Clasper Although certainly not pre-eminent as a competitor during his rowing career, 'Our Harry' became a genuine folk hero in his own lifetime due to his tenacity and fairness as a racing man, together with his prowess as a boat-builder. His boats, or 'claspers', enjoyed huge popularity being sold from his several boatyards many years after his death by sons, sons-in-law and grandsons, the last of which, a coxed pair, were reputedly rowed in the Boston Marathon by a Derwent Rowing Club crew in 1956. *1841* 1 match in Durham (no win); *1842* Matches in Newcastle and South Shields

90

(£5); *1843* 5 matches in Newcastle (£100); *1844* 5 matches in London and Newcastle (£155); *1845* 5 matches in London, Liverpool and Newcastle (£300); *1846* 3 matches in Newcastle, Durham and Manchester (£135); *1847* 3 matches in Durham, London and Newcastle (£70); *1848* 4 matches in Durham and London (£150); *1849* 4 matches in London, Durham and Stockton-on-Tees (£140); *1850* 10 matches in Carlisle, Newcastle, Stockton, Manchester and Durham (£270); *1851* 6 matches in Henley, Carlisle, Newcastle and Durham (£85); *1852* 9 matches in Nottingham, Manchester, Carlisle and Chester (£190); *1853* 11 matches in London, Durham, Nottingham, Manchester, Chester and Glasgow (£280); *1854* 10 matches in Newcastle, Durham, Carlisle and London (£290); *1855* 4 matches in London (£20); *1856* 8 matches in Newcastle, Durham and London (£115); *1857* 3 matches in London and Manchester (£120); *1858* 4 matches in Durham, Newcastle, Glasgow and Loch Lomond (£370). *A career total in 18 years of £2,230.*

James Renforth Unlike his British predecessors, Renforth was lucky enough to be competing at the height of commercial interest in professional rowing. He was heavily sponsored by Newcastle backers and became the only 'home-grown' international superstar of the Victorian era, a fact amply reflected in his earnings. *1867* 5 matches in Newcastle (£300); *1868* 5 matches in Durham, Sunderland, Leeds, Chester and London (£210); *1869* 5 matches in Newcastle, Kings Lynn, Hull and London (£500); *1870* 3 matches in Lachine (Canada) and Newcastle (£1,400). *A career total in 4 years of £2,590.*

59. *British Rowing Almanack*, 1892 'Review'.
60. Conversation with Harry Read, Poplar, Blackwall and District Rowing Club, 15 Sept. 1985.
61. Derwent Rowing Club, account book 31 July 1872.
62. Worcester Rowing Club, minutes, AGM (March 1898).
63. Kingston-on-Hull Rowing Club, minutes (7 May 1893).
64. Bideford Rowing Club, minutes (20 May 1903).
65. *The Times*, Obituary (22 Oct. 1941), 12e.
66. W. Lawson, *Tyneside Celebrities* (Lawson, Newcastle, 1873), p. 74.
67. K. Gregson, *The Songs of Tyneside Boat Racing* (North East Labour History Bulletin, No. 16, 1982).
68. Conversation with John Bishop, Hexham Boat Club (15 Nov. 1985).
69. Agecroft Rowing Club, minutes (23 June 1939), referring to the 1880s.
70. 'Bristol Ariel R.C.', *Illustrated Bristol News* (July 1961), 20.
71. *Aquatics* by an Amateur (Whittaker & Co., 1851), p. 71.
72. Records of the Nautilus Crew (12 Aug. 1855).
73. Bradford Rowing Club, minutes (20 March 1868).
74. *Bell's Life* (20 July 1870), 15.
75. J. Jeffrey, *Rowing* (Dean & Co., 1897), p. 103.
76. Berwick-on-Tweed Rowing Club, minutes (11 Oct. 1872).
77. *The Times* (11 Jan. 1933), 13f.
78. K. Gregson, *The Songs of Tyneside Boat Racing* (North East Labour History Bulletin, No. 16, 1982).

5

Recreationalism

What can be more amusing than Searle's yard on a
fine Sunday morning? It's a Richmond tide, and
some dozen boats are preparing for the reception of
the parties who have engaged them.

(Charles Dickens, *Sketches by Boz* (1835), Ch. X)

Throughout the periods when trade, commercialism and professionalism dominated the rowing scene there was continual activity
in recreational boating which sought to minimise competition,
fostering the notion of taking to the water for pleasure alone. If we
are to believe Strutt then this tradition began when King Edgar
embarked on the River Dee in AD 983 since he alludes to the event
as a 'mere frolic' while, at the same time, accepting the evidence of
William of Malmesbury in concluding it to be the 'earliest record of
such a pastime'. Pepys' Diary often mentions parties of pleasure
boaters voyaging on the River Thames frequently making for the
Three Pigeons Inn at Brentford and Monsieur Misson describes the
many household barges as 'pleasure boats' in his *Memoirs and
Observations* of 1719, while Defoe, in his *Tour* of 1726, comments
on the habit of fashionable ladies of using the pleasure boats at
Hampton Court and the proliferation of such craft between London
Bridge and Blackwall.

The fashion for such boating among the wealthier classes is well
attested by William Hickey who commenced boating as a child at
Westminster School and in 1768 became one of the owners of an
eight-oared cutter which required the services of a 'waterman in rich
livery' as a steersman on the regular long rows in which the crew
tested their strength and stamina.[1] Like all fashions among the
genteel classes, that for pleasure boating soon waned and in 1773
Hickey maintained that 'rowing ceased to be the fashion and was
supplanted by sailing'.[2] However, the newly renovated Ranelagh
Gardens extended the vogue by incorporating a boating canal which
served as an aquatic Rotten Row for those inclined to use it, but by

1788 Ranelagh itself was 'fast on the decline and must soon make its exit from the circle of fashion'.[3]

By this time recreational boating had taken hold at Oxford and Cambridge universities, having been introduced there by ex-Westminsters and Etonians, but only on the desultory basis of undergraduates renting six-oared boats from local watermen to use as picnic transport, a habit which became so popular in Oxford that the Boathouse Tavern on Folly Bridge began renting out pleasure craft on a regular basis as did Cross from his boatyard in Cambridge. Such boats returning from a day out would vie with one another to be first back to the boatyard and thus a competitive element was introduced into an activity which ultimately became 'bump' racing in which winning boats make physical contact with those in front of them.

In the beginning, such racing was very informal with boats being rowed without their full complement of oarsmen and frequently under boat names in preference to college colours. Each boat continued to carry 'a tin panthermaticon containing all possible materials for a slap up pic-nic' and each steersman was 'equipped with a bugle to send notes of defiance to rival crews',[4] a situation which still prevailed in 1842 when Thomas Hughes described the bumps in *Tom Brown at Oxford* as a 'hurly burly of delirious joy'.

It was against this background that the first university Boat Race was suggested by Charles Wordsworth, who recalled the occasion many years later as only one of many 'trifling and insignificant' sporting events which he had helped to organise while at college,[5] explaining his involvement as the result of acquaintanceships with both Oxford and Cambridge undergraduates derived from inter-school cricket matches. Living in Cambridge and studying at Oxford, he used his schoolboy contacts to promote the first university cricket match, the success of which prompted him to suggest to his Cambridge friends the possibility of a boat race, an idea taken up enthusiastically and resulting in the initial verbal challenge to Oxford University Boat Club.

Not only does this explanation of events justify Wordsworth's inclusion in the Oxford crew though not a specialist oarsman; it also accounts, as he says, 'for the discontinuation of the cricket match and boat race for six years after I had taken my degree in 1830'[6] and indicates the purely recreational nature of such activities far removed from the 'professionalism' of their present-day counterparts.

From Charles Wordsworth at Oxford, we can turn to William

Wordsworth in Windermere where pleasure boating had recently caught on and which the poet featured in 'Rival Oars' of 1798 when describing friendly competition between boats 'sweeping along the plain of Windermere'; with similar recreational boating being common among the leisured classes, wherever suitable water was to be found, even to the extent that its popularity prompted the wealthier landowners to include boating lakes in the landscaping plans for their country houses.

Such 'genteel' boating had been customary from the early eighteenth century and consisted of rowing or sailing small craft carrying three or four persons; towards the end of the century, members of elite Liverpool society were to be found doing just this on the River Mersey[7] as part of a recreational life which would have included other activities such as cricket and bowls. The boating was consolidated into more formal occasions during the first half of the nineteenth century, although an increase in river traffic brought about a decline in pleasure boating as such and the venue changed from open river to Birkenhead Float, a sheltered inlet on the Wirral side of the river where the new industrial class hired out boats to row deep into the countryside. Such activity had become so popular by the 1870s that it was quite common to see 'scores of people pulling up the Float on a Saturday afternoon'.[8] On the other side of the water in Sefton, the local authority frowned upon the prospect of pleasure boating of any description with the local park regulations of 1864 stating that 'no boat, other than a model yacht, shall be allowed on any of the lakes without the specific permission of the corporation', an exclusion explained perhaps by the desire of a middle-class council to prevent the incursion of the rowdier elements of society who had begun to row as a rural relief from city drudgery.

No such exclusion was enforced at Birkenhead where the new park of 1844 featured a large boating lake boasting a magnificent boathouse costing £600 together with a wide range of pleasure craft for anyone paying a few pence.[9] In Manchester, the proletarian boating man had been well catered for since 1839 when Mary Ann's boathouse opened near Victoria Bridge, soon to be joined by many others on the River Irwell. The most significant of these was that run from the Standard Hotel by Jack Parkinson since it provided storage space for the racing craft of the semi-professionals while also housing the many pleasure boats used by the inn customers. The local tradition of pleasure boating was consolidated by the development of Pomona Gardens in the 1850s and of Trafford Park in the 1890s both of which catered for the casual boater.

So popular was boating that it was possible to see, at least until the First World War, 'three, four and even five hundred people on Trafford Park Lane on a Sunday afternoon'.[10] The interest it generated was so great that a local hirer, Will Crookes, thought it worth while to lease a shop on Deansgate for the whole of one summer to sell his range of canoes, sailing boats and rowing boats.[11] In Preston on the River Ribble, similar prosperity prompted John Crook, the local hirer, to join a consortium of businessmen in pressing for a weir 'for the retention of water at Avenham' so that his boating firm could continue to grow despite the onset of river silt[12] and James Sladen's fortunes at Hollingworth Lake had been founded on the huge influx of day-trippers using his boats, eventually allowing him to purchase the prestigious Beach Hotel, thus diversifying into other forms of entertainment.

In other central Lancashire towns, the authorities had provided parks with lakes and we find pleasure boating in fashion in the 1880s and 1890s at such exotic spots as Queens Park Lake in Blackburn and Roughlee Pleasure Gardens in Burnley. The latter town had provided its workers with boating opportunities since 1829 at Pendle Bottoms and on the local canal at Nelson House where Goodchilds hired out boats.

Elsewhere, the existence or provision of artificial waters encouraged recreational boating as in Nottingham where as early as 1780 William Elliott laid out a pleasure garden and boating lake for the people of the city, which was generally used by the more genteel class of person. This became redundant after the Enclosure Act of 1845, which facilitated the establishment of more central recreation grounds, and its lake was filled in to provide a railway siding for the new railway station. Ironically, the railway in Bedford actually stimulated the growth of pleasure boating in the town since, when it arrived in 1846, it took trade from the river carriers thus reducing water-borne traffic and allowing the expansion of boat hiring from Chetham's yard with demand producing first the yard of Goatley and Biffen and later that of Foster and Bryant.

Almost at the same time in 1842, the Severn Navigation Act was passed, allowing the construction of locks on this fast-flowing river which further encouraged the pleasure boating already well established by 'the young men of Shrewsbury School who generally give an annual gala in the month of June,[13] where racing played a very minor role compared to the 'great amount of eating, drinking and listening to bands'.[14]

This element at galas and regattas was mainly responsible for their huge popularity, as those who attended did so less to watch any aquatic activity than to eat, drink and be merry, to which may be added the factor of fashion which undoubtedly affected the fortunes of Henley Regatta, swamped as it was by hordes of water-borne picnickers who reduced the racing events to a mere sideshow.[15] The *Lock to Lock Times* for 5 July 1888 compared that day's influx of train excursionists travelling in to the regatta which numbered 6,768 with a normal Saturday's toll of 1,000; many would have strolled the few paces from the station around the corner to Hobbs' boatyard to hire some form of craft in which to disport themselves to the utter dismay of the regatta officials.

While steam trains promoted the spread of boating in this way, the steam launches were generally reviled as 'a terror to pleasure boats and a source of danger to all who row'[16] with the early Thames steamers of the 1840s and 1850s forcing many boating enthusiasts to seek calmer waters upstream at places like Kingston. Together with general crowding and water pollution, they were responsible for pushing some holiday trade off the river altogether and on to less congested streams like those at Huntingdon where there was blessed 'freedom from the great crowds one gets on the Thames'.[17]

Some organised rowing clubs took advantage of the fashion for pleasure boating by buying recreational craft and renting them out to augment club funds as did Talkin Tarn RC near Carlisle which, in 1907, raised £119 this way indicating some 9,000 casual users[18] while the Vectis club on the Isle of Wight made its boats available to holiday trippers by offering cheap temporary membership during the same year.[19] The success of this approach lends some support to Lady Bell's contention that there was at this time 'in all classes an increasing and often unreasonable demand for pleasure'.[20]

Although the First World War caused a substantial decline in boating activity, it re-asserted itself in the post-war period with a vigour suggesting a strong desire for normality and reflecting a change in its very nature from one of 'pleasure pure to one of pleasure as a rapid and restless escape from work in offices and shops'.[21]

This escape from the drudgery of long hours worked in shops, offices and factories had begun more than a century before with the help of several groups of well-meaning, middle-class people who were interested in cultivating the education and manners of the working class in order to facilitate a peaceful and ordered society. The first Mechanics' Institutes for working-class education were established in the early years of the nineteenth century, but being rather too academic failed to retain the interest of their pupils and were gradually subscribed by the emerging white-collar workers, while the prohibition of political discussion encouraged the true mechanic to espouse the overtly political and socialist Working Men's Associations.

By the 1840s, the Christian element of the Institutes had met the political element of the Associations in the form of the Christian Socialists, led by F.D. Maurice of King's College, London, who were committed to 'lifting up' the working man both morally and materially to which end they established various co-operative movements and, in 1848, the Working Men's College in Great Ormond Street. One of the features of the new organisation was its emphasis on sociability, so that tea parties and excursions were as great a part of the whole enterprise as academic study, with the element of recreation receiving particular attention in order to avoid what was thought to be 'intellectual priggism'.

Among the first college clubs to be formed was the Maurice Rowing Club, whose founder and leading light was Frederick Furnivall, a recent Cambridge graduate embarked upon a lifetime's task of compiling the definitive English dictionary and an amiable eccentric who experimented in rowing-boat construction while also organising trips up river for Mission Society children. He established regular Sunday picnic excursions from the club's Hammersmith boathouse to Canbury Island and was continually harassing people for donations to buy equipment,[22] much of which, in fact, he provided himself. For example, in 1904, being a fierce advocate of sculling as the purest form of the sport, he bought a fine eight-oared boat from New College, Oxford and converted it into the only known octuple sculler for use by the girls in the club.[23]

Whether through middle-class promotion or working-class emulation, many artisan clubs appeared throughout the country during the second half of the nineteenth century, such as those on the River Lea in north London and on the Isle of Dogs, where the inhabitants were 'admirers of muscular Christianity practising boat-racing, footracing and other athletic sports' combining such activities with the more rational recreation of playing in brass bands.[24] This combination of 'rational' and 'muscular' was quite common and in the greater Manchester area the Free Trade Hall concerts, together with innumerable brass bands and choral societies, existed alongside several working men's rowing clubs such as Ringley, Irwell and Ellesmere.

At Saltaire, near Bradford, Titus Salt's model village provided

10. Members of the Hammersmith Rowing Club for girls in the octuple sculler, steered by Frederick Furnivall in 1906.

ten societies including those for madrigal singing and brass bands but also a boathouse so that 'mill workers from Saltaire or Shipley, or shopmen and lasses out for the day could make the voyage to Hirst Mill and back.'[25] Elsewhere in the north of England, the rowing club at Talkin Tarn, already a strictly teetotal organisation, was joined by other facilities in Brampton like the Temperance Society, the Literary Society and the new Reading Rooms, all of which were deemed to promote a sober and industrious approach to life while over the fells in nearby Tynedale there had grown up many small rowing clubs, 'established for the commendable purpose of affording healthful recreation for hundreds of the local youth'.[26]

Much of the rowing activity of young men in the middle and later years of the century was promoted by their employers and given active support by existing clubs. In Oxford, for instance, the Albion Rowing Club was established by the drapery firm of Ellistons, and St John's College gave vital support to the fledgling working men's club of St Philip and St James by making available the college barge for its use.[27] The university itself had already sponsored the formation of the Oxford University and College Servants Rowing Club in 1850 in emulation of the Oxford University Boat Club which inaugurated an annual 'servants' race' between the universities.[28] Bathursts, the firm of boat-makers in Tewkesbury, sponsored the local regatta of the Working Men's Club in 1891, the success of which resulted in the inauguration of a rowing section[29] while the Worcester Rowing Club espoused the cause of local groups of aquatically inclined grocers who trained regularly at the club under the supervision of its professional trainer.[30]

Back in the 1850s, working men's rowing was, as we have seen, partly professional in origin, but at the same time, there existed purely recreational clubs such as that produced by the locomotive and carriage depot of the Shrewsbury and Hereford Railway which was 'set on foot entirely for the benefit and amusement of the employees'.[31]

It was just these reasons that determined Thomas Gradwell of the Barrow-in-Furness foundry to establish the Gradwell Rowing Club which became the Barrow Working Men's Rowing Club in 1876.[32] 'To develop the pastime of rowing between the different business houses of the city' was the avowed intention of the Norwich Rowing Association in 1898, which sought to regulate the boating of several 'house' clubs such as the Norwich Warehouse Company Club which had been formed in the 1880s simply to provide a healthy outdoor diversion for employees. Had it not been for such actions on the part of employers, it is quite likely that during a period when the social exclusivity of many sporting clubs was absolute, the employees would have found it almost impossible to participate in rowing.

In Bristol, for instance, the working man who wished to row was practically forced to do so in the dock areas since the pleasanter up-river locations were overutilised by the middle-class clubs[33] and even in Lincoln where the favourite summer pastime was boating 'which prevented our hard working sons of toil from public houses and dram shops', the artisans were required to show a degree of circumspection in the organisation of their regatta in order to avoid 'placing themselves in antagonism with the gentlemen of the rowing club whose countenance and assistance they hoped would be extended'.[34] Nevertheless, where there was adequate water and local industry, the working man did receive reasonable boating provision as on the River Trent at Burton where the large brewing families of Bass, Allsop and Worthington liberally patronised the working-class Trent Rowing Club and the local regattas while effectively bringing about the formation of Burton Rowing Club in 1863.[35]

Similar commercial backing for working-class rowing was provided by the Vulcan Engineering Works and the Royal Porcelain Company in Worcester, and even in a relatively sleepy market town like Evesham the formation and success of the local club owed much to the Smith family who established the *Evesham Journal* in 1862 and helped form the club in the following year, promoting it widely through its columns while also encouraging its own staff to take up the sport.[36]

This policy of encouraging healthy outdoor recreation led directly to the establishment of working men's rowing clubs throughout the country during the second half of the nineteenth century and was one symptom of the ethic of muscular Christianity, so well-learned and propagated by the public school and Oxbridge graduates who lent their support to this expansion of rowing.

Social philanthropy and aquatic zeal combined equally in the personality of John 'Rob Roy' MacGregor, an ex-Cambridge oarsman who was responsible both for establishing many 'ragged schools' for the hordes of London street children and for popularising rowing and canoeing through his adventurous river trips in Europe and beyond. As a Christian missionary, he spent much time in the East End of London and therefore joined the only gentlemen's rowing club in the region, the Curlew Club, whose minute books indicate his religious commitment, describing how he was moved to row down Blackwall Reach peddling Bibles to the local sailors, the sale of which, together with income from lecture tours and books, raised many thousands of pounds for his schools.

With men like Fred Furnivall and John McGregor active in the boating world, it seems clear that 'aquatics' during the 1860s and 1870s was, appropriately, very much in the main stream of philanthropic developments and their influence can be inferred from the *Rowing Almanack*'s contention in 1867 that the 'sport, despite unfavourable elements, has been fostered to no mean extent by the increased faith in the tenets of muscular Christianity'. However, contemporary Christian principles did not extend to welcoming the less privileged into the establishment fold; rather they tended towards the production of strictly separate institutions for working-class activities. This 'apartheid' strengthened with the formation of the Amateur Rowing Association in 1882, which obliged those excluded from the rowing scene to establish the National Amateur Rowing Association, among whose objectives was 'the promotion of the sport and recreation of rowing to all members of the community without prejudice to the generality of that object'.[37]

The Christian ethic became very deeply imbued in the sport of rowing at club level throughout the country, being disseminated and consolidated by seemingly endless supplies of ordained oarsmen coming down from Oxford and Cambridge colleges, settling into their new parishes and preaching a combination of rowing technique and religious virtue.[38]

The Reverend Dr Mackinder of Gainsborough Rowing Club spoke in 1875 of boating as 'productive of high physical development, strong moral courage and highly cultivated mental activity', creating a 'sportsmen's spirit'. Further reference to this was made by Reverend Whincup nearly fifty years later at Bradford Rowing Club on the occasion of the unveiling of the club's war memorial, when he remarked that the fallen had 'gone forward in the sportsmen's spirit like Our Lord, for the war was a sportsmen's game and our men played it even with our enemies'.[39]

During the 1850s the Norwich Rowing scene was so full of ordained activists that a popular poem of the time was used to describe various local races: 'A Canon to the right of them, a Canon to the left of them ...' while in Evesham one of the rowing club's three ordained committee men of 1882 was moved to remark that 'Mother Church has shown her wisdom in giving this sport her blessing and her sons have been wise in becoming its devotees'.[40]

The practical application of the Christian principle continued to find expression in the rowing world well into the 1930s when the Deal and Walmer Rowing Club was formed expressly to 'do something to keep the lads off street corners'[41] and Ian Fairbairn was allowed by the Henley Stewards to erect a tent in the regatta enclosure for his Working Boys' Rowing Club.[42] Despite this, the principle of separate development continued to produce the 'in-house' regattas of those classes excluded from establishment events, regattas such as the Victoria House Regatta of Sayles and Company in Cambridge[43] and the London Transport events held regularly until the 1950s.[44]

Another effect of the large Christian involvement in the sport was the almost universal application of the 'No Sunday Boating' rule which was quite in tune with the early humanitarian Christian movement which made strenuous efforts to remodel traditional leisure patterns with the establishment of the RSPCA in 1824, the Temperance Movement in 1829 and the Lord's Day Observance Society in 1831. The Society for the Suppression of Vice had already turned its attention to aquatics in condemning the 'shameful practice of rowing machines and boat races on a Sunday',[45] but middle-class attempts to impose its religious and domestic culture on the rest of the country stirred up controversies that influenced important areas of political, religious and social life and certainly affected rowing.

For most working people, even after the reduction of Saturday working hours, Sunday was the only time in the week when they were completely free to indulge in recreational activity, with the 'Sunday' rule effectively banning them from organised club boating and, while this was no problem for the gentlemen's club, it did pose serious problems for those with more cosmopolitan memberships. At Nottingham Rowing Club, which had grown from the trade-based Nautilus Club into a thoroughly middle-class association, the 1862 constitution includes the 'Sunday' rule but also makes provision for the payment of subscriptions by instalments, presumably to cater for a section of the membership on weekly wages;[46] by 1894 this section had grown to be a large and vociferous group who demanded to row on Sunday and openly flouted the prohibition.

The committee naturally took steps to discipline them, demanding an apology which was not forthcoming; consequently, the members concerned resigned from the club in disgust and formed themselves into the Nottingham Boat Club with the emphasis clearly on the recreational side of the sport – Sunday pleasure trips and picnics being high on the list of priorities. Fortunately for posterity and the world of art, one of the club's founder members was Arthur Spooner who recorded the 'First Sunday Outing' on canvas, the sale of which in 1984 for £90,000 at Christie's happily served to secure the club's future which had, at that time, looked uncertain.

Elsewhere, similar dissensions were expressed: the Eton

Excelsior Club actually rescinded their 'Sunday' rule in May 1885, only to be forced to reapply it in June by Eton College, their new landlords, who refused to make any premises available if Sunday boating was allowed; and at the Ancholme Rowing Club in Brigg, the rule was carried only after 'a long and animated discussion'.[47] Quite often the rule prohibiting Sunday activity would be appended to another banning racing for money, as at Nottingham and Bradford where 'no match or race for money amongst members shall be permitted on any pretence whatever'.[48]

This association lends credence to the view that many club committees regarded both forms of activity as somehow unsporting, unChristian and downright unBritish. Although the rule was strictly enforced (witness the expulsion of a Derby Rowing Club member for taking out a boat on the Sabbath),[49] as the end of the century approached it was generally relaxed as more people demanded access to club pleasure craft and many clubs like that at Ancholme allowed pleasure trips but continued to prohibit the use of racing boats for training purposes.

In areas such as the north-east and north-west of England, where there was a tradition of working class membership, the rule was never rigorously applied, although some clubs like Cambois on the Northumberland coast frowned upon Sunday outings which lasted beyond tea-time – but even this condition was withdrawn in the 1920s.[50] Similarly, the rule was being relaxed in the Methodist south-west of England with Poole Rowing Club allowing Sunday boating for the first time in 1920.[51]

The Victorian vogue for boating had various manifestations, one of which was the long river trip immortalised by Jerome K. Jerome in *Three Men in a Boat* (1889), but such tours had been common-place from the 1840s onwards, with the *Norfolk News*, for example, mentioning the feat of two Norwich Rowing Club members in rowing the River Seine in the summer of 1847. Many appetites for such adventure would have been whetted by the publicity surrounding the building and transportation of the new 40ft *Challenger* lifeboat, constructed in Manchester and rowed around the coast and up the River Thames in 1852.

The *Field* began to publish accounts of long touring trips throughout the country as with the 'Boating Tour through the West of England undertaken by Mr Proprietor, Mr Contrary and Mr Enthusiast',[52] while local papers recounted parochial tours such as that of boat-club enthusiasts on a round trip from Lincoln via Gainsborough, York and Hull, a distance of 270 miles.[53]

The fashion for such adventures was given great impetus by John MacGregor who published accounts of his canoe trips in Europe (1865), Scandinavia (1866) and the Middle East (1868) and it is hardly surprising that the *Rowing Almanack* for 1870 incorporated a 'touring information' section for guidance 'when undertaking those agreeable and invigorating tours by water which have become generally popular'. Such trips were purely for pleasure, certainly lacking the austerity of MacGregor's tours, and by the 1880s whole families would embark on the Oxford–London trip using the capacious Thames skiffs specially modified for camping. Otherwise, they would use the conveniently sited riverside hotels, mentioned in the *Dictionary of the Thames* written in 1887 by Charles Dickens Junior, which catered for passengers from the river which 'swarms with boats for four months on end'.

This contention is amply justified by the Thames Conservancy figures for 1898 which show 10,482 pleasure boats registered and 257,307 lock tickets sold. Many clubs up and down the country would organise such touring trips partly as social events and partly as tougheners for their regular oarsmen. Events like Bradford Rowing Club's 'Ousers', which were long rows on nearby rivers such as the Ouse, Wharfe and Derwent, became annual institutions taken together with marathon rows for established crews over courses like Shrewsbury to Worcester and Ruabon to Chester.[54]

Kingston Rowing Club in Hull used similar methods in organising excursions to Driffield, and Selby and Cygnet Rowing Club at Chiswick planned no fewer than 13 up-river trips during the 1890 season, including a three-day tour, while Ryde Rowing Club had the incentive of 'Round the Island' rows to keep them up to scratch, with the record times gradually lowered from 24 hours in 1885 to 10 hours in 1901 and 8 hours in 1964.

As indicated earlier, the rowing at Oxford and Cambridge universities began on a very lighthearted note with the early racing reflecting a long tradition of pleasure boating among the leisured classes, and this exclusively recreational element featured prominently in events around the country which owed more to the fun fair than to serious boat racing. Despite the prejudice felt by some sections of the community against aquatic amusements 'as having an immoral tendency',[55] regattas such as that at Bedford established themselves in the 1850s as a combination of bucolic diversion and genteel pastime which included 'races' commencing at 1.30 in the afternoon and finishing at 5.00,[56] and even Henley Regatta Stewards resolved in 1867 to add some spice to the programme by including a 'land and water canoe race'.[57]

Much of the entertainment available at such events was reminiscent of the rural sports of a century before, with the Ironbridge fêtes of the 1860s providing races for coracles as well as coxed fours; Leeds Fair of 1868 featuring canoe races 'open to all', counterbalancing the professional sculling competition; Poole Aquatic Sports of 1873 sponsoring an aquatic tug of war called 'French and English'; and the Lancaster Quay Sports of 1884 soliciting entries for a 'tub race in casks'.

In country areas, the regattas were a welcome relief from rural monotony and were often promoted in conjunction with other similar diversions like the gymkhanas and Pierrot troupes at Hereford[58] and the flower shows at Evesham regattas where competitors were no more or less than 'duffers whose oars went like the sails of a windmill nearly swamping everybody with the splashing they made'.[59]

During the 1880s and 1890s regatta committees endeavoured to provide 'illuminated processions' or 'Venetian fêtes' to crown the day's festivities as they did at Hampton Court Aquatic Sports in 1888 where 200 illuminated boats took part, with the music being supplied by a military band ensconced on a floating stage, itself festooned with over 600 coloured lanterns. The *Lock to Lock Times* of 24 August 1888 describes possibly the ideal event at Sunbury-on-Thames with its 'cloudless skies, charming costumes, splendid music, good rowing, capital punting, illuminated lanterns and unsurpassed fireworks'.

A particular novelty at this time at River Thames regattas was Dongola racing, named after the flat-bottomed punts used by Lord Wolseley to carry soldiers and supplies en route to relieve General Gordon in the Sudan in 1885. The punts were designed for the shallow River Nile cataracts of Dongola province and were paddled rather than poled, with Wolseley offering £100 to the first battalion to complete the journey in what *The Times* called the 'longest boat race in history'.[60] Dongola racing soon caught on at upper Thames regattas with most events staging a mixed-sex race as a concluding attraction to the day's entertainment which, together with a fashion for 'swanning around' in Venetian Gondolas and pedalling the new fangled water cycle, presented ample opportunity for aquatic society, or what Furnivall called 'the riparian smart set', to indulge their fancy for the exotic.[61]

11. Edwardian eccentricity exemplified by Mr Rowell and his water cycle on the River Ouse at St Ives, 1910.

Perhaps it is not too surprising to relate that such recreational events met with more than a little disapproval from certain quarters since their lack of regulation created great difficulties for organisers, most of whom lived close to the river and worked in the City of London. Gradually, their influence established a serious side to pleasure boating in the inauguration of a skiff championship in 1891 where the traditional touring skiffs were raced in a variety of double sculling pairings. This development inevitably encouraged the 'pseudo-amateur' whose participation was responsible for the formation, at Anderton's Hotel in Fleet Street in 1901, of the Skiff Racing Association 'to maintain the standard of Amateur sport in skiff and kindred races' at five upper Thames regattas.[62]

One of the most important results of the late-Victorian fashion for boating was the introduction of women to aquatics on a significant scale. Before this time the participation of women had been restricted to those working in water trades who regularly took part in rural sports, as at Poulton, Chester and Saltash, or as genteel passengers on picnic trips, for it was the accepted mid-Victorian wisdom that women could not sustain the effort of maturing physically while indulging in strenuous mental or physical activity.[63]

The entry of women to competitive rowing took place at a time when they were achieving intellectual and political emancipation with the Women's Property Act of 1870 and the Matrimonial Causes Act of 1878, and their involvement in racing first occurred in country house crews formed to contest the novelty scratch races at neighbouring venues like Cookham, Wargrave and Marlow, with the first ladies' eight recorded at Wargrave Regatta in 1878.

By 1880 Lady Grenville could write in her *Gentlewomen's Book of Sports* that it was 'essential that every English girl should learn to row since now that everything is changed it is seen to be the very best thing for her' and the upper-class English girl was further encouraged in her rowing at the new colleges for women, particularly Somerville and Lady Margaret Hall in Oxford. Both established boat clubs in 1884 primarily for recreational purposes and the activity was made conditional upon bye-laws which became enshrined in the first rules of the Oxford University Women's Boat Club in 1906, namely:

Rule 1: Young ladies shall take their outings at such times that they do not encounter gentlemen's crews.

Rule 2: They shall have a draw string in their skirt hems so that no ankle is exposed.

Rule 3: If coaching by a gentleman is desired leave must be

obtained from their moral tutors and a gentleman cox must act as a chaperone.

Such rules might be considered over-protective and yet there were occasions at boat clubs when similar regulations might have prevented much unpleasantness; witness the following correspondence culled from the minute books of Bradford-on-Avon Rowing Club:

> There have been rumours going on lately that my daughter (who is now completely ruined) first met her downfall by being enticed to the boathouse ... the boathouse has obviously been used for immoral purposes ... please make it impossible for it to be so used again.[64]

Many club records reveal that committees frequently administered prohibitions to members concerning the use of pleasure craft for the purposes of 'canoodling', a word itself derived from 'canoe' and, without doubt, the freedoms enjoyed in recreational boating did much to foster the mingling of the sexes. The college authorities, therefore, did have some justification for circumspection in relation to pleasure boating but they also refused to sanction any form of competition which was regarded as 'unladylike'.

The new ladies' clubs had to satisfy themselves with time-trialling and rowing for 'style points', a situation which prevailed until the 1920s, but outside the colleges 'the fair sex took to racing at the frequent skiff regattas for which rigorous training is unnecessary'.[65] Before the First World War there was a sprinkling of open ladies' clubs: Clapton Ladies and Cecil Ladies clubs on the River Lea in north London, Derby Ladies Rowing Club and Warwick Ladies Boating Club, which supplemented the competitive involvement of watermen's daughters like those at the Falcon and Neptune clubs in Oxford who had, since 1869, rowed at regattas despite being 'hampered by tight lacing and long skirts'.[66]

The First World War freed many women from earlier restraints, making it possible to take part in 'men-only' activities with many 'Victory Regattas', featuring ladies' races in four-oared boats, most significantly those at Weybridge Regatta in 1919 which attracted four serious entries and resulted in the establishment of a ladies' section at Weybridge Rowing Club in 1920 and a separate club for ladies in 1925. By 1927 the number of clubs in the Thames region, together with those from Reading, London, Oxford and Cambridge universities, was sufficient to hold a timed race for eight-oared boats on the Putney to Mortlake course. The great success of this encouraged the formation of Alpha Ladies Rowing Club at Chiswick, but, more importantly, opened the eyes of many male rowers to the viability of women's rowing which was further confirmed by the success of Amy Gentry's crew at Ostend Regatta in 1930, eighty years after Ann Glanville's Saltash crew took the prize at Le Havre Regatta.

Despite the lead set by the south, the majority of ladies' rowing remained purely recreational with only a few provincial regattas incorporating 'serious' races for them while most would include 'novelty' races only, such as that sponsored by Rowntrees at the York Regatta of 1922. Following the failure of the clubs at Derby and Warwick, no further clubs or sections were formed until the 1950s, despite isolated pockets of enthusiasm such as those at Bewdley Rowing Club which turned out a succession of ladies' crews from 1936 onwards and at Dartmouth where women's rowing started in the same year, even though 'women were not allowed in the boathouse and the men carried the boats in and out for them'.[67]

The progress of rowing for women was undoubtedly hampered by the male establishment view that it was unbecoming and likely to result in a deterioration in club discipline, and ladies were often barred from attending even social occasions such as the annual 'water parties' held by Cambridge Town Rowing Club with club members voting unanimously that 'ladies not be invited'.[68] Although the Derby Ladies Club flourished for a few years during the Edwardian period, it made the mistake of taking a hut immediately below the Derwent Rowing Club boathouse and using 'their' stretch of water so that 'serious' rowing at Derwent was dislocated, with club officers considering that 'it would have been conducive to better rowing on the ladies' part (and on D.R.C. members) had they located themselves elsewhere'.[69]

The inevitable result was that the ladies were eventually forced to move to a less disruptive, and attractive, venue. Even the Skiff Racing Association, which regulated the type of rowing most favoured by women, remained ambivalent towards them, unable or unwilling to sanction a ladies' double sculling championship to rank alongside the men and perennially complaining about the 'costumes worn by the ladies which were unnecessarily scanty'.[70] This complaint was often levelled at oarswomen obliging them to 'clad themselves most circumspectly in long black stockings – since white suggested underwear – black shorts, long socks, voluminous tops with sleeves covering the arm pits and berets which covered long hair'.[71]

12. A typically all-male water party of Nottingham and Union RC members indulging in some 'dry-land rowing', 1908.

The Amateur Rowing Association decided as early as 1907 that it did 'not legislate for ladies and therefore could not affiliate clubs containing ladies',[72] thus effectively barring them from all its member clubs in exactly the same way that it excluded manual workers. The result of this exclusion was the establishment of the Women's Rowing Association in 1923, following a lead given by Amy Gentry of Weybridge Ladies Rowing Club, which signalled the transition of women's rowing (as opposed to 'ladies'' rowing) from the recreational to the competitive arena.

The prejudice against women rowing was only one symptom of a running battle between the advocates of 'rowing' and 'boating' with the former arguing that competitive rowing should take precedence over what they regarded as simply 'messing about in boats'. Until the mid-nineteenth century the term 'rowing' was often confused with the adjective 'rowdy' and so 'boating' was generally employed to avoid ambiguity or unpleasant associations, but as 'scientific oarsmanship' became the fashion following professional improvements in the sport, 'rowing' became the accepted nomenclature, with 'boating' remaining to represent more leisurely aquatic activities.

Many of the early clubs began for almost arbitrary recreational purposes as in Lancaster where 'the propriety of the cricket club becoming a boating club' was duly discussed and sanctioned.[73] Boating was frequently only one of several activities offered by the clubs, e.g. cross-country and boxing (Thames RC), swimming (Bridgnorth RC), fishing (Folkestone RC), tennis (Warwick BC). Nevertheless, the tension between the two aquatic factions was recognised as early as 1856 when the newly established London Rowing Club made it an article of policy to 'keep as many boats as possible so that racing and pleasure can co-exist'.[74]

Nottingham Rowing Club was 'divided as to what object the club should have',[75] finally deciding that it should concentrate on racing, a policy which eventually resulted in the formation of the recreationalist Nottingham Boat Club. The Nottingham decision probably inclined the neighbouring Burton Leander Club to take racing more seriously and in 1864 it proceeded to sell its pleasure craft, replacing them with modern racing boats.[76]

The general increase in serious boat racing prompted Anthony Trollope to write in his *British Sports and Pastimes* of 1868 that 'sport is being made too much of with men rowing until there comes upon us a fear that they are killing themselves or they are nothing'. Some clubs like those at St Ives, Huntingdon and St Neots contented themselves with club and inter-club scratch racing, while others like Bradford were unable to compete 'due to the want of racing boats',[77] a situation which had hardly improved 20 years later according to the serious oarsmen at the club who criticised the recreationalist committee for 'grudging payment of regatta entrance fees from club funds which is not a good principle on which to run a rowing club'.[78]

Several clubs attempted a compromise between their recreative and competitive members with Worcester Rowing Club setting aside some seasons for 'competitive rowing only'[79] while others were adamantly opposed to pleasure boating in any form, for example, the Britannia Club in Worthing which was described by its chairman as 'the Worthing Racing Boat Club which has nothing whatever to do with pleasure boats'.[80] Both factions became increasingly short-tempered as pleasure boaters condemned regatta racing as 'farcical'[81] or 'monotonous',[82] extolling boating as 'neither the child of the bookmaker nor the pastime of the rowdy'[83] while the Amateur Rowing Association disparaged the boaters as 'those who care nothing for the sport or noble art of rowing'.[84] Bridgnorth Rowing Club appealed desperately for action 'to prevent the club degenerating into a club for pleasure rowing',[85] but did so against a cultural background epitomised by that in Lancaster where members joined the local club 'for the social advantages it afforded rather than rowing'.[86]

Before the First World War, the pleasure-boating faction held the upper hand simply due to numerical superiority which translated into a financial control of most clubs other than the larger racing clubs like Thames, London, Kingston and Leander. The recreational lobby was so powerful in Nottingham that when the Trent Navigation Bill of 1906 made compulsory a levy on pleasure boats using the local locks, the neighbouring boat clubs used the good offices of two influential members, Sir John Turney and Sir Samuel Johnson, to persuade the Navigation Company to exempt club rowing boats altogether.[87]

There was a resurgence of boating enthusiasm after the war, particularly, it seems, on the River Avon at Warwick where it became 'so congested with pleasure boats during the season that serious rowing was no longer possible and the local club, therefore, tendered its resignation from the Amateur Rowing Association'[88] while carrying on in name only as a tennis and bowling club. A similar fate threatened the Stratford-on-Avon Rowing Club only a few miles down river as the economic depression of the 1930s forced the committee to choose between the capital expenses incurred by the boating section and the competition costs of the rowers, and at a very acrimonious Annual General Meeting in 1937 the boat-racing faction narrowly carried the day with the pleasure boats being sold off to balance the club's books.

The period between the wars saw a general decline in pleasure boating, due partly to the high costs of replacing equipment and partly to the availability of alternative attractions. At the same time, boat racing gained fresh impetus from a new athleticism nurtured by government fitness campaigns[89] and a dawning awareness that national prestige was involved at the growing number of international events including Henley Regatta. After the Second World War, the spirit of internationalism, together with the need for domestic renewal, created an atmosphere entirely conducive to the promotion of organised sport and the serious oarsman benefited accordingly.

Since 1898 when there were 457 clubs nationwide, all of which catered for pleasure boaters and racing men alike,[90] the total dwindled to a mere 100 in 1950 of which only 7 had pleasure-boat sections; while the number of clubs has since more than doubled, the boating presence has decreased even further. Today, the pleasure-boater is reduced to hiring out from commercial firms which operate from the major rivers, seaside resorts and municipal lakes but in some upper Thames clubs it is still possible to encounter the occasional touring skiff tucked away beneath racks groaning with new plastic and carbon fibre racing boats.[91]

Boating for pleasure, or boating 'for the love of it', was merely one expression of the Victorian middle-class desire to confirm social position through tasteful demonstrations of prosperity. The hall-mark of such demonstrations was a leisurely approach calculated to betoken a gentility which was exemplified in the amateur ethic and institutionalised in the amateur club. It is to the evolution of both that we turn in the following chapter.

NOTES

1. *Memoirs of William Hickey*, Vol. 1, 1749–75, p. 95.
2. Ibid., p. 297.
3. *The Times* (17 May 1788), 4a.
4. The Johnian Boat Club, minutes (16 June 1826).
5. 'A Chapter of Autobiography', *Fortnightly Review*, Vol. 40 (1883), 50–97.
6. Ibid.
7. R. Rees, 'The Development of Physical Recreation in Liverpool during the Nineteenth

Century' (MA Liverpool University, 1968).
8. K. Tarbuck, *Liverpool Victoria Rowing Club 1884–1934* (Atherton St., Liverpool), p. 8.
9. Birkenhead Improvement Commission, minutes (29 Jan. 1845).
10. *Trafford Park 1896–1939* (Manchester Polytechnic, 1979).
11. *Manchester Guardian* (17 June 1907), 10b.
12. *Preston Guardian* (13 Oct. 1891), 5a.
13. H. Pidgeon, *Memorial of Shrewsbury* (Eddowes Press, 1837).
14. *Eddowes Shrewsbury Journal* (16 June 1847), 2c.
15. For contemporary photograph see *Victorian and Edwardian Boating* (Batsford, 1987), plate 39.
16. *Lincolnshire Chronicle* (23 March 1887), 4d.
17. *Health Giving Huntingdon* (Huntingdon Chamber of Commerce, 1906).
18. Talkin Tarn Rowing Club, minutes (31 March 1907).
19. *Guide to the Isle of Wight* (Ward Lock, 1907).
20. Lady Bell, *At the Works – A Study of a Manufacturing Town* (Arnold, 1907), p. 7.
21. F.V. Morley, *The River Thames* (Methuen, 1926), on pleasure boating at Abingdon.
22. *Daily News* (13 and 14 March 1885), 8a–c.
23. See *Victorian and Edwardian Boating* (Batsford, 1987) for photo of Furnivall (plate 100).
24. T. Wright, *Some Habits and Customs of the Working Classes by a Journeyman Engineer* (1867, reprinted Kelly, NY 1967), p. 27.
25. W. Cudworth, *Round about Bradford* (1876, reprinted Mountain Press, 1968), p. 7.
26. W. Lawson, *Tyneside Celebrities* (Lawson, Newcastle, 1973), p. 81.
27. *The Record of St. Philip and St. James' Rowing Club 1889–1909* (Blackwell, 1910).
28. *Oxford University and College Servants Rowing Club 1850–1950* (CSRC, 1950).
29. *Worcester Herald* (11 June 1892), 3e.
30. *Worcester Herald* (29 June 1895), 5b.
31. *Eddowes Journal* (19 Sept. 1855), 5a.
32. *Barrow Herald* (6 Sept. 1876). 2c.
33. H.E. Mellor, *Leisure and the Changing City 1870–1914* (Routledge, 1976), p. 235.
34. *Lincoln Gazette* (1 Sept. 1866), 3c.
35. *Burton Weekly News* (27 May 1870), 7a.
36. *Evesham Journal* (27 Sept. 1873), 4c.
37. National Amateur Rowing Association, Constitution (1896).
38. The Christian Ethic found expression in other sporting and recreational activities at the time. J. Ford, in *This Sporting Land* (New English Library, 1977) mentions football clubs such as Aston Villa (Wesleyans), Bolton (Church of England) and Everton (Congregationalists) founded by churches, p. 167. Golby and Purdue, in *The Civilisation of the Crowd 1750–1900* (Batsford, 1984), note Christian origins for walking tours and rail excursions (p. 98) and brass bands and choral societies (p. 106).
39. *Yorkshire Observer* (13 June 1923), 12c.
40. Evesham Rowing Club, minutes (20 Aug. 1882).
41. F.J. Hunt, *Deal, Walmer and Kingsdown Rowing Club 1929–77* (Kent Print, 1977), p. 64.
42. Henley Regatta, minutes (18 April 1936).
43. *Cambridge Journal* (8 July 1931), 15f.
44. District Line Rowing Club, minutes (15 Aug. 1952).
45. M. Quinlan, *Victorian Prelude, A History of English Manners 1700–1830* (Columbia University Press, 1941), p. 64.
46. Nottingham Rowing Club, Rules (5 Sept. 1862).
47. Ancholme Rowing Club, minutes (17 April 1895).
48. Bradford Rowing Club, Rule II (1868).
49. Derby Rowing Club, minutes (23 March 1883).
50. Cambois Rowing Club, minutes (6 Aug. 1925).
51. Poole Rowing Club, minutes (4 May 1920).
52. *The Field* (27 Oct. 1860), p. 15.

53. *Lincoln Gazette* (8 Oct. 1964), 5b.
54. Bradford Rowing Club, minutes AGM (March 1885, 1886, 1887).
55. *Bedford Times* (21 Aug. 1859), 2a.
56. Bedford Regatta cards (1861–68).
57. Henley Regatta, minutes (24 June 1867).
58. Hereford Regatta, programmes (20 July 1899, 22 July 1903, 22 July 1904).
59. H. Williams, *Diary of a Rowing Tour from Oxford to London in 1875* (Sutton, Gloucester, 1982) on Evesham regatta, 5 Aug. 1875.
60. *The Times* (4 Sept. 1884), 8a.
61. *Victorian and Edwardian Boating* (Batsford, 1987), photos of Gondola (plate 94), Dongola racing (plate 97).
62. Skiff Racing Association, minutes General Meeting (10 March 1910).
63. M. Maudsley, 'Sex in mind in Education', *Fortnightly Review*, Vol. XV, 466–83.
64. Bradford-on-Avon Rowing Club, minutes (3 Oct. 1905 and 22 Feb. 1906).
65. 'Review', *British Rowing Almanack* (1900).
66. Neptune Rowing Club, minutes (8 Sept. 1869).
67. Conversation with Len Rey, Exeter Rowing Club (8 Aug. 1984).
68. Cambridge Town Rowing Club, minutes (2 Sept. 1984). For photos of contemporary water parties see *Victorian and Edwardian Boating* (plates 63–64).
69. Derwent Rowing Club, minutes (9 Sept. 1901).
70. Skiff Racing Association, AGM (March 1907).
71. Correspondence with Irene Foley, Alpha Ladies RC, 2 April 1985, with reference to the club's clothing rules for 1936.
72. Amateur Rowing Association, AGM (March 1907).
73. Lancaster Rowing Club, minutes (20 Sept. 1842).
74. London Rowing Club, minutes, Annual Report 1856.
75. Nottingham Rowing Club, first minute (29 July 1862).
76. Burton Leander Rowing Club, minutes (27 June 1864).
77. Bradford Rowing Club, minutes (26 March 1877).
78. Bradford Rowing Club, minutes (2 June 1897).
79. *Worcester Herald* (2 May 1879), 6b, on the rowing club's inaugural event of the season.
80. Worthing Amateur Boat Club, AGM (April 1895).
81. *St. Stephen's Review* (10 Aug. 1889) on Richmond Regatta: 'Since all interest seems lost in this kind of meeting as far as rowing is concerned would it not be more satisfactory all round to give up the farce of rowing and convert them into what they really are, "Water Galas"'.
82. S. Crossley, *Pleasure and Leisure Boating* (Innes & Co., 1899), p. 28: 'The Henley Regatta of 1899 had a larger number of supporters among boating men than among rowing men and there was a monotony as regards the majority of events which fails to interest the average pleasure boater'.
83. Ibid., p. 5.
84. 'Review', *British Rowing Almanack* (1901).
85. Bridgnorth Rowing Club, minutes (19 April 1902).
86. John O'Gaunt Rowing Club, minutes (21 March 1907).
87. Nottingham and Union Rowing Club, letters (29 Jan. 1906, 9 Feb. 1906, 13 Feb. 1906, 16 and 17 Feb. 1906).
88. 'Proceedings', *British Rowing Almanack*, 1927.
89. Many clubs received advice from the newly formed (1937) National Fitness Council and several, including Poole RC (see AGM, March 1939) and Ancholme RC (see AGM, 1937) actually received substantial grants towards the costs of renewal. In 1939 the National Advisory Council for Physical Training appointed a full time National Organiser for rowing.
90. G.T. Rees, *The Rowing Club Directory of Great Britain* (Lock to Lock Times, 1898).

91. The traditional Thames Skiff continues as a collector's item; note the auction of two such at Malmesbury in 1985 for £1,000 each.

6

Amateurism

The outsiders, artisans, mechanics and such like troublesome persons can have no place found for them. To keep them out is a thing desirable on every account ... no base mechanic arms need be suffered to thrust themselves in here.

(*The Times*, 26 April 1880)

During the nineteenth century, pleasure boating provided the genteel classes with a recreational haven from open competition and any contact with the less desirable social elements for, as Sydney Crossley maintained in the introduction of *Leisure and Pleasure Boating* in 1889, 'the professional in the rowing world is a thing apart from his fellows and it is not even necessary to consider his existence when dealing with boating as a pastime'. However, for those middle- and upper-class 'aquatics' who chose to race boats rather than simply 'mess about' in them the situation became vastly more complicated from the 1830s onwards as regattas proliferated and began to attract an increasingly wide social diversity of entries, encouraged by lucrative prize funds and ever more convenient rail travel.

Initially, much of the gentlemen's rowing had been in closed competition between schools or colleges but after graduation, when the oarsmen returned home, they found ad hoc local events organised in very haphazard fashion which made few allowances for a gentleman's 'status' and the new clubs of the time were established to maintain a tradition of gentlemen's rowing away from the professionals and artisans by inaugurating new regattas which excluded these groups. Those who formed the clubs and introduced the new racing regulations usually cited three overriding reasons in justification: first, that any professional involvement in rowing would encourage cheating; second, that the 'spirit' of the sport would be lost; and third, that professionals or manual workers would outclass the amateurs due to their extra training and superior strength.

A fourth, rarely expressed reason was that of plain snobbery. The overwhelming majority of middle-class oarsmen learned to row at public school or university where they also learned a classical view of society which encouraged them to believe that human beings are 'naturally' classifiable into at least three types, the production of which was determined, to an overwhelming extent, by heredity. Such a view was amply supported by the current theological teachings with which they would also have been fully conversant and which were plainly expressed by the Warden of Radley College, itself a rowing school since 1849, in the following words:

> A gentleman both knows and is thankful that God, instead of making all men equal has made them all most unequal. Heredity, rank, nobility of blood is the very first condition and essence of all Christian privileges and woe to the man who will honour no one except for his own merit and his own deeds.[1]

The years when professional oarsmen were emerging from working environments around the country also saw a burgeoning socialism with the repeal of the Combination Acts and the establishment of the Trade Union movement whose first strikes took place in Manchester in 1829 and Newcastle in 1831, and which persuaded the government to extend the franchise in the Reform Act of 1832.

To 'respectable' society, socialism spelt disaster: a letter published in *The Times* and signed by 40 clergymen from Chester on 13 April 1840 probably voiced the fears of many middle-class folk when it proclaimed 'alarm at the fearful progress of Socialism, a system which tramples all decency underfoot and sets lawful authority at defiance and would turn this happy land into a scene of bloodshed, anarchy and ruin'. Perhaps it is not surprising that the first exclusively gentlemen's rowing club in the north of England was established in Chester in 1838, and it seems more than likely that at least one of the anonymous letter writers was involved with its formation.[2]

This trend towards 'anarchy' continued during the middle years of the century through further political, social and educational reform: the Ten Hours Act of 1847 which freed, for the first time, many workers for recreational activity on a Saturday;[3] the Reform Acts of 1867 and 1884 which greatly extended the franchise; the Union Chargeability Act which finally detached the labourer from his place of settlement and created mobility of labour; the establishment of the Labour Representation League in 1869 which promoted working-class MPs; and the Newcastle Commission of 1861 which presaged an enormous expansion of popular education beginning with the Education Act of 1870.

This general advancement of the working class caused consternation among many, with the *Saturday Review* concluding that 'the great working class as a body becomes every day a firmer phalanx not really impressible or subject to change'[4] and Robert Lowe actually went as far as to say that 'one class may swamp the other',[5] while even Mrs Beeton noted that the introduction of cheap silks, cottons and tweeds had 'removed the landmarks between the mistress and her maid, between the master and his man'.[6]

The gradual destruction of the cultural and political privileges of the old school was compensated by an increase in social exclusiveness which was marked in rowing by the 'black-ball' system of membership election to clubs, an increasingly prohibitive definition of the term 'amateur', the encouragement of fragmentation and separate developments in the sport, the codification of strict racing regulations and the establishment of the Amateur Rowing Association in 1882 which institutionalised and vigilantly policed the foregoing until the 1950s.

The cultural derivation of the term 'amateur' stems from the eighteenth-century connoisseurship of the fine or polite arts enjoyed by the gentlemen of leisure and taste who dabbled nonchalantly in many activities and whose dilettantism explains their disdain for excellence in performance, a view perfectly reflected by Trollope when he features billiards as an example: 'To play billiards is the amusement of a gentleman; to play billiards pre-eminently well is the life's work of a man who in learning to do so can hardly have continued to be a gentleman in the best sense of the word'.[7]

This prejudice against efficiency of performance, allied to that felt for the artisan which derived historically from the ancient Athenian snobbery against trade, was mixed with Victorian religious orthodoxy to produce an amateur ethic which proposed the exclusion of the professional at any cost. For many establishment figures, this became a moral crusade with much being made of the 'cleanliness' of amateur sport and its encouragement of self-control, self-reliance and good fellowship, moral qualities alongside which were often ranged more pragmatic considerations, such as the advantages to be gained in the 'work of life' by an involvement in sport.

This point was particularly well made in the introduction of the

Badminton *History of Athletics* where sporting activity is commended as 'an opportunity for making lasting friendships and connections which are often of the greatest value in later life'.[8] This element of the 'old-school-tie' approach is well represented in the rowing world and given voice in the Eton Boating Song whose refrain boasts that 'We'll row for ever, steady from stroke to bow, and nothing in life will sever the chain that is round us now.'

As class lines became more difficult to maintain during the second half of the century, the screening capacity of the ruling cliques was severely reduced and ex-public school men faced a takeover by the lower-middle-class tradesman and clerk, a situation which provided the stimulus for a stricter definition of 'amateur'. The true cultural derivation of this definition was finally and publicly admitted when the athletics correspondent of the *Saturday Review* of 20 April 1867 confessed that 'the facts of his being civil and never having competed for money are *not* sufficient to make a man a gentleman as well as an amateur'.

This sentiment was well understood by the rowing establishment whose gentlemen administrators had made the distinction between 'gentlemen amateurs' and 'amateurs' at regattas for the previous 25 years at least and whose patrician attitudes had been learned at school and university at a time during the first quarter of the nineteenth century when these institutions were filled with the most socially exclusive class of students ever.[9] It was this generation of students which was responsible for the establishment of the first rowing clubs with the first entry in the Eton Boating Book in 1812 mentioning the Monarch ten-oared boat and the 'Laws of the Monarch Boat Club' being recorded by ex-Etonians at Trinity College, Cambridge during 1825.

These laws make provision for fining crew members who 'speak after silence has been called' or 'neglect to wear the proper uniform' and similar regulations occur in the earliest Oxford club at Exeter College in 1830 where fines extended to 'anyone who swears or uses bad language'. These habits of internal hierarchies, petty disciplines and 'correct' dress had been well learned at school and were religiously repeated in college boat clubs, and well-drilled crews in the 1841 inter-university race moved the correspondent of *The Times* to congratulate the manly efforts of the 'young patricians who are the future aspirants to fame and fortune in the pulpit, at the bar, in the senate and at the cannon's mouth'.[10]

It was such aspirants to fame who first dispensed with the services of the professional watermen in the pursuit of fair competition following the 'fouling' victory of Leander Club over the Cambridge University Boat Club in 1838 and that year's varsity race was stipulated as a strictly no fouling match to be steered by gentlemen. Partial explanation of this and subsequent exclusions can be found in the records of the Oxford University Boat Club for April 1846 where Arthur Shadwell, an ex-Eton and Oxford coxswain, is quoted as saying that a 'coxswain ought to be a thinking, reasoning being in a higher degree than any waterman has yet shown himself to be'.

Nevertheless, fouling continued in the race due to the instructions given to the crews by their professional trainers, particularly Robert Coombes of Cambridge who was universally blamed for Oxford winning on a foul in 1849 which, together with other perceived shortcomings, led eventually to Tom Egan, an ex-Cambridge University coxswain, taking over the coaching and making the point at the time that the style and polish of rowing was more important than winning for a sectional interest.[11]

Apart from feeling that watermen were socially and intellectually inferior, it was also felt that they were simply technically incompetent so that, after a few years of unsatisfactory imitation, the gentlemen introduced a more scientific approach which was, according to Archibald Maclaren who was the director of the Oxford Gymnasium, 'particularly marked in men who passed through public school and university life' whose improvment in technique was 'so great that little is left to be desired'.[12]

At the same time as university oarsmen discredited and marginalised the professional watermen, they also sought to apply their new rules concerning amateur status and racing practice further afield. Initially, this was achieved in the Grand Challenge Cup at Henley Regatta in 1839, where the principles of no fouling and steering by amateurs were adopted along with a definition of eligibility which entailed membership of Oxbridge colleges, London University, Eton, Westminster, the Household Cavalry or similarly constituted clubs – which, at the time, effectively meant the Leander Club.

Further modifications of these rules restricting the power of professional umpires and more closely defining 'fouling practices' were effected ten years later, again by delegates from Oxford and Cambridge University boat clubs and Leander Club, chief among them Arthur Shadwell and Tom Egan.

A similarly constituted committee called together in 1872 by the Thames Regatta secretary, himself an ex-President of Cambridge University Boat Club, finally settled the thorny problem of a boat's correct course during a race which had been the cause of most fouling since, according to the editor of the *British Rowing Almanack*, 'professionals particularly were quite unable to comprehend which was and which was not their proper course after water had once been taken after the start'.[13]

The editor of the time, E.D. Brickwood, was also *The Times*'s rowing correspondent and represented London Rowing Club on the committee, reiterating on its behalf the establishment's faith in the current convention that 'amateurs may be divided into two classes viz. gentlemen amateurs and tradesmen amateurs and it is not desirable that barriers between them should be broken down'.[14]

It is, therefore, hardly surprising to find that the *Almanack* during the 1860s and 1870s editorialised extensively on the nature of 'true' and 'pseudo' amateurism while incorporating huge amounts of copy on Oxbridge and Henley rowing. The last vestigial professional connection with the varsity race was severed in 1877 when 'Honest John Phelps' judged a 10 yard Oxford victory as a dead heat and it was decided that no waterman should ever again act as a judge.

The process of applying 'Varsity' and 'Henley' rules to rowing activities in general was continued by university graduates throughout the country with the first provincial application of the 'gentleman amateur' principle applied by the Chester Victoria Rowing Club following the Chester Regatta of 1837 in which there was an event for amateurs from which manual labourers were specifically banned. The 1838 event, in honour of Queen Victoria's Coronation, included the Coronation Cup 'to be rowed and steered by amateurs being persons not normally employed in manual labour'.[15]

The success of the event determined various local aquatic gentlemen to form a club, the success of which was felt to be assured by 'the high patronage which is promised for the undertaking' including Lord Grosvenor, Sir Philip Malpas, Sir Richard Bulkeley and Sir George Back,[16] all Oxbridge men. These amateur aquatic gentlemen continued to row for money, however, as in the race between the 'Chester Deva' and 'Liverpool Crusader', 'whose crews will pull against each other for £100 a side over a 3 mile course',[17] and it seems reasonable to conclude that the demarcation between competitors within regattas organised by such gentlemen was based on social rather than financial considerations.

In Lancaster, there had been for many years 'a day set aside for racing boats but always on so paltry a scale that instead of a day of amusement and recreation the time was spent in riot, and drunkenness'[18] so that when Edmund Sharpe came down from St John's

College to return to the city, he and a few friends set about establishing a club and regulating the regatta.

Following an initial effort in 1843, the new club and regatta became a fixture of the local scene with the success of the 1844 event attracting a huge attendance of local gentry which had been notably lacking at the previous boat races held in the dock area of the town, and the club's relocation in the rural setting of Halton Waters enhanced its position in society to such an extent that it soon became the area's leading social organisation numbering aldermen, councillors and mayors among its membership.

At the same time, further north at Talkin Tarn, the traditional land and water sports began to be supplemented by 'gentlemen's' events due to the influence of James Howard, the Duke of Carlisle's son, already used to boating from the family boathouse on the tarn, and recently returned from Trinity College, Oxford. Many existing 'boat races' and 'sports' were considered by the newly graduated gentlemen to be 'background disreputable affairs got up by publicans and garden owners for their own profit' as with the first Manchester and Salford Regatta,[19] yet even when their own influence was exerted, as at the Worcester Regatta of 1845 when three 'reputable' stewards were engaged, there remained the taint of cheating as a result of heavy wagering.[20]

This reputation was gradually expunged, partly due to the presence of the Oxford Worcestershire Boat Club whose university student members located its headquarters in the city in 1847. Elsewhere, returning graduates were able to initiate rowing from scratch, for example in Gainsborough, where the first paddle was dipped by Henry Stavely, down from Trinity College, Cambridge in 1844 and where racing was established in 1853 by Philip Moore, an Oxford Blue. Similarly, rowing was first introduced to Tewkesbury when Cheltenham College boys returned to the area after graduating from Cambridge University in 1853.

By this time, Henley Regatta was firmly established as the gentlemen's regatta *par excellence* with its standards openly admired by influential aquatics like Francis Playford, a founder member of London Rowing Club in 1856, who wrote to the Henley Stewards to the effect that their event proceeded successfully 'without the aid of tavern or public house which explains the thoroughly gentlemanly character of the regatta'.[21] The closer regatta venues were to Henley or Oxbridge, the greater was the likelihood of emulation, like Bedford where the rather bucolic racing of previous years had become regulated by a succession of university boat club presidents, with the result that it became almost exclusively a gentlemen's regatta. Silver cups replaced the usual money prizes to the extent that the local paper was moved to comment that these 'were of no use whatever to the Bedford working man'.[22]

Oxbridge theological graduates set up clubs during the 1860s at Greenwich (Rev. Miller), Evesham (Rev. Strong) and St Ives (Rev. Goldie), the last of which was consolidated by the founder's son, J.H.D. Goldie, a Cambridge University Boat Club president, with the further clubs of Burton-on-Trent and Stratford-on-Avon being established by newly returned graduates of wealthy local families such as Archie Flower of Flowers Brewery in Stratford and Harry Nadin, a Cambridge Blue of 1868, of Eversheds Brewery in Burton.

There was a considerable Oxbridge influence even further afield with local families contributing their university-educated sons to Barrow Rowing Club,[23] to Middlesbrough Amateur Boat Club, where 'dress' and 'undress' uniform was compulsory for rowing members,[24] and to Ryde Rowing Club where a telegram communicating the dead heat of the 1877 University Boat Race 'caused considerable excitement all over town'.[25]

One result of this Oxbridgisation of rowing in the regions was some social disruption, for it was for the first time during the early and middle years of the century that many middle-class families sent their sons to public school and on to university from which they returned speaking almost a different language from most of the inhabitants of their native towns. Having formed friendships at college which loosened parochial attachments, they made little contact with fellow townsmen further down the social scale with whom their fathers and grandfathers had probably mingled freely in their schooldays at the local grammar school.

In rowing terms, this encouraged the growth of exclusive clubs and the separate development in each area of other clubs for those less socially acceptable, a trend which was generally justified by the establishment as necessary to prevent the incursion, however slight, of the professional element. Brickwood, in his *Boat Racing* of 1876, included some 'draft rules for any amateur club', prime among them being one which stipulated that 'the objects of this club shall be the encouragement of rowing amongst gentlemen amateurs' and another that 'one black ball in five shall exclude from membership'. Naturally, not all clubs could sustain such regulations but the metropolitan clubs certainly could and in 1879 formed themselves into the Metropolitan Rowing Association for the purposes of maintaining the standards of amateur oarsmanship and facilitating the selection of representative crews, objectives determined by a committee of 25 members, 23 of whom were either Oxford or Cambridge men.

In certain areas of the country, the enforcement of the strictest amateur regulations was extremely difficult, leading to many misunderstandings and unpleasantnesses, particularly in the north-west of England where the traditions of trade, commerce and professionalism had produced a unique blend of rowing activity. The age-old Chester Regatta incorporating fishermen's races was effectively taken over by the city's gentlemen in 1840 and immediately suffered financially as the regular sponsorship declined, while the new stewards were unable to solicit sufficient funds from a gentry disinclined to contribute to an event formerly given over to what they regarded as the worst excesses of commercial exploitation.

The local paper weighed in on the side of the committee declaring that it saw no reason why such support should be withheld since rowing 'is a true and manly sport deserving the encouragement of the inhabitants generally'.[26] Gradually, subscriptions materialised in emulation of Lord Grosvenor's noble patronage in donating a special prize in honour of Prince Albert, an action which not only helped to save the regatta but also allowed the newly formed club to apply successfully for royal designation. Similar problems of transition occurred at nearby Warrington, where the old annual boat races from Fiddler's Ferry into the town centre[27] had been appropriated by the local gentry and transformed into a society event with exclusive grandstands erected as enclosures adjacent to the finish line at Warrington Bridge. The effect was to push the rural sports element of the original event on to the following day, a separation which caused considerable upset in 1844 as the secretary of the regatta explained in a letter to his chairman on 14 August:

> My attention has been arrested with a placard as large as life of rural sports with my name as one of the stewards, this will undoubtedly militate against the good opinion of our regatta subscribers who disapprove of the sports, the results being evident.

Such opinions might have been expected since the gentlemen of Warrington had been among the first to promote racing for 'gentlemen amateurs', despite early local resistance in 1841 when a move to open up the 'Silver Sculls' race to 'all classes' was 'negatived by a considerable majority after a stormy meeting'.[28]

WARRINGTON REGATTA.

On Thursday July, 22nd, 1841.

PATRONS:

SIR RICHARD BROOKE, BART.
J. I. BLACKBURNE, ESQ. M. P.
THOMAS LYON, ESQ.
JOSEPH STUBS, ESQ.

JOHN WILSON PATTEN, ESQ. M. P
GEORGE C. LEGH, ESQ.
HOLBROOK GASKELL, ESQ.
WILLIAM STUBS, ESQ.

STEWARDS:—JOSEPH PERRIN, ESQ. & RICHARD S. NORRIS, ESQ,

UMPIRE:—JAMES DAVIES, ESQ.——*The Rowing Matches to start at Ten o'clock.*

The Stewards' Ordinary, *will take place immediately after the Regatta at the FEATHERS' INN. For Tickets apply at the Bar.*

ROWING MATCH FOR WORKMEN OF WARRINGTON, for four-oar boats for a Sweepstakes of 15s. each boat, and £8. added, over the cup course, second boat to save his stake, not less than three to start:—all watermen, fishermen, or others connected with the river to be excluded. 23 ft. keel.
1 Mr. Mc. Knight's Mermaid, J. Tomason, J. Langley, J. Cartwright, Hugh Gore, John Mc. Knight, Cx. *blue and fancy caps*
2 Mr. Sanderson's "Wha'd o' thought it," E. Grainger, — Miller, — Barnett, — Sharpe, —————— Cx, *black and white ball.*
3 Mr. Thewlis names Pearl, J, Mather, P. Naylor, — Clatworthy, W. Bradshaw, — Rogger, Cx. *blue and white.*

A SAILING MATCH from Fiddler's Ferry to Warrington, for Warrington Boats, not exceeding 21½ ft. keel, for a Sweepstakes of 10s. each, with £3. added. Four to start or the £3. will not be given. The second boat to have stake returned, Entrance 3s. 6d. To start from opposite the Ferry house, and terminate at the winning flag opposite the Grand stand.
1 Mr. Heath's Vulcan, Mr. Heath, Coxswain, *yellow.*
2 Mr. Bayley's Majestic, Jas. Pye, Coxswain, *scarlet.*
3 Mr. Thewlis's Phœnix, ———— Coxswain, *crimson and white.*
4 Mr. Stirrup's Victoria, Mr. H. Stirrup, Coxswain, *blue.*
5 Mr. T. Johnson's The Snake, Mr. T. Johnson, Coxswain, *red and white*
6 Mr. Jones's Miss Sankey, Richd. Wilcock, Coxwain, *orange and light blue.*

THE OPEN STAKES.—A Sweepstakes of £3. each boat, with £20. added from the fund, for Amateurs the members of any established club in Warrington, Liverpool, Chester, Runcorn, Dublin or the Clyde, to be rowed in four-oar Gigs over the cup course. The winner to pay £4. to the second, and the third boat to have entrance money returned. Four to start or no race. Entrance £1. each boat.
1 The Mersey R. Club, Mersey, A. Littledale, W. Eaton, H. Royd, H. Crewe, ————Cx. *blue flag, M. R. C.*
2 The Royal Chester R. Club, Princess Royal, H. Potts, C. W. Potts, T. Dixon, C. Walker, John Massey, Cx. *blue flag, and white.*
3 The Royal Chester R. Club, Deva, J. Dutton, E. Moss, J. Challoner, R. Catherall, W. Walker, Cx. *blue flag, and white.*
4 The Crusader Club, Crusader, J. Swinton, T. Stirrup, J. Ridgway, Bernard Dromgoole, William Worthington, Cx. *scarlet and gold.*
5 Warrington Victoria Club, The Corsair, J. Phillips, T. Johnson, W. Woods, J. Woods, Mr. William Heath, Cx. *blue and white, "Corsair."*
6 The Thetis Club, The Thetis, Edw. Blundell. Shaw Thewlis, G. Venn, J. S. Mather, Mr. Heath, Cx. *blue and white.*

A SET OF SILVER SCULLS, for Gentlemen Amateurs of Warrington, pulling a pair of sculls and two oars, in Wherries, to a boat moor'd in the river below Tom Paine's Bridge, and back to the Winning flag. Entrance 15s. each. Three boats to start or no race.
1 Mr. W, Wagstaff's Water Witch, *red.*
2 Mr. Joseph Litton's Zephyr, *blue*
3 Mr. J. F. Marsh's Gazelle, *white*
4 Mr. H. Stanton's Pearl, *green*

THE WARRINGTON CUP, of not less than £20. value, added to a Sweepstakes of £2. each boat, to be rowed for by Warrington Amateurs, Tradesmen, and Tradesmen's Sons, not being employed by any except their parents, in four-oar Gigs, from the starting place, opposite the Grand stand, through the Lancashire arch of the Railway Bridge and back

through the Cheshire arch to the winning flag: the second boat to receive
£4. and the third boat to save entrance money.   Entrance £1. each boat:
three boats to start or no race.

1 Mr. J. Smith names The Neptune, J. Alderson, J. Whittle, H. Franco J. Pickmere,
  Mr. Smith, Cx. *blue.*
2 Warrington Victoria Club, The Corsair, W. Woods, W. Gibson, J. Gibson,;J.;Woods,
  John Phillips, Cx. *blue and white*
3 The Crusader Club, The Crusader, W. Stirrup, T. Stirrup, J. Swinton, B.;Dromgoole,
  W. Worthington, Cx. *white body, crimson and gold caps.*
4 The Thetis Club, The Thetis, Edw. Blundell, Shaw Thewlis, Geo. Venn, John;Mather,
  Mr. Heath, Cx. *blue and white.*

A ROWING MATCH, for four-oar boats open to all classes; for £3.
—15s. to second boat: Cup course, three to start or no race, 23 ft. keel.

1 Mr Mc. Knight's Mermaid, Jas. Langley, Jas. Cartwright. John Tomason, Hugh Gore,
  John Mc. Knight, Cx. *blue and fancy caps.*
2 Mr. Middleton's Pearl, Thos. Mason, Thos. Mason, Junr. Robt. Mason, John Mason,
  Mr. Middleton, Cx. *union jack.*
3 Mr. Bayley's Majestic, James Pye, James Hill, James Cartwright,; James;Lomax,
  Joseph Pye, Cx. *scarlet.*

THE STAND PURSE of 20 Guineas, given by Gentlemen of War-
rington, to be rowed for by Warrington Amateurs, in four-oar Gigs or
Wherries, over the cup course, entrance £1. the winner of the Warrington
Cup to give two boats length, the second boat to receive £2.

☞ The entry for this Race to close at 9 o'clock on Wednesday Evening, at the Bridge
Inn, Latchford.

A SWEEPSTAKES, of 10s. 6d. with £10. added, to be rowed for by
Amateurs of Warrington, in six oar Gigs or Boats, over the Cup Course.
The winner to pay the second boat £2.   Three to start or no race.
Entrance 10s. 6d. each.

1 Mr. Bayley's Majestic, Jas. Pye, Jas. Cartwright, Jas Lomax, Jas, Hill, Wm. Jackson,
  Saml. Jackson, Joseph Pye, Cx. *scarlet,*
2 Mr. Jones's Sons' of the Mersey, S. Hewitt, Wm. Hewitt, Jos. Phillips, Wm. Grainger,
  Henry Unsworth, Joseph Leftwich, Cx. *orange and light blue,*
3 Mr Thewlis names Psyche, Edw. Blundell, Shaw Thewlis, Geo. Venn, John Mather,
  John Phillips, John Pickmere, Mr. Heath, Cx. *white and blue edges, "Psyche."*

Regulations:——Every boat to have a Coxswain, and to row in colours. All disputes to be settled by the Stewards.   No fouling will be permitted.   The contesting boats
to keep above the Bridge Mill Pier, and the crews to muster there prior to starting on the
ringing of a bell.

☞ As the different boats pass through the Railway Bridge, a gun will be fired, and the
number of the first boat hoisted in front of the Grand Stand.

J. N. GARDNER, *Secretary.*

13. Annual boat races in Warrington.

Once such rules were in place, there remained the difficulties of
enforcement, not only in 'gentlemen's' events but throughout the
complex fragmentation of events for other categories, and regatta
committees often needed to refer to the establishment of the day for
a ruling, as at the Lancaster Regatta of 1846 when the stewards took
exception to a Manchester crew containing known tradesmen which
had won an amateur race. The stewards were inclined to disqualify
them but wrote for clarification to the editor of *Bell's Life* magazine
in London, Tom Egan, the future Cambridge University Boat Club
president, who replied that

> if the oarsmen in question were journeymen or mechanics they
> should be defaulted and this difficulty can be avoided in future

by stipulating that gentlemen amateurs should be members of some regularly constituted club as at Thames and Henley Regattas.[29]

Similar difficulties over eligibility caused much ill feeling at Preston Regatta in the same year when aggrieved parties refused to join the sports or attend the regatta dinner at the White Hart Inn which eventually attracted a paltry 20 people.[30]

Wrangles over status qualifications continued for decades in the area with John Crook Junior, of the Boathouse Inn at Preston, actually being taken to the County Court in 1875 by his opponent at the local regatta after winning a gentlemen's sculling race though himself in trade as a boatbuilder. The local sporting newspaper volunteered the opinion that 'persons of Crook's class should not be allowed to claim the privileges of amateurship and the conduct of the Ribble Rowing Club in admitting him to membership and attempting to override long established principles cannot be too severely reprobated'.[31]

A similar disqualification had followed the victory, during the previous year, of the Bolton and Ringley Rowing Club crew of working men at the Agecroft Regatta, eliciting the enquiry from the club secretary, 'Is not a working man who is honest in all his dealings as much a gentleman as a man with a good coat on?'[32] Even Henley Regatta stewards found it difficult to apply the social definition of 'amateur' to 'foreign' or provincial crews, of which they knew little or nothing, and the John O'Gaunt Rowing Club's entry in the Stewards Cup of 1870 was objected to on the grounds of its trade connections, only for it to be reinstated when the Mayor of Lancaster, himself a club member, telegraphed his confirmation of its genuine status.[33] The Henley authorities were, however, not averse to bending their own rules when it suited their purposes, as in their acceptance of a French entry from gentlemen oarsmen who openly admitted having rowed for money and against artisans.[34]

Soon after the first Henley Regatta in 1839, the 'Henley Rules' separating gentlemen competitors from the rest were applied in the Thames Grand Regatta which included races for 'Gentlemen', 'Watermen', 'Landsmen' and 'Apprentices' with the gentlemen stewards offering to 'return entrance money to the watermen should their demeanour and conduct be orderly and respectful but should they be guilty of any fouling or foul conduct their names will be at once expunged'.[35] Such inducements obviously had their effects since the following year the regatta attracted many competitors who were 'roughs of the first order but who rowed well and conducted themselves properly'.[36]

Where gentlemen oarsmen and administrators were readily available to oversee rowing events directly, as on the River Thames at Putney, then social amateurism was enforceable and it was even possible in remote areas like the north-west of England where there were concentrations of gentry as in Chester and Lancaster. Naturally, in Oxford and Cambridge, the new social tone of rowing was vigorously promoted at club and regatta levels, with the old Oxford watermen's regatta becoming the Oxford City Regatta at which 'no booths or stalls of any description will be allowed and the public is cautioned against trespass with police on duty to enforce the regulations',[37] while the rules of the new Cambridge Boat Racing Club of 1844 stressed that 'no person connected in any way whatsoever with any boatyard be allowed to pull or steer on any race nights'.

In other, less gentrified, areas the new rules tended to disrupt existing organisations such as the old established Northern Rowing Club in Newcastle-on-Tyne which had progressed contentedly with a socially mixed membership until 1869 when it stumbled over the new definition of 'amateur'. This was applied when the local regatta entry qualifications were tightened up by the organising committee from the Tyne Amateur Rowing Club constituted by the 'upper class of amateurs'.[38]

The immediate result was that the amateur members of the Northern club were adjudged to have been tainted by association with their 'professional' colleagues and refused admission to the regatta unless accredited by a bona fide amateur club, something which the Tyne club itself was unwilling to do and so a third club, the Newcastle Amateur Rowing Club, was established to offer sanctuary to those unfortunates deemed to be neither fully amateur in the best social sense of the word, nor fully professional.

Further guilt by association revealed itself in Nottingham during 1862, when the committee of the Nottingham Rowing Club enquired of *Bell's Life*, 'Does a club of watermen and amateurs qualify to send an amateur crew to row for an amateur prize?', receiving the inevitable reply that this would be 'quite unsatisfactory'. The result was that the committee felt it expedient to 'request those gentlemen who are strictly watermen to withdraw their names'[39] – an interesting form of words which indicates the confusion which many must have felt in situations like this.

The 'gentlemen' watermen, who probably worked on the Colwick steamers and were, therefore, wholly amateur as far as the sport of rowing was concerned, were thus forced out of an amateur club and into clubs like Trent Rowing Club which had been established for the very purpose of boat racing for money. This state of affairs continued until the formation of the Nottingham Britannia Rowing Club in 1869 which, like the Newcastle club, accepted the wider definition of 'amateur' which omitted the ban on manual workers.

Other clubs hoped to avoid such drastic action by not adopting the comprehensively exclusive social definition, and the Tweed Rowing Club at Berwick, having written – as many provincial clubs did – to London Rowing Club for advice on a constitution, came to the inescapable conclusion that 'the London rules would require some modification for our use', the modification being that 'amateur' was defined as 'one who has never rowed for money'.[40] Nevertheless, this meant that Tweed Rowing Club members were excluded from the '*purely* gentlemen amateur' events at the annual Berwick Amateur Rowing Club regattas.[41]

The Norfolk and Norwich Rowing Club rules for 1867 show the same compromise in that they stipulated that the club consist of an 'unlimited number of bona fide members' while allowing that only persons who had competed in watermen's races were actually ineligible, and, whereas those clubs directly influenced by the Oxbridge tradition always insisted upon a membership of 'Gentlemen Amateurs', others were content with simply 'Amateurs'.

During the 1860s and 1870s, this split in definition produced a duality of club growth throughout the country with 'gentlemen's clubs' together with 'amateur clubs' springing up in practically every rowing venue to cater for the social diversity of their catchment areas, but even by 1876 there were still relatively few totally socially acceptable clubs and E.D. Brickwood could name only the following as those which included the 'upper class of amateur': Oxford University, Cambridge University, Eton, Leander, London, Thames, Kingston, Tyne, Chester and Lancaster.[42]

As we have seen, Brickwood also included some draft rules for the formation of a bona fide amateur club and was later instrumental in establishing the Metropolitan Rowing Association in 1879, which extended its self-imposed responsibility for the maintenance of the amateur ethic from London to the whole of the country when it was transformed into the Amateur Rowing Association in 1882. It was felt by the committee that only by such transformation could strict amateurism be ensured in the provinces where evidence of laxity in its application was everywhere apparent.

Furthermore, since the introduction of the new boat-racing legislation in 1872, correspondence had confirmed them in the belief that there were several well-connected clubs around the country which could be relied upon to implement 'correct' procedures at club and regatta levels, viz. Pengwern Rowing Club (Shrewsbury), Worcester Rowing Club, Burton Leander Rowing Club, Royal Chester Rowing Club, Bristol Ariel Rowing Club and Tyne Amateur Rowing Club, a selection which gave them a comprehensive spread of influence. The constitution of the new association continued to reflect the Oxbridge bias in that all the original varsity and London clubs were awarded three votes each, the provincial clubs with the strongest Oxbridge connections, i.e. Royal Chester and Pengwern, were awarded two votes apiece while the rest had only one vote each. The self-appointed management committee, which included only one provincial member from Chester, gave to itself the right to decide which of the affiliated clubs should attend general meetings.[43]

In some areas, the victory over the 'pseudo-amateur' had already been achieved, as at Bedford where in 1882 the local paper lamented the passing of the glorious days of the regatta, commenting that it was currently run for a 'select circle in Bedford, a society function confined to those in rowing circles', where working men were banned from entering due to their 'muscular power against which ordinary amateur gentlemen would find it difficult to compete'.[44]

This argument, like that employed against the evils of rowing for money, was fallacious and often countered by W.B. Woodgate in his *Reminiscences* of 1909, who recalled beating many professional crews in practice while, much earlier, a wager cited in the *Rowing Almanack* of 1861 also called it into question when an amateur easily bettered a waterman's time for four crossings of the River Thames at high tide. While the local rowing establishment in places like Bedford had at last restricted all rowing activity to the right class of people, counterparts in more cosmopolitan areas were struggling to do so and, in traditionally 'mixed' areas like Worcester and Burton-on-Trent, the gentlemen of the local clubs were faced with the dilemma of satisfying the Amateur Rowing Association while, at the same time, continuing to stage the widely popular annual regattas.

The decade following the inauguration of the new association, therefore, witnessed a further fragmentation of the rowing scene as rowing administrators continued to wrestle with problems foisted upon them by an elite group of self-appointed gentlemen sitting in splendid metropolitan isolation. Almost immediately, the Association's committee added a sixth clause to the five-point definition of 'amateur', one which disqualified from Association events any member of any club containing non-amateurs under the exclusive code, a move which as the Midland clubs protested, would 'disqualify half the mixed clubs in the provinces'.[45]

Realising that such a rule could not, as yet, be enforced, the Association withdrew the proposal, replacing it with ever more circular definitions concluding with that of 1889 to the effect that 'no member of the Amateur Rowing Association shall compete at any regatta which is not held under Amateur Rowing Association rules'. This remained open to interpretation, a fact which moved the editor of the *Rowing Almanack* in 1890 to comment that there must be a return to the old practice 'where gentlemen will be able to confine amateur competition in which they take part to their own class and thereby avoid the sport's prostitution in the accursed greed for gold'.

Nevertheless, the 1889 definition was potent enough to produce practical effects: in Burton-on-Trent where the working men's Trent Rowing Club wrote to the neighbouring gentlemen's club asking if it would help in establishing 'another amateur rowing association with a wider definition of "amateur"' to which the inevitable reply was 'that no good end would be attained by attempting to start an opposition association';[46] in Yorkshire where the White Rose Club wrote to the 'amateurs' of Bradford Rowing Club on the same theme only to receive the response that 'the committee wish to express their opinion that they are wholly satisfied with the Amateur Rowing Association definition as it stands';[47] in Worcester where the Provincial Rowing Association was established to ensure the 'retention of the right to include in regattas classes for certain trades and callings';[48] at Talkin Tarn where there was a 'perceptible falling off in numbers of spectators due in great measure to the elimination of the professional rowing contests from the card';[49] in Hastings where the Coast Amateur Rowing Association was formed to provide competition for a wider class of oarsmen;[50] in Newton Abbott where the West of England Rowing Association was established for the same reason;[51] but the most significant of all effects was the inauguration, through the efforts of F. J. Furnivall, of the National Amateur Rowing Association in 1890, which championed the cause of rowing for all by excluding from membership only those who rowed for money.

The National Amateur Rowing Association was established by Furnivall to counteract what he believed to be the 'hypocrisy' of the university attitude towards working men, which patronised them in many walks of life and totally excluded them in rowing. His belligerence unfortunately caused the first meeting between the two governing bodies to result in a 'widening of the breach rather than a widening of the amateur definition'.[52] This breach was confirmed and extended in 1894 when the Amateur Rowing Association finally pushed through the sixth clause of its already exclusive amateur definition, confident in the knowledge that any club which was unable or unwilling to meet the new restrictions could find a home with the National Amateur Rowing Association.

Even this expedient often failed to clarify the local situation: Trent Rowing Club in Burton was, quite naturally, one of the first clubs to affiliate to the National body, having been practically ostracised from the Burton rowing scene by the gentlemen of Burton Leander and Burton Amateur clubs, an exclusion which these clubs wished to extend to the local regatta itself. However, the event had been organised by all three clubs since the earliest days, before social divisions had assumed such importance, and Trent Rowing Club had participated fully in the proceedings, whereas after the establishment of the Amateur Rowing Association the club was barred from entering what was, in effect, its own regatta.

The Burton Rowing Club minutes show the many inter-club letters relating to the matter together with the advice given by the Amateur Rowing Association's headquarters, and on 27 March 1893, there was a special meeting to decide the issue, one which included many community-based, non-rowing regatta committee members who felt that the two gentlemen's clubs had purposefully conspired to exclude the working men's club from participation. The result was that Trent Rowing Club was allowed, by a substantial majority, to compete at the event in a way which was quite contrary to the wishes of the amateur establishment.

Neither the local gentlemen's clubs nor the Amateur Rowing Association could ignore this blatant flaunting of the rules and after three years of further squabbling, the Association finally wrote to say that it would be acceptable for Burton Regatta to hold races for National Amateur Rowing Association clubs or those of any unaffiliated organisations, as long as this was 'clearly stated on posters and programmes by the inclusion of "not under Amateur Rowing Association rules" '.[53]

In Worcester, where the same dilemma existed between traditional popularity and contemporary exclusivity, another compromise allowing a similar dispensation had been worked out with the formation of the Severn and Midland Rowing Association which later became the Provincial Rowing Association, and throughout the country regatta organisers were quick to establish their own local rowing associations which promoted selective events or applied the 'Non-A.R.A.' wording to existing fixtures.

By the end of the century there were additional rowing associations on the River Lea, in the West End of London, in Hammersmith, in Southampton where the Amateur Rowing Association accepted all the local clubs including the working men's clubs, and in Cambridge where the local association actually upheld rather than relaxed the amateur definition, a move which resulted in the formation of the new Cambridge Rowing Club which welcomed working-class members.

As at Cambridge, so at Oxford, where the strict definition was fiercely enforced even to the extent of disqualifying the winner of the ladies' sculling event at the town regatta of 1896 since, as a waterman's sister, she was adjudged to be ineligible for the prize, a ruling which prompted the local paper to exclaim that 'it seems to be a dreadful thing to live in the same street as a professional ... Bah ...'.[54] Happenings such as these continued to aggravate the editor of the *Rowing Almanack* who, in the 1897 edition, continued to promote the establishment view that

> there is an inclination to kick over the traces in the provinces where some very crude notions of amateurism and sport still prevail and if this latitude is overlooked the amateur question in rowing is likely to fall into the same slough as in athletics, cycling and football.

The 'Review' section of the same edition, and many others, was given over to the difficulties of applying the new rules to recalcitrant organisations. R.C. Lehmann, the Amateur Rowing Association's secretary, took up the debate on strict control in his book *The Complete Oarsman*, published in 1908, in which he cites the arguments on both sides.

Against the strict definition he cites the following: the advantages of brute strength are not proven; the definition is arbitrary in its exclusions (banning carpenters but not drapers, for example); the number of working men who can afford the leisure to pursue rowing cannot be great and would be easily controlled; and no other country apart from Germany demands similar prohibitions.

In favour of strictness, he cites the following: amateurism in rowing has been maintained because of the ban against manual workers; that allowing the admission of those who might be tempted by money would simply be the thin end of the wedge; there had been no demand from the National Amateur Rowing Association for any relaxation of the controls; and 'they are happy'.

Strictly speaking, the National Association was not at all happy, having solicited the Amateur Association on many occasions for further talks without success; nor were regatta organisers who complained of falling entries and of support leaching away to 'more popular branches of athletics',[55] while an overt ban on working men was superfluous at a time when the entrance fees and subscriptions to Amateur Rowing Association clubs and events often represented a month's wages for them.

The weight of Lehmann's argument, therefore, taken together with contemporary evidence, would lead an objective observer to conclude that little else but social antipathy towards those involved in menial duties informed the Amateur Association's attitudes at this time with such attitudes actually hardening during and following the First World War. Even stalwart supporters of the Amateur Association, like the Reading Regatta committee, appealed for relaxation in the dark days after the war complaining that 'unless the Amateur Rowing Association were to relax their rigid rules about amateur status, no viable regatta entry could be foreseen'[56] and the Association's refusal to do so appeared to be simply one more example of the post-war 'class cleavage from which the country is now suffering'.[57]

The *News Chronicle* picked up on this theme when it featured 'Snobbery in the Rowing World', reporting that the Mayor of Chester had declined to act as President of Chester Regatta in 1934 since as 'a plumber's apprentice he had been barred from rowing at the event himself', and further informed its readers that the Royal Chester Club 'interpret the Amateur Rowing Association's laws to the letter'.[58] This story and others like it began to attract widespread criticism at a time when the role of physical recreation was coming under scrutiny with a House of Commons debate in 1937 dwelling for some time on the unjustness of the Amateur Association's rule 'that a man who earns his living by his hands is not eligible. There are many Honourable Members in all parts of the House who would like to see that rule revised.'[59]

Not surprisingly, perhaps, the Amateur Rowing Association dropped the offending rule within a matter of weeks of the debate allowing numerous clubs to affiliate almost immediately.

Many of them, like the John O'Gaunt Club in Lancaster and the Northwich Club in Cheshire, had waited many years for the opportunity of doing so.[60] Nevertheless, the Association continued its ban on 'those who worked in or about boats' – a rule which held up the affiliation of the Cambridge Rowing Club in 1951 until the club expelled an offending member who happened to be a college boatman. It also maintained its antipathy towards trade, denying affiliation to the Metropolitan Vickers Rowing Club of Trafford Park, Manchester in 1958 due to its 'association with commerce'.[61]

By 1956 there remained so few who were engaged 'in or about boats' that the prohibition citing them became irrelevant and the rule was finally repealed, leaving the way open for the amalgamation of the two major rowing associations. This produced, in theory at least, an organisation combining the 'grass roots' intelligence of the provincially orientated National Amateur Rowing Association with the efficient administration of the metropolitan-based Amateur Rowing Association.

Throughout the period when the Oxbridge establishment was seeking to exclude the professionals and multifarious 'pseudo-amateurs' from the sport, there were other factors at work which resulted in the reduction of the numbers working in water-borne trades, many of whom were made redundant by a succession of technological innovations. John Taylor, the Waterman's Poet, complained as early as 1622 in *The Arrant Thief* that 'all our profit was running away on wheels' as more sophisticated carriages became available but there remained, according to records at Watermen's Hall, some 3,000 registered watermen in London in 1820 and it was not until the 1840s that new bridges combined with passenger steamers to reduce that number by half.[62]

By 1901 Forster in *Down by the River* had to conclude that 'the oar plays a humble part in the heart of London, a battered skiff or sturdy police boat is all that remains' while further downstream were the Gravesend watermen: 'a brave and resourceful set of men are being driven from the bosom of the Thames'.[63] By 1935 Harry Harris in *Under Oars* notes that there remained 'little if any under oars work anywhere on the London river'.

Elsewhere, the same contraction of water trade can be traced as in

Cambridge where the River Cam had been used extensively for the supply of coal, food and materials until the 1840s when the advent of better roads and rail connections, together with an increased demand due to large population increases, led to the eventual demise of the canal/river trade. Between 1851 and 1900 the numbers of watermen employed on the River Cam fell from 387 to 73[64] and an exactly similar demise in Oxford is described by Mary Prior in *Fisher Row*.

The story of Runcorn Ferry on the River Mersey in Cheshire will stand as an example of numerous others around the country with its decline originating in the opening of the local railway in 1831 and its subsequent purchase by the rail company, shortly after which a footbridge was built and in 1905 a road bridge which killed the ferry trade completely.[65] Around the coasts, the fishing industry was considerably rationalised by the introduction of steam trawlers in the 1870s and 1880s with many men made redundant.

So it was that during the middle years of the century, many watermen began to seek employment in allied occupations with those having specialised rowing knowledge becoming professionals whose activities peaked in the 1870s and whose skills, as seen above, were utilised by many amateur clubs. Although the clubs were more than happy to employ professionals as trainers on several pounds a week and 'winning' bonuses, they continued to seek their total exclusion from competition itself, but found it difficult to do so with the first and second generation of such practitioners.

As the water trades contracted and the supply of skilled men began to diminish, the new rowing associations began to find it easier to squeeze out the professional and semi-professional elements in the sport and we can see how the clubs used those made redundant from full-time employment. As early as the 1850s the London watermen suffered redundancies but had always found opportunities for earning money in cash events at local regattas, even at Henley, but in 1867 Henley Regatta discontinued the watermen's race with the proviso that 'the sum of ten pounds in addition to the twenty pounds paid to them be allowed for their attendance'.[66]

From this time onwards, the watermen, often Doggett's Coat and Badge winners, were used to marshal the course[67] and service the select enclosures, likewise at the large metropolitan events whose accounts show expenditure set aside to employ 'Coat and Badge men' to act as waiters and doormen.[68] Elsewhere, the story was much the same with John Ritchie, a salmon fisherman, first employed in November 1872 by the Berwick-on-Tweed Rowing

14. Berwick-on-Tweed RC, 1881, featuring its gentlemen members and, sitting on the foreshore, its boatman who was paid 10s a week and whose wife was paid 2s a week for scrubbing the clubroom floor.

Club as a boatman at 10s a week;[69] James Mitchell, who doubled as a
municipal boatman and millworker, employed by Bradford Rowing
Club;[70] Jimmy Green who moved up to Chester from Chiswick to
service Royal Chester Rowing Club;[71] Josiah Snape, the local boat
hirer employed by Lancaster Rowing Club for an annual wage of £21
19s 2d;[72] John Tallboys, an Oxford bargeman employed at 5s a week
by the Neptune Rowing Club;[73] an anonymous boat hirer employed
by Warwick Boat Club at 18s a week 'and two pounds a year rent for
16, Mill Street for use by the club';[74] an anonymous fisherman
employed by Ironbridge Rowing Club at a salary of £6 a year;[75] and
Albert Thornborough, a boat builder employed by Hereford Rowing
Club.[76]

Squeezed by the application of an amateur ethic from above and a
diminishing supply from below, the professional element in the sport
of rowing gradually withered and was practically moribund before
the First World War. After the war there remained a few isolated
instances of professional events in otherwise strictly amateur regattas,
as at the Gravesend Town Regatta which was revived after the hostilities in 1925 with a programme much reduced due to the contraction of
the local river trade but with several races for small cash prizes or gift
vouchers.

In the north of England the Gateshead Christmas Handicap
spluttered to an end in 1938 while the one remaining professional
event at Durham Regatta came to an end in 1947 when the competitors themselves expressed the desire that 'the name "Professional
Four Oared Handicap" be dropped in favour of the "Northern Rowing Association Four Oared Handicap" since it was their intention to
become amateurs'.[77]

The final victory for amateurism came, ironically, at Gravesend
where in 1698 the first professional racing had taken place: in 1950
Eric Phelps and Eric Lupton competed there for the last professional
European Sculling Championship under the conditions, as expressed
in the programme, that 'they row today for the love of rowing and
without definite promise of any particular prize.'[78]

The continuing application of the amateur ethic during the nineteenth century was directly responsible for the formation of
hundreds of clubs throughout the country which were established
either for the purpose of maintaining social exclusivity or providing
those excluded with the means of carrying on organised activities.
The fortunes of these clubs were subject to a host of determining
factors, an investigation of which is the subject of the following
chapter.

NOTES

1. Quoted in G.L. Guttsman's *The English Ruling Class* (Weidenfeld & Nicolson, 1969), p. 207.
2. See references to clergymen as founder members of the club in *Royal Chester Rowing Club 1838–1938* (Laver, Liverpool, 1939).
3. 'The Diary of Moses Heap', typescript in Rawtenstall library: 'After the Act we played games on a Saturday which we had never done before' (p. 21).
4. *The Saturday Review* (5 July 1862), 4b.
5. *Hansard* (26 April 1866), c. 2099.
6. Mrs Beeton, *The Book of Household Management* (Longman Green, 1888), p. 1453.
7. A. Trollope, *British Sports and Pastimes* (Virtue & Spalding, 1868), p. 5.
8. M. Shearman, *Athletics and Football* (Longman Green, 1888), p. 7.
9. M. Sanderson, *The Universities in the Nineteenth Century* (Routledge, 1975), p. 17.
10. *The Times* (15 April 1841), 5a.
11. *Bell's Life* (10 April 1852), 7b.
12. A. Maclaren, *Training in Theory and Practice* (Macmillan, 1866), p. 43.
13. 'Review', *British Rowing Almanack* (1873).
14. London Rowing Club, minutes (20 March 1872).
15. Chester Regatta, poster (28 June 1838).
16. *Chester Chronicle* (12 Oct. 1838), 7a.
17. *Liverpool Albion* (28 July 1840), 4c.
18. Lancaster Rowing Club, minutes (20 Aug. 1843). Also, from the same source, the view of a Gentleman Amateur on the respective merits of Artisan vs. Gentlemen's rowing:

    17 September 1945

    The Quayside people held their 'Mudlark' regatta today, overhead it rained, underfoot was squashy and around the cold wind swept in gusts. A committee of management (save the mark …) have arranged the races in so comfortable a way that every boat that runs must have a prize either great or small and sundry little dodges are used to make ends meet. Nothing more need be said of this miserable business than that the prizes amounted to £21.7.6. d, that never more than 200 people were assembled to witness the races, that the committee looked like drowned rats from rain etc., etc., and that the only good race in the lot produced a vast amount of Jaw at the riverside and a long letter of complaint in the newspaper on the Saturday. At night, the committee, the competitors and a few 'navvies' got hilarious together but at whose expense this correspondent saith not.

    Tuesday, 22 September

    The club, having now been established comfortably on Halton Water for something like 5 or 6 weeks, this day held their 3rd regatta on that most excellent spot for boating. The course was from just above the aqueduct to a buoy moored opposite Halton Hall, round it and back to the starting point. James Alison of Carus Lodge gave permission to the club to use part of one of his fields for the accommodation of spectators and here the club pitched two tents and placed in them tables laden with a tolerable profusion of good things, Champagne and Venison Pasty forming no small item on the bill of fare. All comers were welcome and not a few availed themselves of the privilege. A brass band and the drums and pipes of the boys of the National School were stationed here, playing in twin appropriate airs. The noble aqueduct bore its crowds of gazers and every good point of view was amply occupied. Mr. Alison at Carus Lodge, Mr. Swainson at Halton Hall and the Reverend Mackereth at Halton Rectory each entertained parties of friends during the day. The weather could not possibly have been more propitious and of the scenery all that can be said is that very few clubs can boast its equal in regatta grounds.

19. Lancaster Rowing club, minutes (7 Sept. 1844).
20. R.J. Davis, *Boating in Worcester in the Nineteenth Century* (Russell, Worcester, 1977), p.5.
21. Henley Regatta, minutes (18 May 1859).
22. *Bedfordshire Times* (16 Aug. 1866), 3d.
23. *Barrow Herald* (15 Sept. 1877), 3a.
24. Middlesbrough Boat Club, minutes (15 Sept. 1866), Rule 12.
25. *Isle of Wight Observer* (31 March 1877), 5b.
26. *Chester Chronicle* (26 June 1840), 4c.
27. Public Notice for an Annual Boat Race. May 1828

> A Rowing match will take place on Thursday next, the first day of May, weather permitting, the boats to start half an hour after flood tide (about one o'clock) from Bank Quay to Warrington Bridge for the first heat; the other heats to be around a boat   that
> will be moored opposite the Black Lion, Wilderspool and back again to the bridge.

Prize for the first boat	A New Boat
Prize for second boat	£1.00
Prize for third boat	£0.10.0
Prize for fourth boat	£0.7.6
Prize for fifth boat	£0.2.6

Boats entered

Henry Duckworth's *Filmert*	colours	Pink
John Ken's *John and Sarah*	colours	Blue
Loden Well's *Wasp*	colours	Yellow
George Richardson's *Betsy*	colours	Green body and pink sleeves
Edward Green's *Alice*	colours	Green body

These races were part of traditional May Day sports and were contested by local watermen and fishermen. They were, however, gradually subsumed under the auspices of the Warrington Regatta from 1840 onwards.

28. Warrington Regatta, minutes (19 Dec. 1841).
29. Lancaster Rowing Club, minutes (22 Sept. 1846).
30. *Preston Chronicle* (12 Sept. 1846), 7a.
31. *The Athlete* (14 Dec. 1875), 4d.
32. Agecroft Rowing Club, minutes (10 Aug. 1874), including the following correspondence: *from the Hon. Sec. Agecroft Regatta, to the Editor of the* Examiner and Times *of Manchester*:

> Will you kindly allow me to state a few facts in reference to the Maiden Four-oared race at this regatta; in the preliminary programme the prize was thus defined 'Maiden Fours Plate, value £10, to be rowed in boats provided by the committee by "Gentlemen" who have never won a four-oared race at a regatta'. From this preliminary programme, a crew entered from the Bolton & Ringley Amateur Rowing Club. We are bound to receive that entry unless we know that they are not actually what they represent themselves to be. They therefore come and row, and in the course of the day it becomes very evident that they are not by any means gentlemen, but sturdy working men of the class known as artisans. They row, or rather pull (under protest) with such power and persistance that, despite the utmost efforts, gentlemen who make the art of rowing a study for their leisure hours are defeated by these men through sheer 'brute force'. In consequence of the protest lodged against them after their victory, the committee withheld the prize in order that the matter might be investigated and after due deliberation the following was resolved upon; that the Bolton & Ringley Amateur Rowing Club be disqualified, it being a mistake that they were allowed to start. Since this mistake did

occur the committee will give them £10 in money although under no obligation to do so since they entered on false pretences. The committee took a broad view of the matter and as it is not unlikely that these men (very decent men in their way) might possibly have misread the qualifications or not have been able to read them at all, it would have been rather inconsiderate to turn them off without anything. We therefore gave them the same amount as the prize in money and as that money has not been returned, we may reasonably suppose it has been accepted.

From the Hon. Sec. Bolton and Ringley Amateur Rowing Club to the Editor of the Examiner and Times:

With your permission I wish to say a word or two with respect to the letter written by the Secretary of the Agecroft Regatta Committee in your Monday's issue. The regatta committee has indeed disqualified our crew but on what grounds it has not told the public; he says £10 has been forwarded to the crew which is true but we cannot accept a money prize since our rules will not allow us to do so since to do so would for ever have excluded us from rowing in another amateur regatta; we have therefore returned the money to the regatta treasurer. The secretary of the regatta states that programmes were sent out and indeed our club received one and also many other invitations to send a crew to the regatta. As to their being bound to accept our entrance, they knew very well that we were working men, for the Agecroft rowers have been up to our club two or three times and rowed with us on different occasions. The two clubs have known each other for two years and they knew very well that we were working men. As to the Agecroft members not inviting us to send a crew, the following is a copy of an invitation from them word for word: 'I enclose a few preliminary programmes for our eighth regatta which you will perhaps post up in a conspicuous place in your boathouse. We shall be most happy to provide boathouse accommodation for crews coming to practise over the course. Boats may be left until August 5th if desired. Hoping your club will honour us by sending us some competitors, Your Obedient Servant, E. Horrax, Hon. Sec. Agecroft Regatta Committee.'

Now, I will leave the public to judge whether the entry from Bolton & Ringley Amateur Rowing Club is a mistake of entry or not.

33. Henley Regatta, minutes (27 June 1870).
34. Henley Regatta, minutes (29 Aug. 1879), together with the rigorous definition of 'amateur' passed by the committee on 8 April 1879: 'No person shall be considered an amateur oarsman or sculler: First, who has ever competed in any open competition for a stake, money or entrance fee; secondly, who has ever competed with or against a professional for any prize; thirdly, who has ever taught, pursued or assisted in athletic exercise of any kind as a means of gaining a livelihood; fourthly, who has been employed in or about boats for money or wages; fifthly, is or has been by trade or employment for wages, a mechanic, artisan or labourer.'
35. *The Times* (6 June 1843), 6a.
36. *The Times* (25 June 1844), 7c.
37. *Oxford Times* (21 Aug. 1841), 2a.
38. *Newcastle Chronicle* (12 May 1865), 8d.
39. Nottingham Rowing Club, minutes (8 Dec. 1862).
40. *Berwick Advertiser* (22 Jan. 1869), 3c.
41. Berwick Regatta, programme (20 Aug. 1872).
42. E.D. Brickwood, *Boatracing* (Horace Cox, 1876), p. 47.
43. 'Review', *British Rowing Almanack* (1883).
44. *Bedfordshire Times* (8 Aug. 1882), 11d.
45. 'A.R.A. Proceedings', *British Rowing Almanack* (1885).
46. Burton Rowing Club, minutes (18 June 1890).
47. Bradford Amateur Rowing Club, minutes (23 July 1890).
48. 'Review', *British Rowing Almanack* (1892).

49. *Cumberland News* (25 Aug. 1891), 4a.
50. 'Review', *British Rowing Almanack* (1900).
51. West of England Amateur Rowing Association, minutes (29 Jan. 1896).
52. Evidence of P.S.G. Propert, co-founder of NARA in *F.J. Furnivall – A Record* (Frowde, 1911), p. 43.
53. Burton Rowing Club, minutes (9 March 1897).
54. *Oxford Chronicle* (23 Aug. 1896), 7c.
55. *Cumberland News* (17 July 1909), 5e.
56. Reading Regatta, minutes (15 July 1922).
57. *The Times* (2 Nov. 1926), 12b. Letter from the Charity Organisation Society.
58. *News Chronicle* (30 July 1934), 7a.
59. *Hansard*, Vol. 322 (7 April 1937), pp. 236–7.
60. John O'Gaunt Rowing Club, minutes (25 March 1938); and Northwich Rowing Club, minutes (28 June 1938).
61. Amateur Rowing Association, minutes (16 June 1958).
62. *Morning Chronicle* (17 Oct. 1850), 3a.
63. *Daily Telegraph* (28 April 1908), 13c.
64. G. J. Greenhough, 'The Present Use of the River Cam' (M. Litt., Cambridge, 1980).
65. For a photograph of the last Runcorn ferryman see plate 24 in *Victorian and Edwardian Boating* (Batsford, 1987).
66. Henley Regatta, minutes (24 June 1867).
67. For the 'Watermen's Procession' see plate 7 of *Victorian and Edwardian Boating* (Batsford, 1987).
68. London Rowing Club, minutes, Annual Report (1877).
69. Berwick Rowing Club, Cash Book (17 Nov. 1872).
70. Bradford Amateur Rowing Club, minutes (18 Sept. 1872).
71. Royal Chester Rowing Club, minutes (16 Aug. 1885).
72. Lancaster Rowing Club, Annual Accounts (1895).
73. Neptune Rowing Club, minutes (12 June 1894).
74. Warwick Boat Club, minutes (9 March 1897).
75. Ironbridge Rowing Club, Annual Accounts (1899).
76. *Hereford Times* (19 July 1901), 10b.
77. Durham Regatta, minutes (30 April 1947).
78. Gravesend Town Regatta, programme (22 July 1950).

7

Club Fortunes

The careers of rowing clubs are very chequered, full
of ups and downs.

(Edmund Sharpe, Jnr at the John O'Gaunt
Rowing Club dinner of 20 January 1920)

Taken over a period of 150 years or so, it is apparent that club
fortunes have been affected by an enormous variety of factors. The
range extends from the obvious considerations of geography
and environment, through those of social culture, politics and
economics to club constitution and administration, each of which
has had its ramifications in advancing or retarding club progress.
The origins of most determining factors were, and remain, part
cultural and part environmental, a truth well displayed at the turn of
the eighteenth century in the Eton Boating Book which cites official
objections to rowing not only on the basis of the practical dangers
presented by water-borne infections but also on the basis of
the moral dangers of association with disreputable waterside
characters.

Despite the complexities involved it is possible, at least,
to identify the availability and quality of water as the dominant
considerations in the development of rowing clubs, fluctuations in
which were subject to both man and nature. Many areas of the
country were simply not sufficiently well endowed with rowable
water to sustain an active club for any length of time and yet so keen
was the enthusiasm for boating that clubs did spring up in the most
unlikely locations.

One such area was Bolton where, by general consent, 'the
facilities for boating are unhappily nil as the River Croal can hardly
be said to be available for the purpose, nor does a spin on the local
canal offer a very tempting prospect' but where, nevertheless, a club
was established in 1865 only to bow to the inevitable and move to the
nearby Rumworth Reservoir four years later.[1] Likewise in Bury,
where the prospect presented a 'very circumscribed scope for

aquatic pursuits lacking a broad, bright bosomed river affording merely a narrow, shallow, zig-zag, inky stream' but where a club and regatta were inaugurated on the local reservoir[2] with both venues eventually closed to recreational use by the city authorities as likely to contaminate the only local supplies of 'corporation pop'.

The use of artificial waters was commonplace particularly in the flatlands of the east of England where meandering rivers had been substantially canalised to take the barge traffic of earlier centuries but whose consequent narrowness restricted rowing activity to timed or 'bump' races. These originated in inter-college competitions at Cambridge but also took place at Gainsborough and at Lincoln where racing was organised along the Foss Dyke with crews rowing at intervals of 100 ft;[3] where canals were wider, as at Boston, club rowing became firmly established and traditional regattas were inaugurated.

Some difficulties, like the distance from the river quoted in the Cheltenham College Boat Book of 1860, proved insuperable even by highly motivated college and university oarsmen while others were overcome by combinations of good fortune and sound management. Boating on the turbulent River Severn was, for example, considerably facilitated by the Severn Navigation Act of 1842, which greatly enhanced the Worcester Regatta by taming the stream with a succession of locks whose provision also encouraged the formation of clubs at Stourport, Bewdley, Bridgnorth and Ironbridge.

Such developments were endorsed by local rowing organisations and often resulted in an expansion of rowing activity like the regatta at Nottingham where, despite the existence of an admirable river 'clean in character, gentle in current and surrounded by rural scenery', there had been no city event due to the obstruction presented by the old Trent Bridge. The new, four-arch Trent Bridge of 1870 entirely removed 'the greatest obstacle to river traffic and stimulated several gentlemen to organise a regatta'.[4] In Birkenhead the new Liverpool Victoria Rowing Club made successful representations to the Mersey Docks and Harbour Board in 1892 to relax its restrictions on boating while also securing a site away from further dock developments which ensured its continuation unlike its many smaller neighbours whose lack of such foresight consigned them to oblivion.

Where similar club spirit existed many, seemingly grievous, difficulties were overcome, no more so than at Bradford, where the River Aire was not only considered 'too narrow for proper racing'[5] but where the club stretch of water was controlled by Saltaire Mills who could 'run it off at their convenience',[6] a situation remedied by several moves upsteam, the last of which necessitated the dismantling, transport and reconstruction of the whole boathouse, brick by brick. Nevertheless, some situations became too fraught and the Lancaster Rowing Club which, like Bradford Rowing Club, had moved upstream from its original site, found later that its new rural location became less accessible as local industry encroached upon it to the extent that the right of way to the boathouse was withdrawn altogether, to be replaced by a toll which, together with other difficulties, brought about the club's demise.[7]

Elsewhere, other clubs in similar circumstances – for example, Bradford RC at Saltaire and Agecroft RC in Salford – secured their positions through the far-sightedness of original trustees who had bought rather than leased their properties. Even this provision failed to save the numerous clubs on isolated and vulnerable sites in areas of Victorian enterprise such as those set aside for dock development in Birkenhead and Manchester.

Not only did industrial development dispossess many clubs, its consequences caused massive disruption: as early as the 1860s the club at Warrington was obliged to cease rowing due to the river-borne pollution produced by the nearby brewery, leather and soapworks while similar effluent produced by the local chemical works pushed the Gloucester Rowing Club off its stretch of the River Severn on to a nearby canal. Even in rural Berwick-on-Tweed, massive river pollution produced by no less than 93 small mills[8] caused the fledgling club to restrict its outings. Mixed with the industrial effluent was raw sewage universally and continuously poured into rivers throughout the land, often with devastating effects for the sport as on the River Lea in north London which had, according to *The Times*, 'all the appearance of a large reservoir of sewage and has ceased to be what it once was, a stream in which it was possible to bathe and on which boating could be had and enjoyed'.[9]

The story elsewhere was much the same: in Cambridge everyone 'had seen the river impassable for foreign bodies'[10] and in Oxford the River Isis was 'little more than an open sewer with the major discharge being at Folly Bridge',[11] the worst possible point for rowing since it was here that Salter's boathouse played host to numerous small clubs; the Leeds Corporation poured sewage entirely untreated into the River Aire, a major factor in forcing rowing off the river on to Roundhay Park Lake where, due to insufficient depth of water, it never flourished; and similar municipal actions throughout the whole length of the rivers Irwell and Mersey only came to an end in 1892 when all the neighbouring authorities joined to counter the overwhelming pollution,[12] the sole rowing survivor of which was Agecroft Rowing Club whose founders had the good sense to choose an upstream site well out of harm's way.

The quality of available water was further affected by the presence of steamboats and barges which presented the greatest hazard to the progress of 'scientific oarsmanship', particularly in commercial centres, and forced the early London clubs upstream to Putney while also pushing the University Boat Race, regattas and Amateur Sculling Championship on to the quieter upper reaches.[13]

As the new suburban rail lines moved westwards gentlemen interested in aquatics took the opportunity during the 1860s to avoid river congestion and establish clubs on the Kingston and Staines stretches of river. The movement 'up-river' was necessary wherever industrialisation brought about domestic or commercial growth and was, therefore, predominantly a northern phenomenon with the wealthier gentlemen's clubs availing themselves of the option, viz. Mersey RC of Liverpool moving to Chester; Agecroft RC to Kersal Vale; Derwent RC of Derby to Darley Grove; Bradford RC to Shipley Glen; Middlesbrough BC to Stockton; Tyne RC to Newburn.

However, we can also see the same trend in the south in Gloucester where the rowing club moved to Hempstead and in Bristol where dock extensions encouraged Ariel RC to move to St. Annes. In practically every case the movement out left behind a poorer club which continued to struggle with the inadequacies of the original site and the majority of these, not surprisingly, eventually ceased operations: Liverpool RC, Nemesis RC, Shipley RC (Bradford), Northern RC (Newcastle), Derby Artisans RC and Avon RC.

Action continued to be taken by those clubs capable of it whenever disruption seemed likely and in 1926 the proposal for a new power station to be constructed on the Dukes Meadow site at Chiswick galvanised all the upper tideway clubs from Kew to Putney into concerted action against the plan. They nominated Julius Beresford of Thames RC to lobby on their behalf. He, in turn, instructed a King's Council to represent their interests at a public inquiry and alerted Sir Henry Moore, MP, who duly brought up the subject in Parliament.[14] The whole plan was viewed with particular apprehension by those interested in tideway rowing since it incor-

15. A central stretch of the River Irwell in Salford, c. 1900, showing the level of congestion which effectively killed rowing on the river. Note a lone Nemesis RC pair-oared boat (*left*).

porated the construction of new coal wharves and envisaged a large increase in barge traffic which would detrimentally affect the activities of 'the well known rowing clubs of London, Thames, Vesta, Auriol, Kensington and Anglian together with those of many colleges and schools, banks and business houses'.[15] The plan was dropped.

The enormous growth in the number of rowing clubs during the middle years of the nineteenth century and the consequent fragmentation within the sport exactly mirrored the dislocation of contemporary society, one which was caused by the relocation of a rural working class into towns followed by a middle-class retreat into suburbia. Some areas of the country were more affected than others by this migration but nowhere remained completely untouched, for, as Paul Mantoux has observed, the early development of Manchester and Liverpool 'sucked in such a mass of population from other regions that the whole demographic balance of the country was upset'[16] and this was followed by extensive industrial developments in the north-east, the Midlands and London itself.

While such developments were responsible for mass incursions to specific locations of people whose very presence encouraged the commercial provision of recreational facilities, they also created cultural and economic fluctuations, which directly determined the fortunes of many rowing clubs throughout the country. In the Manchester area, there were some dozen independent clubs together with further 'one-boat' clubs using the established public-house facilities which also hosted the professional class and the Manchester and Salford Regatta, one of the earliest in the country established in 1842, provided separate races for every conceivable class of oarsman 'so that no youth inclined to boat racing had any difficulty in finding encouragement'.[17]

Indeed, the north-west of England which cradled the Industrial Revolution and suffered the over-population that went with it also nurtured some of the earliest clubs and regattas in the country with Warrington RC (1840), Mersey RC (1840), Nemesis RC (1847), Broughton RC (1848) and Bury RC (1853) all easily pre-dating the first properly constituted metropolitan club, the London RC of 1856 and even Leander Club which only ceased to be a 'one-boat' club when it moved from commercial premises to its own boathouse in Putney as late as 1866. The same trend is discernible in the growing industrial areas of the north-east with Tyne RC (1852) and the Midlands with Burton Leander RC (1847) and Derwent RC (1857).

At the same time as these clubs were developing in the industrial regions, others were established in the county towns by the local gentry, viz. Royal Chester RC (1836), Vigornia RC (Worcester, 1841), Lancaster RC (1842), Gloucester RC (1846), Huntingdon RC (1854), Shrewsbury RC (1857) and Hereford RC (1860), all of which were formed as socially exclusive members' clubs by people who wished to maintain the tone of their home towns against the possible intrusions of the commercial and industrial classes. In Chester, for example, it had been for generations 'the deliberate policy of the citizens to ignore and thwart any exploitation of the city's economic potential',[18] an attitude which also informed the membership rules of the Royal Chester Rowing Club and one equally matched by the Shrewsbury club whose members were recruited exclusively from the 'Nobility, Gentry and Clergy' elements of society.[19]

Despite efforts to keep the cultural effects of economic development at arm's length, it was impossible for many clubs to avoid the repercussions of fluctuating economic fortunes and nowhere is this more clearly demonstrated than in Lancaster where lapses in the regatta exactly coincide with the failure of the local cotton markets,[20] which caused the subscription lists to wither away completely. Some clubs managed to weather such storms due to the benefaction of local patrons which was more commonly forthcoming in the smaller market towns like Gainsborough, where the local club prospered through all the periodic depressions of its first fifty years due to the support of Major Marshall of the town's agricultural engineering firm which provided subscriptions, personnel and premises to the extent that it was 'not possible to estimate the great advantage to the rowing club of such a connection'.[21]

In Stratford-on-Avon, the patronage was extended by the club president, Sir Arthur Hodgson, a local landowner who, despite the agricultural depressions of the 1890s, continued to solicit support for the club with the result that it was 'more generously assisted than any other club in the borough'.[22] A similar story can be told of James Williamson who, as president of the John O'Gaunt Club in Lancaster, ended years of uncertainty by donating its site to club members in perpetuity for the annual rent of just 2s 6d.[23] Where individual sponsorship was unavailable for a town club, as in Cambridge, the local shopkeepers frequently came to the rescue in times of economic depression, particularly in order to revive an annual regatta, and in 1899 the regatta organisers thanked the local employers not only for providing prize vouchers but also for allowing their assistants to leave work early in order to compete for them.[24]

This 'double' sponsorship was also provided on a much larger scale by the Players' Company in Nottingham, the Wills Company in Bristol and the Midland Railway Company in Derby. Certain areas of the country were more susceptible to the vagaries of economic fortunes than others and the north-east in particular was badly hit by the succession of depressions experienced throughout the country during the second half of the nineteenth century and the first of the twentieth, in contrast to the relative prosperity enjoyed in the south of the country. While the General Strike of 1926, for example, called as a countrywide demonstration against the government's economic policies, endangered the very existence of some northern clubs such as those at Blyth and Cambois whose members were excused subscriptions 'until the first pay day after the strike',[25] its results in the south were mild indeed.

Typical of these were the inconveniences produced by the strike and suffered by one Cambridge college crew whose 'coach was on duty constabular with cox giving lessons vocabular'.[26] Later still, in 1939, the London Rowing Club Annual Report stated that the main disruption to its activities derived from the high incidence of marriage among its members, together with the loss of many others to medical school. Further reading of club correspondence at this time reveals a continual loss of active members to colonial service abroad.

The availability of workers for participation in rowing was a prime determinant in the growth of clubs, since, before 1878 and the Factories and Workshops Act, employees were unable to row except on Sundays and summer evenings. Many organisers of early regattas only managed to secure mass support for their events by prevailing upon the local corporation to award special half-day holidays so that workers could attend if not actually compete. Conditions of work varied considerably from one area and industry to another and it was as early as 1861, for instance, that the hosiery manufacturers in Nottingham replaced the mid-week half-day holiday with a regular Saturday afternoon break, which prompted the establishment of the Nottingham Rowing Club in 1862, while the heavy engineering centres like Derby had to wait until 1878 for similar dispensation, immediately reflected there in the formation of Derby Rowing Club in 1879.

In London, the 1878 Act spawned literally scores of company or trades clubs[27] whose existence encouraged the rowing establishment to tighten further the rules excluding working men from rowing, a development which culminated in the formation of the Amateur Rowing Association in 1882 and the subsequent formation of various Trades Rowing Associations throughout the 1880s and the National Amateur Rowing Association in 1890.

Ever since the beginning of organised rowing, the difficulties presented by declining interest had attracted the attention of commentators, the first of which in *Aquatics* of 1851 bemoaned the marked falling off in rowing activity which he ascribed to the expense connected with the sport in clubs which often restricted membership to the number of boat seats available, dividing all necessary expenditure accordingly. The numerous London Tideway clubs of this era were too small to be either financially viable or competitively successful, with the result that the level of aquatic activity declined dramatically during the 1850s.

This situation prompted the establishment of London Rowing Club in 1856 which welcomed an unlimited membership at a reasonable subscription of one guinea which immediately resulted in a thriving club with competitive success at the Henley Regatta of 1857 attracting a further supply of new members. The importance of competitive success was well understood by club and regatta officials alike and the stewards of the Manchester and Salford Regatta of 1858 endeavoured to ensure a healthy entry by stipulating that 'all crews contesting and not winning a first or second prize will have their entrance fees returned',[28] sure in the knowledge that crews who had paid to lose were unlikely to return the following year. Many regattas suffered from the competitive weakness of local crews and a constant refrain was that 'home grown skill should, after all, be a great if not chief object of regatta committee care'[29] which led, often counter-productively, to the inclusion of events closed to all but local entrants and to joint crews made up from several clubs.

In some instances, the strength of 'out-of-town' competition killed regattas completely, as in the case of Derby Regatta in its early years, and the lack of local rowing enthusiasm was blamed for the failure of numerous regattas in Reading during the last quarter of the nineteenth century. This was explained by the 'difficulty of getting men together due to the prosperity of Reading and the many other things to do in the town'.[30] The racing success of a club would attract competition from other areas to its home regatta which helps to account for the blazing success of the events in Bedford whose local club had 'by its rowing success placed itself on a par with the best clubs in England'.[31] While this effect was well noted, it was not always possible for clubs in remoter areas to take advantage of it, although Norwich oarsmen finally managed to bring back prosperity to their area following almost a century of parochial contests by dint of 'competing away and convincing clubs that they had a regatta worth visiting with stout local defenders of the Yare Championship'.[32] We can also see how Bideford Rowing Club's success at south coast regattas pulled in quality competition to its own, hugely popular events during the 1920s and 1930s at a time when clubs such as Poole RC and Worthing RC were suffering from exactly the opposite condition.[33]

Competing away was not always straightforward and was mostly determined by the availability of suitable boat transport provided, during the nineteenth century, by rail networks which, when well developed, allowed clubs to compete at 'foreign' regattas and facilitated reciprocal visits. As we have seen, the earliest regattas occurred in the newly industrialised areas of the north-west and north-east where there already existed extensive rail networks which encouraged the development of substantial events at Chester, Durham, Newcastle, Warrington, Liverpool, Lancaster and Preston in the 1830s and early 1840s, while the Midlands were opened up by links between Derby, Burton and Nottingham in 1846.

Early rowing on the River Thames was strengthened by the close proximity of clubs to one another and the ease with which crews could simply row up or down river to neighbouring competitions but the venues of the newer Metropolitan clubs were determined by the periodic westward advances of new or improved rail extensions which created the new suburbia: London RC at Putney (1856), Kingston RC (1858) heavily dependent on members from expanding Surbiton, Twickenham RC (1860), Molesey RC (1866), and Staines RC (1866). The fast city services were also utilised to the full: witness the notice of 1861 from Thames RC at Putney which encouraged attendance at training by advertising the 'rowing train which leaves Waterloo at 6.34 p.m.; crews will be formed at 7.00 p.m.'.[34]

In the east, the Broxbourne club on the northern reaches of the River Lea was one of the first 'commuter' clubs established in 1847 on the first London to Cambridge rail connection while the working men's club of Clapton Warwick was formed nearly 30 years later close by the new Lea Bridge station, soon after the opening of the Chingford Line which was pushed up the Lea Valley by the Great

Eastern Railway to facilitate the growth of the local brick-making industry.[35] Similar developments can be seen elsewhere, particularly in Cambridgeshire where the establishment of Huntingdon RC in 1854 and St Ives RC in 1860 immediately followed the arrival of rail links providing easier access to neighbouring rowing areas and on the Isle of Wight where clubs at Shanklin (1875) and Ryde (1877) were formed only after rail connections to the ferry terminus opened up the prospect of competition at various south coast events.

The earliest railway companies positively welcomed boat freight which they transported on flatwagons but rates varied considerably with clubs in the remoter areas suffering inflation, typical of which was the £5 3s 6d paid by Lancaster Rowing Club for the carriage of a four-oared boat to Preston Regatta and back in 1847[36] despite the club chairman's position as a director of the rail company. The larger companies actually sponsored events as did the London and North West Rail Company in conveying 'boats *free* of charge to and from' the Bedford Regatta of 1864[37] being fully aware of the enormous commercial potential of such events in filling holiday 'specials'.

The size and number of regattas increased noticeably during the 1870s, almost certainly due to a vast new excursion business generated by a series of measures leading to a widespread expansion of free time and, the more this business grew, the less inclined were the rail companies to carry boats at all, initially relegating them to carriage roofs where they became covered in soot and later introducing prohibitive freight charges. Clubs began to complain about the situation, particularly those with large distances to travel, and Ryde Rowing Club, together with other south-coast clubs, 'memorialised the local rail companies in the hope of obtaining more advantageous terms' without success,[38] while Kingston Rowing Club in Hull was unable to send any crews away during one season due to 'the enormous cost of taking the new Clasper'.[39]

In 1911 Hereford Rowing Club represented the provincial point of view to the Amateur Rowing Association by drawing its attention to the exorbitant freight rates and sought its intervention with the rail companies only to learn the following year that the companies 'were unable to accede to a reduction in carriage rates for boats',[40] an outcome resulting in regatta committees providing boats on site which gradually had the effect of depressing the standard of rowing in the provinces.

When clubs managed to travel and compete but consistently

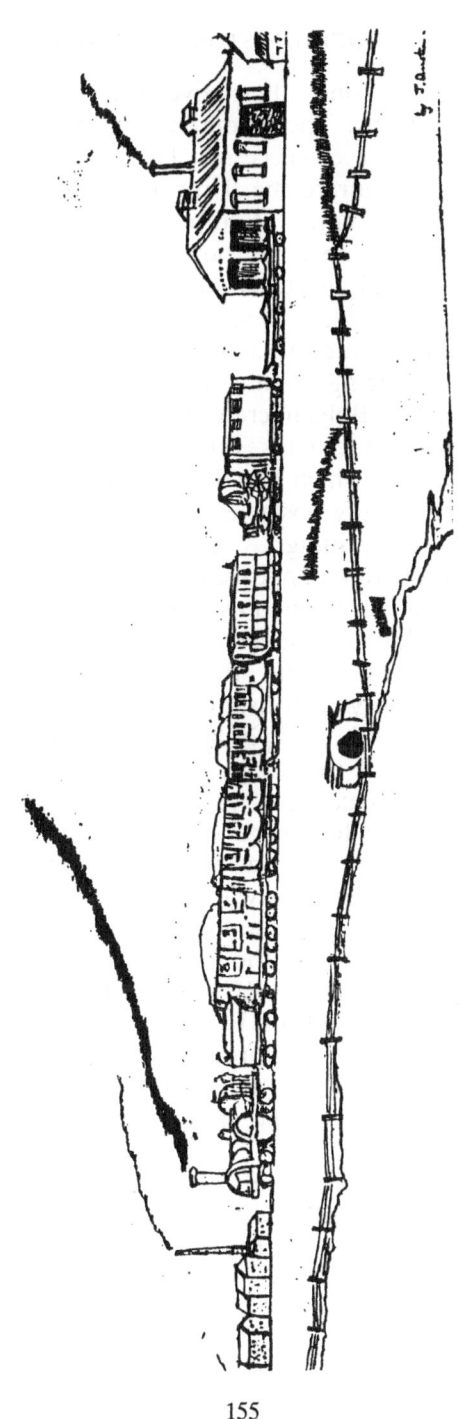

16. Lancaster Rowing Club's boat, *Lune No. 1*, being pulled out of Lancaster station en route for Chester Regatta, August 1845. Many boats were transported on flat wagons, as here, in the early years of the railways, but were gradually banished to carriage roofs and ultimately banned altogether as uneconomic.

failed to win, one alternative was to poach better oarsmen from other clubs. The prime culprit in this respect was Leander Club, whose lack of success at Henley Regatta prompted the club officers to inaugurate the 'University Qualification' in 1890 which encouraged the entry of 'top oarsmen from the universities or those who seem specially desirable to the committee',[41] a policy which often rendered the best men unavailable to the smaller, less successful clubs. Despite such efforts to concentrate rowing talent on the London tideway at Putney, it became obvious that British rowing was lagging behind the foreign competition with Leander Club losing to a Belgian crew at Henley Regatta in 1907 and defeats at the hands of Germans, Canadians and Americans in subsequent years, a decline which the *British Rowing Almanack* of 1911 attributed to the 'many obstacles in the way of getting the City man to devote time to training'.

What, at the time, appeared to be the final insult was the crushing defeat of Leander Club in the 1914 Grand Challenge Cup at Henley Regatta by Harvard University which resulted in the insertion of the following lament in the 'In Memoriam' columns of *The Times*: 'In loving memory of British Rowing which passed away at Henley on Saturday, July 4th. Deeply lamented by many sorrowing followers who hereby place their regret on record'.[42]

During the next five years similar, black-bordered columns expanded to fill whole pages of newspapers around the country with the names of the dead and missing, among whom were enormous numbers of rowing men with most clubs closing down throughout the hostilities simply due to the lack of membership. Clubs often lost every active member to the forces, for example John O'Gaunt RC, Bradford RC, Neptune RC, Nottingham RC, Poole RC, Lincoln BC, and Eton Excelsior RC, and the national average mortality rate for club members approached one-third, figures which certainly support the contention found in Neptune Rowing Club's Annual Report for 1914 that 'the great sport of rowing proves that it is a breeder of patriotism'.

The habits of daring and endurance exhibited by officers and men had often been attributed to the 'manly sports of Britain' since the time of Waterloo and were alluded to in regard to the Crimean War by J.H. Walsh in his *Manual of British Rural Sports* in 1856, in which rowing figures prominently, while perusal of rowing club membership figures during the Boer War period indicates the extent to which those hostilities affected clubs up and down the country.[43] In the immediate post-war years there was an astonishing revival of rowing fortunes as many clubs and regattas achieved record levels of participation, due to a steady accumulation of funds and careful stewardship during the war combined with a universal feeling of release after years of restraint.

Regattas on the River Thames showed a particular resurgence since it was possible for clubs on the river simply to row to the various venues of competition, but elsewhere transport difficulties allied to delays in the return of active members precluded an immediate revival. Typical of many provincial regattas was that at Durham whose secretary received the following replies to his inquiry concerning possible entries for the 1919 regatta: Ryton RC (returned undelivered), South Shields RC ('failed to see how they could manage to send a crew'), Tynemouth RC (no reply), Tees RC ('no fine boat rowing possible owing to transport difficulties'), Sunderland RC (returned undelivered), York RC ('a tentative "yes"'), and Talkin Tarn RC (no reply); needless to say there was no regatta in 1919.[44]

Nevertheless, as more men returned to civilian life, even the regions resuscitated and, certainly by 1923, the *Rowing Almanack* could truly observe that 'there were more men participating in the sport than at any previous period', a post-war revival that was repeated in practically every detail after the Second World War, albeit with a smaller number of clubs, since the reduction brought about by the economic depression in the 1930s more than compensated for the upturn in fortunes enjoyed during the 1920s (Appendix 2).

The depressed 1930s saw many smaller clubs fail through want of support and in some areas the contraction of activity was particularly noticeable, as in Manchester where six predominantly working men's clubs went defunct leaving only Agecroft Rowing Club, a trend also discernible elsewhere: in Chester where 8 clubs were reduced to 3, Newcastle (5 to 2), Oxford (9 to 3), Cambridge (7 to 3), Worcester (5 to 2), Southampton (5 to 1) and York (6 to 1), with all the failed clubs being trade- or works-based organisations such as Armstrong RC in Newcastle, Pearl RC in Oxford and Midland Railway RC in Worcester which had been too reliant upon a closed and steadily reducing membership.

In most cases, those interested in continuing to row simply joined, where possible, a neighbouring 'open' club and so several clubs around the country gained extra support from unexpected quarters: Grosvenor RC took the members from Chester's defunct clubs since Royal Chester RC would not accept them; similarly in the case of Derby RC and Derwent RC; Agecroft RC benefited from Manchester's contraction and Liverpool Victoria RC from the demise of Liverpool RC and the removal of Mersey RC to Chester; in Newcastle the dispossessed were more likely to join Tynemouth RC than the more socially exclusive Tyne RC whereas in Oxford, they had all three remaining clubs to choose from (Falcon, Hannington and Neptune); in Cambridge, national affiliations continued to divide the domestic scene and most working men gravitated to Rob Roy RC while in Southampton, the Coalporter's Club welcomed all comers as did the city clubs in York and Worcester.

In some locations the most suitable response to the depression of the 1930s was to join forces with a nearby club which often meant in practice that a strong club took over a weak one as Burton Leander RC did with Burton RC, Eton Excelsior RC with Eton Victoria RC, Kingston RC (Hull) with St George's RC, Kingston RC (Thames) with Kingston Town RC, Tees RC with Middlesbrough BC and John O'Gaunt RC with Lancaster RC, all of which resulted in stronger organisations in terms of membership, finance, premises and boat stock. In areas where rowing was a marginal activity at the best of times and the options of contraction, amalgamation or takeover were unavailable, clubs disappeared entirely as at Didsbury, Warwick, Kings Lynn, Lincoln, Sunderland, Preston and Tewkesbury.

The element of amalgamation or takeover had been present practically from the very first moment in the history of club development, indeed the coming together of the Star and Arrow boat crews to form a more competitive Leander crew may be regarded as the first such example of acquiring strength through unity. With each economic depression, which happened every twenty years or so, we can see smaller clubs amalgamating in order to combat the harsh financial realities of increasing costs and diminishing incomes. The process began in the 1850s when the myriad small London boat clubs dissolved and were effectively re-formed as one substantial London Rowing Club which immediately attracted 140 members with the object of 'restoring that spirit and emulation amongst rowing men which once made the oarsmen of London both watermen and gentlemen, the most renowned in the world'.[45]

Its subsequent success was attributable to its decisions to have no limit on size of membership, to abandon the contemporary club system of fines for petty infringements, to limit members' financial commitment to annual subscriptions only and to hold regular scratch races and winter meetings in order to maintain enthusiasm throughout the whole year at a time when normal procedure was to close clubs completely during the winter months. During the next period of economic depression, in the 1870s, there were similar consolidations in Worcester where the Sabrina, Leander, Argonaut, Vigornia and Nil Desperandum rowing clubs amalgamated to form the Worcester Rowing Club in 1874 and in Lincolnshire where the Eagre, Eclipse and Trent rowing clubs coalesced into the Gainsborough Rowing Club during the same year, a club which doubled its membership to over 100 over the following six years, justifying its founders' intention that it should become a 'more virile organisation' than any of its predecessors.[46]

Once again, twenty years later in the 1890s, the trend was towards amalgamation as many smalll clubs formed rowing associations in order to benefit from much needed economies of scale while also representing members' interests in negotiations with the two new governing bodies. These associations often resulted in club consolidation as in Norwich where the local 'business house' clubs of Greens, Chamberlains, Hope Brothers, Curl Brothers, Buntings and Norwich Warehouses became Norwich Rowing Club while in Oxford the local rowing association proved to be the catalyst which reduced the host of River Isis clubs to three only.[47]

Such amalgamations were often facilitated by the joint use, by many clubs, of commercial boatyards as headquarters at a time when the majority of rowing clubs continued the original expedient of hiring a set number of boats for specific periods throughout a whole year at a set price, a procedure particularly common in Bedford (at Chetham's), Oxford (at Salter's), Nottingham (at Radford's), Kingston-on-Thames (at Messenger's), Cambridge (at Foster's), Eton (at Goodman's), Putney (at Thompson, Bowers and Simmons) and Shrewsbury (at Pengwern). This method of organisation did, however, have its drawbacks as the original members of Liverpool Victoria Rowing Club found when pelted with mud by local 'roughs' on their regular runs between their headquarters at the Egerton Hotel and the distant boatyard.[48]

Apart from the obvious inconvenience, the cost of using commercial yards tended to become prohibitive as boat-hirers realised that they could make more money by releasing 'club' boats to the general public and began to increase their rates accordingly, and we find this happening in Windsor where Goodman's new and 'miserable' charges squeezed the finances of the Eton Excelsior Club to such an extent that 'it was impossible for the club to boat there again'.[49]

Certain clubs were able to build or buy their own premises almost immediately as in the county towns where subscriptions were readily forthcoming and when this happened, for example in Shrewsbury with Pengwern Rowing Club, they soon became the most successful, attracting high levels of membership.[50] Similarly, in Oxford and Cambridge the larger colleges simply bought out the commercial yards and constructed their own elegant headquarters in their places.

The financial strictures of hiring frequently required clubs to think hard about their futures and as early as 1873 the Nottingham Rowing Club committee was discussing the advisability of further continuing the club, bearing in mind that its subscription income barely covered its account with Radford's.[51] The result was that the club resolved to build its own premises close by, following, as we have seen, precedents set by other gentlemen's clubs at Agecroft, Derby, Bradford, Middlesbrough, Newcastle and Bristol.

Where individual clubs were unable to purchase premises, it became necessary for several to co-operate in the venture, an early example of which was the combination of all classes of clubs in the construction of the Manchester and Salford Regatta Club boathouse. This was built in 1842 on the banks of the River Irwell near its confluence with the River Medlock and housed the sixteen boats, chiefly owned by local working men, used as 'committee boats' in staging the annual regatta. Similar shared premises were made available by other early 'regatta' clubs elsewhere, notably at Newcastle, Derby, Lincoln and Tewkesbury, and working-class solidarity can be discerned in the purchase of a long lease on Biffen's at Hammersmith by the West End Association of Trades Clubs, promoted by the National Amateur Rowing Association in 1895.[52]

While it was often the case that financial and economic factors encouraged closer co-operation between some clubs, it was also true that social and cultural factors had decidedly the opposite effects. As we have seen, the strict application of the amateur ethic caused untold trouble in various areas of the country, like Shrewsbury where the original boat club was so socially exclusive that it fostered the establishment of the more cosmopolitan Pengwern Rowing Club in 1871 which supplanted it completely by the turn of the century. Likewise in Chester, the Royal Chester Club, with its 'blackball' system of membership election, fostered the formation of the Grosvenor Rowing Club in 1869 which was specifically inaugurated for 'the use of clerks and assistants in the city'.[53]

In Lancaster, events took an exceptional turn during the parliamentary elections of 1865 when it was found that Tories and Liberals had spent some £7,000 each on bribing the electors,[54] many of whom belonged to the well-established Lancaster Rowing Club whose secretary, John Hatch, was implicated in the scandal along with other members. Following these disclosures in the Report of the Bribery Commission in 1867, extensively published in the local papers, the club dissolved in order to re-form as the new, Tory-orientated Lancaster Rowing Club, expunged of the dissident Liberal elements.[55] These, in turn, formed themselves into the less exclusive John O'Gaunt Rowing Club[56] which, led by the same John Hatch, proceeded to purchase the original boathouse leaving the Lancaster club to move across the river to build new premises.

As in Shrewsbury, Chester and Lancaster, so it was that social considerations produced club duplication throughout the country (Appendix 3) while the social constitution of a club often determined its fortune since gentlemen's clubs invariably counted the more influential members of local society as subscribers. When in financial difficulties, such clubs could frequently obtain sympathetic treatment from banking members like J.B. Wilson of Bradford Rowing Club who, as manager of the Craven Bank in Shipley, arranged the £100 overdraft which enabled the club to extend its social facilities in 1892, thereby securing its future prosperity.[57]

Many clubs sought to improve or consolidate their positions by assiduously cultivating the 'Establishment', whether at the local level as in the case at Nottingham where the whole city council was invited to the annual Nottingham Rowing Club dinner in 1895, held significantly in the Masonic Hall, or nationally when clubs like Royal Chester, Cambridge '99 and Nottingham sought royal approval by telegraphing the Palace with loyal support at every opportunity, a ploy which nevertheless failed to gain Nottingham Rowing Club the royal designation for which it twice applied in 1902.[58]

Similar activity around the country elevated the standing of many rowing clubs in the local community to the point where they became the natural meeting place for the leading social, political and commercial elements, fulfilling the role arguably provided today by golf clubs. By the beginning of the First World War there would have been many eminent personages prepared to agree with the Lord Mayor of Lancaster when he opined that 'there were two positions that any man might desire to occupy in the town, the Mayoralty and the Captaincy of the rowing club'.[59]

17. The John O'Gaunt RC on the occasion of unveiling the club's roll of honour on 5 July 1921. The second row includes the current Lord Mayor and several past mayors, in addition to aldermen and councillors at a time when the club was the most prestigious social institution in Lancaster.

162

Ever since the first Henley Regatta in 1839, there had been an inexorable trend towards fragmentation in the organisation of rowing, caused by a social divisiveness which culminated in a split at national level with the inauguration of the National Amateur Rowing Association in 1890. By that time separate allegiances had become well established both locally and regionally. This separateness was nowhere more apparent than in Cambridge where the traditional tensions between 'Town and Gown' only served to complicate those caused by class distinction to the extent that the town's Rowing Association was not only unable to guarantee the affiliation of local clubs but refused to join either of the national governing bodies which it regarded as opportunist upstarts.

Nationally, the situation was not dissimilar as the *Rowing Almanack* indicates in its 'Club Directory' of 1892, which shows that there were 36 clubs affiliated to the Amateur Rowing Association, 30 affiliated to the National Amateur Rowing Association, 24 to the Tradesmen's Rowing Association and 21 to the Coast Rowing Association leaving as many as 100 clubs totally unaffiliated except to unofficial parochial bodies which responded sympathetically to the diversity of local requirements.

There continued to be arguments against the artificial barriers in the sport which set apart blue- and white-collar workers despite the consistent failure of any evidence to show 'that the clerk has to give way to the engineer in rowing supremacy'[60] and yet the separate development continued. This often created a strong community spirit among those excluded from the mainstream, such as that experienced in the Lower Tideway Trades Rowing Association in the 1930s whose members were barred from the Amateur and National Amateur bodies alike as professional watermen. On their stretch of the river, all competitive rowing was carried out between relatively few clubs with regattas providing 'committee' boats to encourage participation and always featuring the 'Lighterage Fours' as the main event of the day, a combination which produced, according to those who took part, an 'esprit de corps which has not existed in the rowing world since then'.[61]

As the Second World War approached, the 'amateur' criteria became less strictly enforced at club and regatta levels, and in 1939 the secretary of the National Amateur Rowing Association, Charles Tugwell, was appointed by the National Advisory Council for Physical Training to be National Organiser for rowing with the task of 'furthering the interests of rowing clubs and helping rowing under whatever organisation it is carried on'.[62] This appointment, made with the full approval of the Amateur Rowing Association, signalled the beginning of all modern developments in the sport by unifying, in name at least, all its disparate elements under one agent. This unification was recognised constitutionally only in 1956 when all rowing activity finally came under the jurisdiction of the Amateur Rowing Association after many years of negotiations between the two governing bodies. The next chapter seeks to continue the review of club fortunes with reference to those determining factors already mentioned and to extend it, through 'unification' and other post-war developments, to the present day.

NOTES

1. *Bolton Chronicle* (22 June 1869), 5c.
2. *Bury Times* (12 Aug. 1870), 3c.
3. 'Lincoln Rowing Regatta', *Bell's Life* (4 Aug. 1855), 5a.
4. *Nottingham Journal* (12 Aug. 1870), 7b.
5. *Bradford Observer* (9 Oct. 1883), 2e.
6. Bradford Rowing Club, minutes (2 April 1900).
7. Lancaster Rowing Club, minutes (27 April 1926).
8. *Berwick Advertiser* (1 Oct. 1869), 3d.
9. *The Times* (1 Sept. 1869), 3d.
10. *The Times* (3 Oct. 1884), 9a.
11. Falcon Rowing Club, minutes (17 April 1869).
12. N.J. Frangopolo, *Tradition in Action* (EP Publishing, 1977), p. 197.
13. *The Times* (4 Aug. 1849), 5c.
14. *Hansard* (18 Nov. 1926), c. 1950.
15. *The Times* (2 April 1927), 11c.
16. P. Mantoux, *The Industrial Revolution in the Eighteenth Century* (Methuen, 1964), p. 350.
17. J. Corbett, *The River Irwell* (Heywood & Son, 1907), p. 70.
18. M.J. Kingman, 'Chester 1801–1861' (MA Leicester University, 1972), p. 45.
19. Club names match with those in *Slaters Directory of Shropshire*, 1857.
20. M.M. Schofield, *The Economic History of Lancaster* (Lancaster Historical Society, 1973), with reference to 1850–56 and 1860–65.
21. Puckering and Dawber, *A Short History of Gainsborough Rowing Club* (John Bellows, Gloucester, 1923), p. 28.
22. *Stratford-on-Avon Herald* (6 April 1894), 6c.
23. Conveyance document in Lord Ashton's Papers (18 April 1904).
24. *Cambridge Gazette* (26 Sept. 1889), 4b.
25. Cambois Rowing Club, minutes (23 May 1926).
26. R.E. Swartout, *Rhymes of the River* (Heffer, Cambridge, 1927), p. 47.
27. *The Rowing Club Directory of Great Britain* (Lock to Lock Times, 1898).
28. Manchester and Salford Regatta, programme (27 Aug. 1858).
29. *Lincoln Gazette* (29 June 1868), 3d.
30. *Berkshire Chronicle* (3 Feb. 1877), 4b.
31. Bedford Rowing Club, minutes (9 March 1889).
32. *Eastern Daily Press* (21 July 1936), 10e.

33. *Worthing Gazette* (25 Feb. 1931), 7c; and *Bournemouth Evening Echo* (29 April), 5b.
34. The preamble to the second minute book of Thames Rowing Club indicates that the club was established to provide 'organised pleasure boating' for the clerks and salesmen of the drapery firms around Fore Street, and St Paul's Churchyard.
35. *The Times* (1 Sept. 1884), 9d quotes the contemporary music hall song about this area: 'wiv a ladder and some glasses mun could see to 'Ackney marshes if it wasn't for the 'ouses in between'.
36. Lancaster Rowing Club, accounts (17 Nov. 1847).
37. Bedford Regatta Notice (July 1864).
38. Ryde Rowing Club, minutes (4 June 1888).
39. Kingston Rowing Club, minutes, Annual Report (1893). Note that some idea of the cost of carriage may be gleaned from the purchase of a new Four by Lancaster Rowing Club and its delivery from London in 1903: cost of boat £33 15s 0d; carriage £7 13s 4d; a relationship which, when translated into modern terms, indicates a transportation charge of £500.
40. 'Proceedings of the A.R.A.', *British Rowing Almanack* (1913).
41. Burnell and Rickett, *A Short History of Leander Club* (Leander Club, 1968), p. 18.
42. *The Times* (6 July 1914), 10b.
43. A. White, *Efficiency and Empire* (Longmans Green, 1901) makes the point that 10,000 men offered to join up in October 1899 in the Manchester area alone but 8,000 were found to be unfit for active service and only 1,200 attained even moderate military standards of physical fitness. Under such circumstances it seems reasonable to conclude that rowing club members (and those of other sports) would be among the most acceptable recruits being above average fitness.
44. Durham Regatta, minutes (10 April 1919).
45. London Rowing Club, minutes, Annual Report (1856).
46. Gainsborough Rowing Club, minutes: 1874 (55 members), 1876 (67), 1878 (81), 1880 (102).
47. Neptune Rowing Club, minutes (17 May 1893).
48. *Liverpool Victoria Jubilee Souvenir History, 1884–1934* (Dabell Buck & Co., 1935), p. 9.
49. Eton Excelsior Rowing Club, minutes (18 May 1885).
50. *Eddowes Shrewsbury Journal* (27 Sept. 1876), 4b.
51. Nottingham Rowing Club, minutes (17 Dec. 1873).
52. For a contemporary photograph of the premises, see *Victorian and Edwardian Boating* (Batsford, 1987), plate 85.
53. *Chester Chronicle* (31 July 1869), 4a.
54. *Report of the Lancaster Bribery Commission* (HMSO, April 1867).
55. *Lancaster Guardian* (14 Sept. 1867), 3a.
56. *Lancaster Guardian* (21 Sept. 1867), 5a.
57. Bradford Rowing Club, minutes (1 Sept. 1892).
58. Nottingham Rowing Club, minutes (15 July 1902 and 15 Dec. 1902).
59. John O'Gaunt Rowing Club, minutes (23 March 1909).
60. *The Times* (12 Jan. 1920), 6c.
61. Letter from Harry Read of Poplar, Blackwall and District RC (2 Dec. 1986).
62. 'A.R.A. Proceedings', *British Rowing Almanack* (1940).

8

Post-war Developments, 1945–91

> In the long history of the Amateur Rowing Associa-
> tion, there has been no year to compare with 1973
> which saw us stepping from the known domestic
> scene into world rowing.
>
> (*A.R.A. News*, January 1974)

Immediately following the Second World War, in October 1945,
Britain successfully applied to host the first Olympic Games to be
held for twelve years and the Olympic regatta was held at Henley
where, in 1908, rowing had been officially included in the games for
the first time. So successful had this venture been, that all the
arrangements were studiously copied in the organisation of the next
games in Stockholm in 1912, and by 1913 the Amateur Rowing
Association was congratulating itself on the fact that all its recom-
mendations 'concerning the management of future Olympic
regattas have been adopted by the various foreign rowing authorities'.[1]

So confident was the British rowing establishment in its continuing international leadership of the sport, that it declined to affiliate
to the world governing body, La Fédération Internationale des
Sociétés d'Aviron established in 1892, due to the Henley Regatta
stewards who insisted upon a maintenance of their independence
from outside forces which has survived to this day, with Henley
Regatta being the only event on the international calendar outside
FISA control.

The spread of amateur rowing as an organised sport throughout
the world was brought about in large part by expatriate British
oarsmen on colonial duty and by the 1860s there were clubs in South
Africa,[5] Calcutta, Canton, Ceylon, Hong Kong (2), Shanghai,
Buenos Aires, Australia (16), together with the first continental
club in Hamburg formed with the help of resident British businessmen. All the newly established national rowing associations of the
1880s and 1890s sought advice on constitutions initially from the

Henley stewards and later from the Amateur Rowing Association itself.

Nevertheless, the promotion of international rowing on a regular basis was sponsored by FISA which inaugurated the European Championships in 1893 and was subsequently recognised by the Olympic authorities as the official rowing organisation for all competitive purposes with the result that the Amateur Rowing Association was constrained to affiliate in 1947 in order to host the Olympic regatta the following year.

At the Olympic regatta of 1948, the British crews won two gold medals, thus maintaining a tradition of success stretching back to the original 1908 event. It was, however, apparent to the authorities that the foreign competition was becoming so strong that future domestic policy would need to promote the selection and preparation of greater numbers of international standard crews. With this end in view, the movement towards the amalgamation of the two rowing associations was given greater impetus by the establishment of a 'merger' sub-committee in 1949, whose remit was to facilitate a unification producing larger numbers of oarsmen eligible for international selection.

Heightened international aspirations encouraged the Amateur Rowing Association to send away, for the first time, two fully representative 'Eights' for competitive experience in 1950, a move which was amply reciprocated with a record 22 foreign entries to the Henley Regatta of that year. This trend continued and a watershed in British rowing occurred in 1954 when Russia brought a fully integrated national team to compete at Henley, an action which more than any other elevated the whole level of international competition to the realm of national prestige.

The nearest that Britain had ever come to a national team was Leander Club but failure at the Helsinki Olympic regatta in 1952, together with the rise of the Russian squad system, made it apparent that a far more rigorous approach to training and selection would be necessary to regain former glories. Thus, in 1955, an International Fund was opened to receive monies raised by direct taxation on domestic regatta entries, a system known everywhere as the 'Bob-a-Nob' levy and generally welcomed by grass-roots oarsmen who wished to see a strong British presence at international level.

This taxation initiative, together with the existing club registration fee, proved to be the final incentive for the Amateur Rowing Association to push for amalgamation with the National Association since by merging it would incorporate hundreds more clubs and regattas, thereby doubling its income. So it was with some relief that the *Rowing Almanack* of 1956 announced the long awaited merger as 'by far the most important event of the whole year'. The 'successful conclusion of negotiations'[2] provided for new divisions around the country to accommodate the new clubs without upsetting local loyalties, the co-option of two National Association committee members to assist in transition, the absorption of the National Association regional and national championships into existing Amateur Association events and the opening up of National Association regattas to 'former Amateur Rowing Association clubs who will now be able to enter without loss of face'.[3]

The organisation which the National Amateur Rowing Association had thus effectively joined was not a democratic body, consisting as it did of 11 members nominated by the 9 founder clubs, 6 members elected by the same clubs with a further 9 elected to represent the remaining 150 clubs. It was common practice, for example, for a new member to be proposed and seconded by existing members, a tradition only broken by Thames Rowing Club in 1950 in proposing a non-Establishment candidate, thus forcing a genuine election and eliciting the criticism of 'unsporting behaviour' from at least one committee member.[4]

On the other hand, the National Association had always been scrupulously democratic at its local and regional levels, avoiding centralisation except for a small secretariat. Its concentration on regional events contrasted with the far greater emphasis placed by the Amateur Association on international representation which had, after all, been its initial *raison d'être* as the Metropolitan Rowing Association back in 1879, and so there remained within the new association a fundamental dichotomy of principle and practice. Dominated, as it continued to be, by the Henley, Oxbridge and London connections, the new Association proceeded to advance the international cause by maximising 'in-sport' taxation during 1958 and, following upon the failure to find suitable water at Boston, Manchester, Chester or even Henley, setting up a sub-committee to press for the construction of a full international rowing course admitting that 'Great Britain must have such a course before she can play a full part in international rowing'.[5]

It was fully allowed that such a policy of 'one track intensity of purpose' resulted in many provincial clubs becoming 'very uneasy partners in the new association',[6] especially the coastal clubs whose problems were so different from those experienced by river clubs. Nevertheless, it was felt that the only chance that provincial clubs were likely to have of breaking the 'Tideway barrier' into top-class rowing was to overcome their reluctance to move further than their local regattas.[7] The institution by FISA of an annual World Championship in 1962 encouraged the Amateur Rowing Association in its preparations for a national squad which was established in 1965 following a dismal Tokyo Olympics. It also encouraged the authorities to redouble their efforts in pursuit of an international course which finally became a reality ten years later with the help of Nottingham City Council and the Sports Council, at Holme Pierrepont where, as a sign of international acceptance, the World Championships were held in 1975.

In order to qualify for financial assistance from the newly established Sports Council, the Amateur Rowing Association had undergone a democratisation process in 1966. This resulted in the formation of 25 regional 'divisions', each electing a representative to sit on the central 'council' which was to meet monthly at the London headquarters and while Oxford and Cambridge universities, Leander, London and Thames rowing clubs retained the right to nominate a representative, it became possible for the first time to vote down, if necessary, the Establishment point of view.

At the same time, the Association's administration improved noticeably, culminating in the organisation of the World Championships which in the official view brought it to 'a degree which is comparable to other major governing bodies in this country, a process which has taken twenty-one years', a commentary concluding with the judgment that 'in the long history of the Amateur Rowing Association, there has been no year to compare with 1973 which saw us stepping from the known domestic rowing scene into world rowing'.[8] Following the appointment of Bob Janousek, a Czechoslovak international, as full-time national coach and the institution of rigorous and professional squad training based at Hammersmith, British crews began winning medals again both at the World Championships and, after six fallow Olympics, at the Games of Montreal and Los Angeles where the first gold medal for 36 years was won.

The concentration by the Association on international rowing over the past 30 years has caused some concern domestically which has centred on the taxation levied by it on clubs, regattas and oarsmen to finance the preparation and servicing of national squad crews. The first murmurings of discontent were heard in 1974 when a general hue and cry was raised in protest against the doubling of the regatta levy, together with an increase of 30 per cent in

169

individual contributions and a further increase of one pound in the club affiliation fee, all of which were designed to pay for the World Championships the following year. Despite this, a policy of 'in-sport' taxation has continued unabated ever since, culminating in the recent introduction of an annual £15 registration fee for every adult rower with the overwhelming percentage of total income being spent on the international side of the sport.[9]

As a response to this, several provincial rowing councils have suggested a regionalisation of the centralist governing body and the East Midlands division has gone so far as to establish, in conjunction with other like-minded parties, the Nottinghamshire Rowing Association in 1981 to provide high-class training facilities for local oarsmen who might be unable or unwilling to attend regular sessions at Hammersmith. The North West Rowing Council has recently inclined towards an absolute declaration of independence from central control (Appendix 4) while the independent *Rowing* magazine has consistently argued that 'the Amateur Rowing Association must move out to the regions and develop a truly national policy not a Hammersmith based policy'.[10] Such criticism has brought about a measured response in the recent appointment of three regional development officers funded directly by the Sports Council to service the clubs in the north, north-west, and east divisions, inspiring the hope that a thorough-going regionalisation on the National Rowing Association model financed by an equal distribution of national assets might be a future possibility.

While the governing body concentrated on cultivating the international potential of the sport, the clubs in the regions busied themselves in reviving domestic rowing activity, always aware of 'how difficult it was to row at all in an age of austerity epitomised by petrol rationing'[11] which obliged many clubs 'to spend an undue proportion of their time scrounging for funds'. It also encouraged adjacent regattas to run two-day events, the communal use of boat transport, much 'cobbling up of cars for carrying boats' and the introduction of sectional boats designed for ease of carriage.[12] Thus, the domestic scene generally continued to be one of changing fortunes as clubs sought, with varying degrees of success, more efficient means of operation in the unpromising economic climate of the post-war years.

Town rowing at both Oxford and Cambridge, always the poor relation to college rowing, finally entered the modern era as Neptune Rowing Club became the first town club ever to have its own boathouse which it erected in 1958, and Cambridge Rowing

Club, perennially known as a 'charity club' from its use of others' premises, coincidentally moved to its first permanent home in the same year when Banham's Estate was finally sold. Neither club, however, prospered in isolation and both were constrained to amalgamate with others to form viable units, in Cambridge particularly where as late as 1982, the Mayor was saying that 'if permission to build [a communal boathouse] is not given I'm afraid that some clubs will go to the wall'.[13]

Meanwhile in Oxford the post-war plague of vandalism had hit the Neptune Club so badly that only extra resources released by the merger of the Neptune and Hannington clubs to form the City of Oxford Rowing Club in 1968 allowed the construction of a secure building which nevertheless continued to be 'victimised by riverside hooligans'.[14] Vandalism became widely recognised as a severe problem for rowing clubs in the 1960s at a time when the post-war baby boom had produced a generation of adolescents who found perfect targets for their destructive inclinations in the often isolated riverside premises of clubs throughout the country.

Attacks often caused major disruptions as at Bradford where a destructive fire prompted an unsuccessful resolution suggesting 'the winding up of the club and disposing of the assets' at the Annual General Meeting of 1963 and in Lancaster where, after many years of constant vandalism, it began to 'threaten the very future of the club,[15] while in Wigan, the boathouse became so unsafe following attacks on it that it had to be demolished by club members who then dissolved the club.[16] In Hammersmith, no less than five trade-based clubs foundered following the sale of the West End Boathouse Company in 1970 for property development, and many clubs which owed their existence to municipal authorities were in danger of similar dispossessions of prime riverside sites since it was certainly true that 'the price of such property is well beyond the slender means of rowing clubs'.[17] Elsewhere, neighbouring clubs sought security of tenure through mergers which consolidated precious assets on one site.[18]

Much financial support was given after 1965 to clubs up and down the country by the Sports Council through its policy of providing a pound of grant aid for every pound raised by club members, a scheme which galvanised many committees into a level of fund-raising previously unheard of in the sport. Ironically, the insurance pay-outs on the vandalism at Bradford and Lancaster enabled those clubs to begin their fund-raising from positions of strength from which they soon progressed to brand-new facilities. So too did

Cambois Rowing Club in Northumberland, which was literally saved from extinction by council grant aid enabling it to relocate from the harbour in Blyth to the newly boomed estuary of the River Wansbeck a few miles further north,[19] leaving behind the traditionally 'professional' Blyth Rowing Club to reflect the surrounding economic fortunes in its decline and ultimate demise in 1985.[20]

In the vast majority of cases it was necessary for clubs to rewrite their constitutions in order to meet the egalitarian conditions of grant aid imposed by the government-sponsored Sports Council, so that rules providing for the majority election of members were replaced by those stipulating that membership was 'open to all', while some clubs such as Boston Rowing Club were compelled to expunge clauses excluding those 'making a living by manual means' and, in this way, club democracy was gradually advanced.[21]

New facilities for a club frequently meant a new lease of life, as evinced by the opening of the Whitby Friendship Rowing Club's new clubhouse in the Outer Harbour which immediately resulted in 'a tremendous awakening of interest in membership which soared to four hundred',[22] a reaction replicated throughout the country as facilities improved during the 1970s to the extent that the slogan 'Rowing is a Growing Sport' was adopted by the Amateur Rowing Association as an advertising gimmick during this period.

Not only was recruitment of members a result of successful fundraising but it was also, more often than not, a prerequisite, with smaller clubs, therefore, finding it virtually impossible to grow into viability despite the herculean efforts of a few club officers. This dilemma prompted many clubs to establish separate sections for women, an innovation considered not only unnecessary but unthinkable before the war. Although there were, by 1956, some 40 women's clubs affiliated to the Women's Amateur Rowing Association, these were mostly college clubs with only 10 genuinely 'open' clubs being represented, and the post-war trend was for such clubs to be absorbed by neighbouring men's clubs,[23] leaving only two specialist clubs for women, in Bedford and Weybridge, together with the closed but powerful Civil Service Ladies Rowing Club, to carry on into the present day.

The first women members of formerly all male clubs were hardly made welcome and the conditions of membership laid down by Star Club of Bedford for the members of Bedford Ladies Rowing Club were symptomatic of the male attitude towards oarswomen generally in that 'women must make alternative changing arrangements, boat when the men do since we cannot provide separate keys and keep nothing other than boats and blades in the boathouse'.[24] Nevertheless, the economies of scale which prompted the first mixed amalgamations became ever more attractive during the inflationary 1960s and 1970s and the overwhelming majority of clubs admitted women to membership during this period.

They realised that without the additional income brought in by women through their subscriptions and fund-raising, not to mention the boost their presence gave to male recruitment, they would have suffered increasing financial hardships at a time when new technology was producing vastly improved but enormously expensive equipment, and successive assessments forced club rateable values towards commercial levels. Usually, the admission of women members saw an immediate improvement in club fortunes, as with Bradford Rowing Club whose overall membership subsequently doubled in the years 1968–78 accompanied by a substantial increase in bar profits enabling the club to buy new equipment, which in turn attracted new competitive members resulting in 'the most stable and successful period in the club's history'.[25]

The more traditional gentlemen's clubs took longer to be convinced of the wisdom of the 'open-door' policy and the Curlew Rowing Club at Greenwich only succumbed to the inevitable female invasion in 1980, admitting that 'at no time or nowhere can rowing be offered economically at current subscription rates and there is need for financial backing from friends, sponsors and social activities'.[26] Poole Rowing Club was the last club to admit women in 1985, leaving Leander Club and London Rowing Club significantly as the only clubs which continue to exclude them, together with Henley Regatta as the only event to do so.

As rowing for women became more established domestically through greater representation at club and regatta levels, it began to expand into the international arena and in 1954 a women's coxed four won a bronze medal for Britain at the first European Championships for women held at Macon in France. The Women's Amateur Rowing Association hosted the event at Willesden in 1960 when a promising young sculler called Penny Chuter managed a creditable fourth place. The inauguration of the Women's World Championships in 1974 prior to the inclusion of women's events at the 1976 Olympic Games prompted the merger of the Women's Association, established in 1923, into the Amateur Rowing Association in order to facilitate the formation of a women's national squad which then joined those already dealing with junior, lightweight and heavyweight men.

Despite enormous efforts the British women have found it extremely difficult to compete successfully against their larger and better financed sisters from the Eastern Bloc countries, winning only one gold and two silver medals in the last twenty years. However, women's rowing today enjoys unprecedented popularity and widespread support throughout the country with females comprising 35 per cent of all active rowers[27] and the international squads often finding it easier to secure commercial sponsorship than their male counterparts, while the principal national coach, whose main role is the selection of all international crews both male and female, is one Penny Chuter.

Since the war, most clubs have sought to secure their competitive futures by establishing links with local rowing schools or by encouraging non-rowing schools to include the sport in their activities by providing equipment. Such links were being discussed in the years between the wars as a means of replacing the many experienced oarsmen lost in the First World War and the first such 'official' approach to a school was that made by F.M. Grant to Wallasey Grammar School in 1922. He persuaded the school authorities to establish a boat club as a junior section at Liverpool Victoria Rowing Club, an arrangement he later described as a 'source of valuable recruiting and of considerable benefit to the club'[28] and one copied later in Lancaster with the Royal Grammar School and in Crosby with Merchant Taylor's School.

The club in Ironbridge was saved from collapse by a similar approach to local schools which produced 40 members in 1964, following a meeting which revealed that there were simply no active members remaining within the club.[29] The contribution made by the Abbott Beyne comprehensive school to the fortunes of Burton Leander Rowing Club in 1975 proved equally efficacious since parental involvement produced social and financial benefits which secured the club's future prosperity.

Many of the older clubs have been sustained from the beginning by a steady flow of oarsmen from neighbouring public schools and such links remain well established today, viz. Kings School and Royal Chester RC, Cathedral School and Hereford RC, Shrewsbury Royal Grammar School and Pengwern RC, Kings School and Worcester RC, Durham School and Durham RC, Bedford School and Bedford RC, Tiffin School and Kingston RC, while many such public schools maintain the exclusivity of their rowing activities by providing 'old boys' clubs closed to all but former pupils, viz. Cheltenham College (Caterpillars BC), St Paul's School (Colet BC), Emmanuel School (Dacre BC), King's School, Chester (Rex BC), Shrewsbury Royal Grammar School (Sabrina RC), Radley College (Radley Mariners BC), Eton College (Eton Vikings BC), Tonbridge School (Tonbridge Boarsmen BC), Bryanston School (Bryanston Buffaloes BC) and Windsor School (Windsorian BC).

Since the Second World War, club/school partnerships have flourished in the maintained sector of education with grammar schools at Liverpool, Lancaster, Bradford, Hull, High Wycombe, Newcastle, Reading, Oxford, Weybridge, York, Maidstone and Wallingford feeding local clubs, all of which have been supplemented recently by comprehensive schools fulfilling the same function in Ealing, Clapton, Norwich, Hexham and Chester. At a time when discussion of the North/South divide is current once again, it is instructive to note that of the 35 schools which have established boat clubs since 1945, 10 are situated north of the Severn/Wash axis while in total this area accounts for 26 clubs including 7 at public schools; the area south of this axis accounts for 73 school clubs of which 35 are at public schools heavily concentrated in the Home Counties.

A similar survey for 'open' clubs reveals that the North accounts for only 8 of the 55 post-war clubs together with 59 from an overall national total of 205. Such figures seem to indicate not only a higher level of prosperity in the South but also a much faster rate of post-war revival than that experienced in the North, and the current period of economic recession has depressed rowing fortunes there even further with clubs failing at Chester-le-Street, Ebchester, Preston, Hull, Middlesbrough, Liverpool, Birkenhead, Fleetwood, Goole, Grimsby, Runcorn and, as we have seen, at Blyth as recently as 1985.

The majority of these clubs were trades clubs affiliated to the National Dock Labour Board which used to hold annual regattas at Putney, hosted at London Rowing Club, to which all member clubs were invited and for which a record entry of 82 crews from 17 ports was received in 1955[30] but from this peak, entries consistently declined until the Board discontinued the event in 1977 following the demise of so many dockers' clubs due to port closures and redundancies.

This reduction of port activity is only one example of a general contraction of water-based trade which has effectively drained the traditional pool of skilled watermen from which so many oarsmen flowed into the sport, a situation illustrated by the action of the Watermen's Company in opening up the 'Coat and Badge' race to all apprentices following its failure to produce sufficient numbers of its own.[31] The decline was symbolised in 1986 by the ceremonial rowing of the last ever crossing of the medieval Hammerton Ferry near Richmond-on-Thames, by waterman Sandy Scott, followed by the poignant donation of the 24 ft skiff to the Docklands Museum.[32]

The gentrification of Doggett's Coat and Badge race, begun less than 50 years after its inauguration, is now complete as the traditional cash prizes have been replaced by 'donations made to the rowing clubs of the men competing subject to such conditions as are required by the Amateur Rowing Association to preserve their amateur status'.[33] Moreover, even old Etonians have won the event twice in the last seven years[34] and every year now there is widespread evidence of the curious role reversal of amateur club men being called in to coach competitors.[35] Despite this decline, there remains a tenuous link between the Watermen's Company and the mainstream of British rowing in the person of Tim Keech, a Woolwich ferryman, whose family have been watermen for 500 years and who represented Great Britain at the 1987 World Championships in Copenhagen.[36]

Elsewhere, watermen's traditions are continued notably at Gravesend where the first organised racing is commemorated annually at the Town Regatta by races in old-style, heavy skiffs now worth some £1,500 each, and in Cornwall, where there has been a resurgence of gig racing led by members of Newquay Rowing Club suitably supplied with racing gigs by Ralph Bird of Devoran, who continues to build them after the style of the originals produced by generations of the Goss family at Calstock.[37] Such racing has become so well established in the far south-west that the 1986 Cornwall Gig Championships attracted 25 crews from clubs in the Isles of Scilly, Newquay, Cadgwith, Truro, St Mawes and Looe, with a particular feature of the event being the 'instant' programme displayed on blackboards to allow for the return of fishermen who stay out at sea if the fishing is good, only to return at the last minute for the racing.[38]

If the influence of trade upon present-day rowing is negligible, having become either totally redundant or of simply token or marginal importance, let us look at those other original elements of rowing activity, recreationalism, commercialism and professionalism to see if they continue to figure in the current aquatic scene. During the eighteenth century, recreational rowing was the province of the genteel classes who had the money to excavate boating lakes and the time for leisurely indulgences, but during the nineteenth century, urban development promoted the commercial provision of boating facilities for the masses. This encouraged the aquatic gentry to withdraw into select boating clubs while the rise of the professional class of oarsmen from the rural sports tradition only served to confirm them in their seclusion.

The sons of the gentry continued to boat for pleasure at Oxford and Cambridge universities but the nature of the water there, together with the influence of Etonians and Westminsters, caused them to introduce a competitive element which they soon transferred to their home waters when they graduated. From the mid-nineteenth century onwards, boat racing began to oust pleasure boating from the club scene throughout the country to such an extent that by the end of the century there were only a very few clubs retaining a recreational section.

Today, there is only one club which considers itself 'mainly concerned with social rowing' and that is the Falcon Rowing Club in Oxford which 'would like to become a skiff and punting club',[39] while the regatta at Hemingford Grey near St Ives is the sole remaining example of the Edwardian 'garden-party'-style regatta. Pleasure boating has thus passed entirely out of the realm of private clubs and into the public domain, a development nowhere better illustrated than at Talkin Tarn, near Carlisle, which was originally used by the dukes of Carlisle as a boating lake. It was later developed as a commercial boating station by the local rowing club 'at considerable expense as an investment for income'[40] only to have it designated a country park in 1973 by Cumbria County Council who now operate the pleasure boats as a public amenity, having compensated the club with new premises.

The same trend is discernible on Lake Windermere, which in earlier times was just 'a playground for a privileged few' whose shores featured many elaborate private boat chalets, but which has developed during the twentieth century into 'a vast area for the recreation of an affluent society'.[41] On the River Thames, and a whole century after the publication of *Three Men in a Boat*, the 'original activity holiday for individuals or groups of up to four', using a camping skiff, remains a popular holiday choice for many during the summer season.[42] The fashion for boating at seaside resorts and on municipal lakes continues, as reflected in the recent provision of a recreational lake in the huge Metro City development at

Gateshead,[43] and there are moves towards impounding the waters of the River Ribble with new weirs to enable a revival of the immensely popular boating facility in Avenham Park,[44] while the range of recreational participants can be seen in the light-hearted Queen's Silver Jubilee Regatta on the River Thames which included 'crews' from offices, shops, public houses, schools and youth clubs.[45]

The demand for recreational facilities brought about by increasing leisure time and a 'sport for all' ethic, has introduced an unprecedented level of commercialism into their provision which has inevitably affected rowing at every level. In a competitive climate, it has become vital for clubs, regattas and the Amateur Rowing Association itself to find and develop their own sources of income, a trend begun early in the post-war period by Hereford Rowing Club in the years 1954–61, when it promoted the Wye Guild Football Pool which raised sufficient money to guarantee the club's future from investment income alone, while the Upper Thames Rowing Club was established at Henley in 1962 with the expressed intention of trading upon the international demand for boathouse facilities on the Henley stretch of the river.

Some clubs have been fortunate in securing permanent sponsorship in the form of backing from local brewers, as in the cases of Cambridge '99 Rowing Club and the John O'Gaunt Rowing Club in Lancaster; others have featured in television advertising, notably Rob Roy Rowing Club with Dick Emery, York City Rowing Club with Rowntree's Kit Kat and Kingston Rowing Club with Cadbury's Maltesers, while those clubs with substantial premises rent out their facilities on a daily basis, as does London Rowing Club whose income of £40,000 is made up of one-third each from subscriptions, bar and outside catering and rent of bedrooms.[46]

During the 1970s, despite substantial rises in subscription rates, it became increasingly apparent that income from active members was not sufficient to cover running costs, let alone the purchase of new equipment, and so club committees turned to the development of their social facilities in order to subsidise rowing activities. Prominent examples of this approach can be found widely scattered around the country: in Folkestone, where a permanent steward is employed to service some 650 members who support 150 rowers; in Whitby, where the Friendship Rowing Club has 400 social members subsidising a mere 35 active oarsmen; and in Evesham, where the club has built up a membership of 700 by diversifying, as Warwick Boat Club did a century before, into tennis and bowling, income from which finances the 40-strong boat section. Evesham Rowing

Club's success stems largely from a convenient site near the centre of town, a continuity of influential and generous presidents in the form of the property-owning Rudge family and excellent relations with the local bank, which allows a current overdraft of £40,000 in pursuit of yet further development in conjunction with a new shopping precinct nearby.

Although few clubs can boast such advantages, there is one commercial opportunity that every club enjoys – the staging of an annual regatta. This often represents the largest single source of income during the year, for which cash sponsorship is eagerly sought from local commercial patrons as in the nineteenth century, with the result that many events can now rely upon at least £1,000 to underwrite their organisations. Even those bastions of amateurism, the Oxford and Cambridge university boat clubs, now receive £70,000 each annually from the BBC and Beefeater Gin who recently succeeded Ladbrokes as sponsors of the Boat Race.

Perhaps the most imaginative sponsorship scheme of modern times was that enjoyed by the River Lea Regatta committee in 1986 who managed to interest the Allan Selby Estate Agency in using their event as an attraction for people to 'drop anchor at Watermint Quay and browse around phase two of our Kentish Homes development whilst enjoying Britain's largest growing regatta'.[47] Such a commercial initiative graphically and ironically illustrates Thatcherite principles in promoting local gentrification, with house prices starting at £105,000, at the expense of a working-class neighbourhood community which established and nurtured the rowing club itself.

Regatta organisers of the nineteenth century often eschewed commercial development as vulgar and potentially disruptive but those of the twentieth century have, of necessity, sought to maximise its potential. Thus, events like Burton Regatta have spread activities over two days to accommodate 'stands and stalls from local traders, sideshows, steam engines and fun fairs',[48] while three-day events are held at coastal locations like Dartmouth, which advertises itself as 'much more than just a rowing regatta with something for everyone',[49] and Whitby, where the local tourist board helps to promote the activities which include Red Arrow flypasts, fairgrounds and a fancy dress carnival at which the rowing club collects much of its yearly income directly from the public.[50]

However, the most successful money earner of all is Henley Royal Regatta which has recently achieved a turnover of £1m by rigorously maximising its income from every source, viz. 'guest badge sales, car parking, grandstand admission, steward enclosure admission, bar and catering, programme and memento sales, lottery tickets and mooring leases, all of which have made the future of the regatta immeasurably stronger'.[51] This prosperity enables the stewards to sponsor desirable entries as they did in 1987 in providing £5,000 towards the travelling expenses of the Russian international squad, a subsidy similar to the one which we may remember caused the authorities to disqualify the Vesper Rowing Club of New York in 1905 on the grounds of professionalism.[52]

Changing circumstances have brought about changes in cultural perceptions, with the current international nature of the sport requiring ever higher levels of performance, and introducing a political dimension demanding victories, which can only be delivered at the cost of a total commitment. Such a commitment requires a level of financial subsidy so great that the Corinthian concept of amateurism can no longer be applied and the 'amateur begins to demand a slice of the professional cake'.[53] The commercial incentives of the eighteenth century leading to the emergence of a professional class in the nineteenth century, whose 'accursed greed for gold' was entirely denied by the Establishment, has been replaced in the twentieth century by an insatiable demand for gold medals which has led to the emergence of a class of competitor whose professional attitude is positively encouraged by the Establishment.

The earliest domestic example of such an attitude was the action in 1954 of D.V. Melvin, a sculler with international pretensions, who was enabled by the local sponsorship of Sir Harold Parkinson to transfer his Electricity Board job from Lancaster to Wandsworth so that he could avail himself of the superior coaching facilities at London Rowing Club. These he proceeded to utilise twice a day, having been allotted extended lunch hours by the Board to allow him sufficient training time on the water. The following year he entered and won the Wingfield Sculls becoming 'the first provincial sculler ever to gain the English Amateur Championships',[54] as a direct result of his commitment to higher levels of competition, which also enabled him to gain international selection in subsequent years.

Thirty years later the covert support given to figures such as Melvin has been replaced by overt financial assistance in payment for product endorsements with Steven Redgrave, Olympic and World gold medallist, currently enjoying the status of a full-time professional in all but name, existing as he does on income derived entirely from the sport of rowing. Fully aware of the commercial implications of personality status, the Amateur Rowing Association has recently appointed a Promotions Executive to maximise the advertising revenue following British success at Olympic and World Championships, resulting in substantial sponsorship deals with Leyland/Daf and the Trustee Savings Bank.

In addition, an independent body calling itself Rowing Promotions Ltd has produced, in conjunction with Channel 4, two series of rowing programmes entitled the 'Leyland-Daf Challenge Sprints' which have attracted some three million viewers. Meanwhile, the University Boat Race continues to attract the largest viewing audience of any BBC outside broadcast, the commercial implications of which have elevated the production of suitable crews for the event into a full-time occupation, a fact recognised by that last enclave of amateurism, the Oxford University Boat Club, which appointed its first professional Director of Rowing in 1987.

It would seem that the post-war period in British rowing, like those before it, reflects the capacity of the sport to respond to a variety of societal forces, exhibiting as it does a new commercialism allied to a new professionalism both ideally suited to the new entrepreneurial age. It is to this very responsiveness over the centuries that we shall turn in the next and final chapter with a view to placing the present situation in an appropriate historical context and sketching the scenario for the future.

NOTES

1. 'Proceedings of the A.R.A.', *British Rowing Almanack* (1914).
2. Amateur Rowing Association, minutes (3 Nov. 1955).
3. Amateur Rowing Association, minutes, Secretary's Report (1955).
4. J.H.G. Page, 'Looking Back', *A.R.A. News* (June 1972).
5. 'A.R.A. Proceedings', *British Rowing Almanack* (1959).
6. 'Review', *British Rowing Almanack* (1957).
7. 'Review', *British Rowing Almanack* (1958).
8. *A.R.A. News* (Jan. 1974), No. 23, p. 3.
9. Amateur Rowing Association, accounts for 1986.
10. *Rowing* magazine (Jan. 1985), p. 2.
11. W. Collins, *A Short History of Stratford-on-Avon Rowing Club* (George Boyden, S-o-A, 1974), p. 31.
12. 'Review', *British Rowing Almanack* (1955).
13. *Cambridge Evening News* (14 Oct. 1982), 6e.
14. City of Oxford Rowing Club, Annual Report (1968).
15. John O'Gaunt Rowing Club, minutes, AGM (March 1971).
16. Eye witness account, L. Marsh Esq., West Lodge, Haigh Park, Wigan.
17. *The Times* (6 Jan. 1970), 7c.
18. 'Site' mergers: St Thomas's RC and Port Royal RC into Exeter RC (1946), Middles-

brough BC and Tees RC into Tees ARC (1946), Medway RC and Gillingham RC into Medway Towns RC (1958), Henley RC and Henley United RC into Henley RC (1961), Mortlake RC, Anglian RC and Alpha RC into Mortlake, Anglian and Alpha RC (1968), Bristol RC and Avon RC into Avon County RC (1972), Crowland RC, City Orient RC, Gladstone Warwick RC into Lea RC (1980).

19. Cambois Rowing Club, minutes (15 Oct. 1978).
20. 'Dole's Blyth Spirit', *Guardian* (19 July 1985).
21. Since 1965 some 78% of open clubs have received some financial help from the Sports Council Grants Unit. Those which have not retain selective admission, e.g. Hereford Rowing Club whose Rule I reads: 'Membership of H.R.C. shall be confined to persons whose membership in the opinion of the committee will further the stated objects of the club, the encouragement of rowing at Hereford amongst amateurs.'
22. Whitby Friendship Rowing Club, minutes (10 April 1976).
23. Absorption of women's clubs by men's clubs: Bideford Ladies RC into Bideford ARC, Dartmouth Ladies RC into Dartmouth RC, Stuart Ladies RC into Lea RC, Alpha Ladies RC into Mortlake, Anglian and Alpha RC, Burton Ladies RC into Burton Leander RC, St Neots Ladies RC into St Neots RC.
24. Star Rowing Club, minutes (7 Feb. 1957).
25. Correspondence with Peter Finney, President, Bradford Rowing Club (27 Aug. 1985).
26. Curlew Rowing Club, minutes, Annual Report (April 1980).
27. Women comprise 27% of adult and 47% of junior members in open clubs; 32% of total membership in schools and colleges. For a full participant distribution (1987) see Appendix 5.
28. Letter from F.M. Grant to John O'Gaunt Rowing Club, 3 April 1933.
29. Ironbridge Rowing Club, minutes (14 April 1964).
30. *Sport among Dock Workers* (National Dock Labour Board, 1955).
31. Conversation with D.V. Melvin, an electrical contractor whose son, an electrical apprentice, was approached to row in the race (20 March 1985).
32. *A.R.A. News* (July 1986), p.3.
33. Race Notice (June 1985), Fishmonger's Company.
34. William Woodward-Fisher in 1980 and Charles Woodward-Fisher in 1986, members of a traditional watermen's family of bargemasters whose father, and then mother, was President of Poplar, Blackwall and District RC.
35. Conversation with D.V. Melvin, London Rowing Club international sculler, who is frequently approached by Doggett hopefuls for coaching (20 March 1985).
36. *T & G Record* (April 1987), p.1.
37. For a photograph of a traditional racing gig see *Victorian and Edwardian Boating* (Batsford, 1987), plate 28.
38. 'Ralph Bird's Boat Race', Radio 4 (6 May 1986). Transcript from Alec Reed, BBC Bristol.
39. Letter from R.T. Rivington, Chairman, Falcon Rowing Club (21 Oct. 1984).
40. Talkin Tarn Rowing Club, minutes (11 April 1973).
41. D. Matthews, *Lake Festivals on Lake Windermere* (W'mere Nautical Trust, 1982), p.17.
42. Advertisement for Constable's Boathouse, Hampton (1987).
43. *N. East Rowing News*, No.22 (Northern Rowing Council, 1985).
44. *Lancashire Evening Post* (27 April 1988), 5a. For a photograph of recreational boating on the River Ribble see *Victorian and Edwardian Boating* (Batsford, 1987), plate 60.
45. National Dock Labour Board, regatta minutes (10 July 1977).
46. London Rowing Club, accounts for 1981.
47. Advertisement in the *Guardian* (19 April 1986), 15c.
48. *Burton Observer and Chronicle* (8 July 1977), 6d.
49. *British Rowing Almanack* (1987), regatta advertisement, p.21.
50. North Yorkshire Tourist Board, Whitby Regatta poster (Aug. 1987).
51. Henley Royal Regatta, minutes, letter from the Chairman to all stewards (23 Aug.

1984).

52. For a photograph of the disqualified Vesper crew see *Victorian and Edwardian Boating* (Batsford, 1987), plate 88.

53. *A.R.A. News* (June 1972), No. 20, p. 2.

54. Wingfield Sculls, minute book (Nov. 1955). D. V. Melvin is the current event secretary.

9

Conclusions

There is a need to examine sports from the inside, to inquire into the relation between sport and the participant.

(Braham Dabscheck in Cashman and McKernan (eds), *Sport in History*)

If one fact above all others is evident from a review of sporting history it is that 'no sport can be insulated from the wider society in which it is played',[1] a principle first propounded by Strutt in 1801 in his dictum concerning 'people' and their 'sports and pastimes'. Much sporting literature has reflected this approach in using its subject matter as a basis for social inquiry so that we now have 'social histories' of all the major sports and yet the literature of rowing, which is considerable, has dwelt almost exclusively upon factual reviews of those activities directly or indirectly affected by Oxbridge influences. This may be explained by the traditional authorship of rowing histories (Appendix 1.ii), the 'stranglehold' which Oxbridge graduates have had upon the administration of the sport and their lack of interest in unfashionable and socially questionable provincial matters. Such literature has therefore failed to recognise the unique position held by rowing as, arguably, the finest barometer of social change provided by the sporting tradition.

Rowing is, no doubt, a sport but one of such complex origins that it stretches into many non-sporting corners of the national identity. Its connection with work, production and transport means that its force and place in any description of sport are unique and yet its very complexity fits it ideally for use as a mirror of social and cultural trends. In order to illuminate and exemplify this unique quality it will be necessary to summarise those principles of social inquiry identified in Chapter 1 and relate them directly to the evolution of rowing as reviewed under those themes common in the sporting tradition and featured in Chapters 2–8. The prime motivation throughout will be to follow Dabscheck's example[2] in concentrating on the people directly involved in rowing activity at all levels with a view to formulating some conclusions concerning historical derivations of present-day perceptions of the sport.

This approach will be facilitated by recourse to Berryman's thesis of enquiry which concentrates on the form, participants, facilitators and situations of any activity.[3] Rowing can then be immediately identified as originally an overwhelmingly trade-orientated activity carried on by a wide variety of watermen throughout the country, in ways determined by the quality of available waters. It was facilitated to a large extent by the land- (and water-) owning classes who either employed the watermen directly as 'serving men' or did so indirectly as tenants on fisheries and ferries.

The enormous rise in the population of London during medieval times encouraged the growth of water-based trade nationwide as barge skippers competed to supply the capital with every known product. The London boatmen became adept at cargo handling and the demand for their services as ferrymen and lightermen necessitated the establishment of their company in 1555. The commercial facilitation of rowing continued to grow with the size of London itself and as greater numbers of men became self-employed there evolved a competitive instinct which found expression in professional opportunism and unscrupulous wager racing. Commerce continued to mould events as the new activity of 'stock jobbing' attracted 'a prodigious conflux of nobility and gentry from all parts of England to London' at the beginning of the eighteenth century[4] who, in turn, financed the development of theatres, gardens and clubs.

The watermen received more than their fair share of patronage from this 'conflux' since, before the bridges, they were vital for transport, while their racing provided the gentry with entertainment and the opportunity for betting, both of which were formalised later in the century in a host of sponsored 'matches' and garden spectaculars. It was in London, therefore, that the rural sports tradition of boat racing among water tradesmen was first commercially exploited and where its form evolved from play to profession.

It must not be forgotten that in tandem with the tradition of rural sports there was that of pleasure boating, practised since the earliest times by the leisured classes, which became fashionable on the River Thames during the eighteenth century in such places as Kew and Richmond. Normally, such boating would take the form of elaborate, water-borne picnics but as young gentlemen returned

185

from the Grand Tour, the Italian influence encouraged the development of formal 'regattas' organised as society events under the auspices of neighbourhood nobility and gentry. It was common practice at these events to feature a watermen's race as a diversion and gambling opportunity, access to which was often restricted to an 'enclosure' made up of club and household barges. In this way did the two aquatic traditions coincide and from this point onwards the tension between the two has continually influenced the evolution of rowing throughout the country.

As the gentry facilitated more rowing activity, either through individual wagering or collective organisation, they began to inject an element of ceremony by offering prizes in celebration of royalty, who were often present at the races, and by awarding prestigious coats and badges which usually brought professional preferment with them. This patronage was very gratefully and respectfully received and there are many watermen active on the rowing scene today whose ancestors first gained advancement in this way and who loyally continue to serve their boat club employers. By the end of the eighteenth century, due partly to this mutuality of respect, it had become commonplace for gentlemen to row in crews with working watermen, many of whom had set up boatyards designed to service the needs of aquatic gentry, be they for accommodation, boat rental, boat-building or tuition.

While this remained the situation in London for the next quarter of a century, the rural sport tradition elsewhere had been unaffected by overt commercial or aristocratic influences and continued, primarily in coastal locations, as a holiday recreation involving fishermen intent on supplementing their meagre incomes. However, as London society moved to the coast at places like Dover and Folkestone, these sports became increasingly commercialised, involving gentlemen's crews, often drawn from the Guards' regiments, and encouraging heavy betting.

Indeed, wherever genteel society congregated, there would be an emulation of the London scene in aquatic productions such as those at Derwentwater in 1783 and Stockton in 1788, while simple recreational boating took place publicly where water conditions permitted as in Liverpool, Nottingham and Shrewsbury and privately where family fortune funded the excavation of numerous boating lakes. Thus, the two traditions entered the nineteenth century, the one largely dependent upon the direct or indirect sponsorship of fashionable society and inevitably centred on the River Thames and the other centred on the public house and local community, using indigenous craft such as 'whalers', 'dredgers', 'crab boats' and 'gigs' and popular in areas as widespread as Chester, Falmouth, Gravesend and Norwich.

The first half of the nineteenth century saw radical changes in both the established aquatic traditions, due to influences which had little directly to do with rowing at all. The commercialisation of society during the previous century had produced a new class of wealthy entrepreneurs whose socially ambitious members attended the great public schools and in so doing were elevated to a position of cultural importance not enjoyed for centuries. The first quarter of the century saw the schools admit the most socially exclusive cohorts of pupils of any in their history with the result that those who passed on to Oxford and Cambridge universities during this period were totally imbued with all the Victorian notions concerning the immutability of rank and social status.[5] Those at Eton and Westminster, who had eagerly indulged in the contemporary fashion for boating, introduced it – with competitive modifications – to their colleges.

It was here, for the first time, that watermen were gradually excluded from participation in rowing activity, initially as stroke oars and then as coxswains and trainers. Although most of these 'aquatic' gentlemen returned to London and the Home Counties after graduation, many returned to the provinces where they actively spread the amateur ethic in clubs and regattas. While educational influence encouraged the development of an 'amateur' rowing which owed as much to social engineering as competitive style, other influences were at work sustaining the growth of professionalism within the sport. Industrialisation had caused the growth of great urban centres and where these possessed suitable water, local watermen were able to take advantage of the many commercial opportunities already enjoyed by their London colleagues.

They continued the traditional racing but were now enticed into greater participation by lucrative prize funds sponsored by a wide variety of entrepreneurs all eager to attract mass spectator custom. The coming of the railways facilitated ever greater competitive involvement as boats and oarsmen travelled regularly between the major racing venues, and also allowed huge numbers of people to visit coastal resorts where the traditional sports were transformed into holiday spectaculars. Thus, provincial aquatic culture originating in parochial sports remained overwhelmingly populist, being facilitated by the commercialism of mass spectatorship in urban situations and involving plebeian participants in 'round the turn' and often handicapped racing.[6]

On the other hand, Thames aquatic culture, having derived from the involvement of gentry, became increasingly elitist under the management of socially aspiring Oxbridge graduates, located as it was in rural environments and involving patrician participants in heavily regulated 'straight-away' racing.[7] The determination with which the Oxbridge connection pursued the application of the amateur ethic wherever rowing took place resulted in the establishment of the London-based Amateur Rowing Association in 1882 and, in retaliation, that of the regionalised National Amateur Rowing Association in 1890. These were pre-dated and post-dated by numerous organisations designed to promote and safeguard the sectional interests of their rowing memberships. They all serve to illustrate the fragmentation and dislocation experienced within the sport between the mid-nineteenth century and the mid-twentieth century when practically all of them were incorporated into the ARA.

Some idea of the complications experienced during this century may be gained by reviewing the proceedings, as Walton and Walvin suggested, in terms of 'geography and types of economic and social environment'[8] and in order to expand this approach to allow a more intimate illustration of rowing developments we can utilise those determinants listed in Smith's *Recreation Geography*.[9] It has been shown how movements of people into London and later into provincial conurbations affected the nature of rowing, and this mobility continued to affect the evolution of the sport as factory systems developed throughout the country even in rural areas like Reading and Bradford-on-Avon.

These systems attracted increasing numbers of workers into urban centres, who began to demand greater access to recreational facilities with the result that pleasure boating became as much a feature of nineteenth-century working-class life as it had been of eighteenth-century upper-class existence. Often, such boating took place as close as possible to the factories as in Huntingdon,[10] Bradford and Manchester, but where necessary the railways took the crowds out to the seaside or inland lakes like Talkin Tarn and Hollingworth Lake. Many northern reservoirs were used for recreational boating but as they were gradually closed to popular use they were replaced by more central municipal park lakes, the first of which was excavated in Birkenhead in 1844.

Recreational boating for the working man and woman led to the formation of many clubs for their use, often facilitated by cheap rail access, such as those at Hammersmith, Clapton, Shipley, Ryton-on-Tyne and Littleborough (Hollingworth Lake); similar access allowed the gentlemen rowers to escape further into suburbia and rurality where clubs sprang up practically adjacent to rail termini. Much of this movement was in search of better water resources in terms of access, exclusivity, pleasantness and suitability for competitive rowing, which explains the exodus of many clubs upstream, away from unsatisfactory tidal stretches.

The country has always been very uneven in its provision of rowable water so that those living in the River Thames basin have, apart from those in East Anglia, much greater access to suitable water than anyone else (Appendix 5) since the area contains hundreds of miles of water which are largely free from the effects of tide and flood. Other regions have coasts and hills which often induce devastating tides and high precipitation, which result in flash flooding as in the river basins of Severn, Tyne and Humber. In addition, the length, nature and accessibility of the River Thames itself has promoted the growth of large numbers of clubs whose propinquity has led to the prosperity of many regattas.

The significant use of resources in the evolution of rowing is not confined to natural resources since demography and topography have combined to produce interesting examples of material prosperity – for example, the very desirable site enjoyed by Evesham Rowing Club on a particularly placid stretch of river close to the town centre, and Friendship Rowing Club's prime commercial site in Whitby harbour. However, proximity to London allied to aquatic advantages meant that clubs on the River Thames had the greatest potential for material prosperity, a fact suitably evinced in the public sector by the clubs at Kingston, Marlow and Henley (Leander Club) among many others, and in the private sector by the proliferation of rowing public schools.[11]

These elements of climate, economics, geography, topography and demography illustrate not only Smith's 'use of resources' but also his point about 'area differentiation' and lead on to those cultural differences which, Dunning and Sheard maintained, led to 'rivalries of a mechanical solidarity kind such as those between north and south, London and the provinces, adjacent towns and sections of towns'.[12] It has been shown how strictly the Oxford and Cambridge men controlled the sport at the end of the nineteenth century with the result that considerable hardships were inflicted on local regattas and clubs and how, more than fifty years later, such control was continuing to make many provincial clubs distinctly uneasy. Furthermore, little sympathy was ever expended on clubs which complained of the competitive disadvantage suffered in the provinces, since the conventional reply from the south was that the only way to break 'the Tideway Barrier' was to travel south to compete more often.

These attitudes, combined with the many advantages enjoyed by the southerners, began to bring about an antagonism between the Thames region and the provinces. Elsewhere, rivalries existed between county towns and industrial areas where relative prosperities so affected club growth, and actually within many county towns and country areas where the existence of gentlemen's clubs necessitated the formation of alternative clubs for 'non-gentlemen'. Even in predominantly working-class areas these rivalries occurred, such as that between the rowers of Walney Island and mainland Barrow-in-Furness illustrated by the local professional champion, Anthony Strong, who dismissed a challenge from across the water as laughable and even denigrated 'the garbled talk of the Walneyite'.[13]

Another aspect of area differentiation relevant to rowing development is that of 'political affiliation', much of which is evident in the diversity of club growth within and between areas, and is merely one reflection of local culture. In Lancaster, for example, which evolved during the nineteenth century from county town to industrial centre, political antipathy engendered by the elections of 1865 split the rowing club and produced two culturally distinct organisations. Similarly, it is particularly noticeable that the earliest working men's rowing clubs were established in the politically active areas of Manchester and Newcastle, where strikes in 1829 and 1831 promoted a new 'socialism' which was consolidated, along with much local aquatic activity, during the 1840s.

Chapter 3 sought to demonstrate how 'economic ties among industries' affected rowing as rail and pier companies, garden and theatre proprietors, town councils and chambers of commerce combined with press and publicity organisations to promote rowing as a profitable entertainment. The initial growth and ultimate demise of professional rowing itself was largely dependent upon the strength and prosperity of the many inter-related water trades while the fluctuations of local industrial prosperity often affected that of clubs and regattas.

Of all Smith's determinants, however, it is those concerning 'social organisations' and 'human values' which offer the most scope to any historian of rowing seeking to explain its complexities. Two major human value systems have operated during the development of rowing as an organised sport, one stemming from its origins in trade and the other from its early noble patronage. The first may be typified by Mason's remark concerning football, that 'working people failed to accept notions about what games playing should have meant as subscribed to by middle class opinion'[14] and the second by Brickwood's contention that there are 'gentlemen amateurs and tradesmen amateurs and it is not desirable that barriers between them should be broken down'.[15] In structural terms, these two mutually exclusive systems inevitably led to the growth of sectional interests, each of which was held to have its own immutable place in the pattern of aquatic social organisation.

The application, from above, of the exclusive amateur definition was largely informed by snobbery and what F.J. Furnivall recognised as 'hypocrisy', some of which has been touched upon in the foregoing chapters, viz. the use of denigrated watermen; the use of denigrated professionals; 'amateurs' rowing for money; the use of denigrated 'fouling' manoeuvres; the contradictory attitudes taken to professional competitive superiority; the sponsorship of professionals and working men while continuing to exclude them; the 'volte-face' of Henley Regatta concerning admission procedures and commercialism.

Although these human values, identified by Cunningham as 'unintellectual, combative, manly, Christian and patriotic',[16] found expression throughout Victorian and Edwardian culture, they continued to linger in the rowing world until 1956 when the last 'manual exclusion' clause was dropped from the racing regulations. Such values continued to imbue the rowing establishment for several years after 1956, so that the sport's administration remained wholly undemocratic until 1966 and the Women's Amateur Rowing Association was only incorporated into the governing body in 1974; vestiges of the value system remain.[17] Since the Second World War, the dominant value in the sport has been that of 'patriotism', as the Amateur Rowing Association, helped since 1966 by the Sports Council, has made major efforts to produce medal-winning international crews.

In attempting to draw some conclusions from the foregoing, it is necessary to point out that any historical analysis either reinforces established 'truth' or seeks to initiate change and that while the literature of rowing has fallen firmly into the former category, the present work falls just as firmly into the latter. In choosing to ignore the diversity of rowing's origins and developments, the existing literature has failed to identify the continuous threads of tradition which link the present to the distant past and illuminate current concerns. Practically everywhere the sport is practised today

191

exemplifies this continuity in reflecting those two aquatic traditions originating in eighteenth-century aristocracy and trade (see Appendix 6), and it is this that makes rowing history so relevant today.

Rowing has shown itself to be an accurate indicator of social trends in reflecting eighteenth-century paternalism/commercialism, nineteenth-century professionalism/fragmentation and twentieth-century democracy/internationalism, while many historical themes are well represented in current practice. The eighteenth-century 'stock-jobber' whose prosperity accounted for contemporary commercialisation, has his modern 'yuppie' counterpart whose enterprise encourages the commercial promotion of rowing on television. Eighteenth-century 'trade' professionals gave way to nineteenth-century 'racing' professionals who have, in turn, given way to twentieth-century 'international' professionals and a widespread acceptance of the 'professional' attitude to winning. Eighteenth-century artificial boating lakes designed for a social elite have given way to twentieth-century artificial rowing courses designed for a competitive elite.

The nineteenth-century control of the boating world by public school/Oxbridge men largely continues with immense influence exerted by representatives of the Leander, London, Thames, Oxford University and Cambridge University clubs together with the Henley stewards, not to mention the President of the Amateur Rowing Association, himself an ex-Cambridge man. This point is amply illustrated by recourse to the composition of the Boat Race crews since 1829 which shows that only 16 oarsmen out of 1,588 have been produced by non-HMC schools, a situation extended in the proportion (66 per cent) of all international medals taken by Oxbridge oarsmen.[18]

Eighteenth-century paternalism has its place today in the employment by the larger clubs of watermen's descendants.[19] The club scene continues to be affected by many of the same influences so important in the nineteenth century: although the maps of population change in the 1980s are almost the precise inverse of those in the 1880s, the result of the demographic change has been to disadvantage further many clubs in the inner cites, where government initiatives have been required to redress the socio-economic balance. However, the same changes have aided the development of those semi-rural and suburban clubs first established in the initial, middle-class flight from urbanisation 130 years before.

The underlying historical economic factors which have effectively split the country into north and south, with all the implications for club growth discussed in Chapter 8, continue unabated and possibly exacerbated[20] to the continuing disadvantage of regional development. The processes of eighteenth-century gentrification and nineteenth-century Oxbridgisation are reflected today in the evolution of tradesmen's clubs, like Lea Rowing Club which now attracts doctors, lawyers, teachers and Oxbridge students in search of competitive success.[21] Some factors, like the requirements for a successful regatta, never change, viz. 'rowable water, pleasant situation, convenient communication and influential characters'[22] and these continue to exist, in far greater measure than elsewhere, in the Thames basin. If to these requirements we add the high cost of equipment, the time-consuming nature of participation and the social origins of many oarsmen, it becomes obvious that rowing remains a select sport of privileged access.

The continuity of the above themes into the present day has simply extended the historical tensions between the two aquatic traditions into current rowing politics, and queries such as 'Why can't we all work together?'[23] are common in today's rowing press. Although the eighteenth-century 'class culture' has evolved through nineteenth-century 'cash culture' into a twentieth-century 'competition culture', evidence of both aquatic traditions has remained constant in the dichotomy of noblemen/watermen, amateur/professional and lately, elite competitor/'grass-roots' participant. In each case, the dominant cultural contest has been that between 'prestige' and 'people'. The flamboyance and patronage so beloved of eighteenth-century aristocracy was largely based upon an attitude of 'noblesse oblige', calculated to exhibit and consolidate cultural prestige, an early example of which was the ceremonialisation of Doggett's Coat and Badge race.

This element of outward show was continued in the nineteenth century as gentlemen of the public schools/Oxbridge concentrated upon social hierarchy, dress, etiquette and an inordinate fondness for royalty, which led many clubs and regattas to crave their patronage. According to *The Times*, the Boat Race 'assumed a ten-fold more attractive form in consequence of the patronage bestowed on it by the aristocracy of the country',[24] a connection subsequently extended by the Prince of Wales, whose regular attendance at Henley Regatta confirmed its royal status, first awarded by Prince Albert in 1851. Prestige through aristocratic emulation and royal association necessarily involved national prestige, which first informed the establishment of the Metropolitan Rowing Association in 1879 to select crews for international competition and even the promotion of professionals in the pursuit of international honours. Prestige inevitably became associated with amateurism, nobility, patriotism and competitive success and those elements within the sport which failed to measure up to these ideals were marginalised by the establishment.

Thus, working men were virtually excluded from access to elite competition until 1956 when numerous international failures convinced the authorities that new blood was required; similarly, women were only incorporated into the establishment and recognised as a competitive rowing force when their World Championships were inaugurated in 1974. By extension of the argument, rowing in the regions was regarded as hardly worth serious consideration since it had largely evolved from trade, was carried on by working men and organised by the National Amateur Rowing Association at a competitive level below that achieved on the River Thames.

Since 1985 and the election of N. R. L. Thomas from the Liverpool Victoria Rowing Club as President of the Amateur Rowing Association, the traditional centralist approach has been somewhat relaxed and regional development has been placed on the agenda. As a self-confessed 'grass rooter', Thomas recognises his 'market value as a President who is not from the old guard'[25] having succeeded the long-serving Christopher Davidge (Eton, Oxford and Olympic Gold) and yet even he, as an ex-Cambridge man, remains ambivalent about the sport's future. On the one hand he feels strongly that the sport 'should seek to develop existing clubs, new clubs on new waters and open up to the public more',[26] while continuing to promote the 'show case' events of Henley Regatta and University Boat Race, whose very existence lends credence to the public's perception of the sport as elitist.

This dilemma is aggravated for rowing as a recipient of the largest single grant by the Sports Council, whose charter demands the 'development and enjoyment of leisure among the public at large' while also encouraging the 'attainment of high standards'. Inevitably, the Amateur Rowing Association has found it impossible to service the regions adequately while maintaining elite international standards, a task which has always been given priority for reasons already outlined. To deny the value of gold medals at a time when international sport has reached such global political and economic importance is regarded as unthinkable, particularly in a sport given to the world – and once dominated – by England.

A recent article[27] has suggested that this dilemma might well be resolved by a policy of thoroughgoing regionalisation which would facilitate the realisation of all the seemingly disparate aspirations within the sport. Citing the Nottinghamshire Rowing Association as an example of international success, it makes the point that such independent action could well be used to advantage in other areas of the country such as Newcastle, Manchester, Worcester and Bristol. It maintains that the current annual income of the governing body (£875,000) could be used to finance such regional schemes which would then generate their own impetus, resulting in a much greater public access and, ultimately, an improved standard of excellence. In this way, a serious interest in the 'grass roots' of the sport would pay dividends at international level.

In Berryman's terms such an approach would mark a return to a largely recreational form of rowing, enjoying a more cosmopolitan participation and benefiting from a wider range of facilitators in more diverse situations and thus to a populism featured by Strutt and latterly espoused by the National Amateur Rowing Association. In so doing, the sport's prestigious public image, so well fostered by the selective 'sport in history' tradition, would be modified by one more consistent with the democratic values of the 'sport as history' approach. The coalition could only augur well for the future prosperity of rowing in England. This devolutionary movement has been given substantial momentum by the new Amateur Rowing Association constitution of March 1991 which reduces the number of appointed members of the governing council, restricts voting to registered members only, reduces the number of rowing divisions from 23 to 11 and greatly increases the devolution of administrative functions to the ten regional councils.

NOTES

1. E. Dunning and K. Sheard, *Barbarians, Gentlemen and Players* (Robertson, 1979), p. 175.
2. B. Dabscheck, in Cashman and McKernan (eds), *Sport in History* (University of Queensland Press, 1979), p. 227.
3. J.W. Berryman, *Sport as Social History* (Quest, Summer 1973), see p. 6 above.
4. D. Defoe, *A Tour through the Whole Island of Great Britain* (London, 1726), Vol. 1, p. 336.
5. G.L. Guttsman, *The English Ruling Class* (Weidenfeld & Nicolson, 1969), p. 209: 'A Gentleman both knows and is thankful that God instead of making men all equal has made them all most unequal' (Warden of Radley College, 1849).
6. This exemplified Model I in Lawson and Morford's 'Ideal Typical Models for Sport' (*Journal of Physical Education and Recreation*, No. 50, 1979).

7. This exemplifies Model II as outlined in the same article.
8. J. Walton and J. Walvin, *Leisure in Britain* (Manchester University Press, 1983), p. 4.
9. S. Smith, *Recreation Geography* (Longman, 1983), p. xiii. 'Movement of people, use of resources, political boundaries, patterns of area differentiation, climate, economic ties among industries, patterns of social organisation and human values'.
10. N. Wigglesworth, *Victorian and Edwardian Boating* (Batsford, 1987), plate 89.
11. We have seen in Chapter 8 how such schools proliferate in the Home Counties. Their prosperity is amply reflected in Eton College's stock of boats which in 1934 represented a present-day value of £1m and includes today a sculling boat for every member of school. The provision echoes Mangan's contention concerning playing fields, that such purchases facilitate the 'translation of a value system into a set of actions', J.A. Mangan, *Athleticism in the Victorian and Edwardian Public School* (Cambridge University Press, 1981), p. 99.
12. E. Dunning and K. Sheard, *Barbarians, Gentlemen and Players* (Robertson, 1979).
13. B. Trescatheric, *Sport and Leisure in Victorian Barrow* (Hougenai Press, 1983), p. 12.
14. A. Mason, *Association Football and English Society 1863–1915* (Harvester Press, 1980), p. 242.
15. London Rowing Club, minutes (20 March 1872).
16. H. Cunningham, *Leisure in the Industrial Revolution* (Croom Helm, 1980), p. 116.
17. In conversation with the author in April 1984, the master in charge of rowing at a major public school maintained in all seriousness that the 'working man' was unfitted for rowing since he lacked the self-discipline and application needed for the successful acquisition of the relevant skills.
18. Once again, rowing culture reflects the contemporary scene: a computer study of 4,500 elite positions in British society since 1880 made by Harold Perkin for his *Structured Crowd* (Harvester Press, 1981), p. 154, found that although the working-class element is better educated and has a higher representation in Parliament, the real levers of power remain in the hands of public school/Oxbridge educated men who still form the majority of Tory cabinets and at all times control the financial aspects of society while owning the lion's share of land and property.
19. In a recent obituary (*Regatta* magazine (June 1988), p. 12) P.E. Coni, chairman of the Henley Stewards, writes of P.N. Carpmael, President of London Rowing Club: 'My particular treasured memories of "Farn" included his deep respect and affection for the Phelps family in particular and the Thames watermen as a body'; he continues to say that his other memories concern Carpmael's enjoyment of Henley Regatta and the splendid party he gave in the Casino at Boulogne.
20. *Regional Trends*, Central Statistical Office (HMSO, 1988).
21. *Regional Trends*, Central Statistical Office (HMSO, 1988).
22. Until the 1960s the various clubs on the River Lea in north London were predominantly peopled by small local tradesmen and businessmen. Due to economic circumstances they amalgamated into the Lea RC in the late 1970s. The enterprise culture of the 1980s has transformed the club's immediate neighbourhood and consequently its social constitution with the effect that it has been the most competitively successful club in the country for the last eight years.
22. *Yorkshire Gazette* (19 Aug. 1865), 7f.
23. Columnist in *Rowing* magazine (May 1988), p. 6.
24. *The Times* (15 April 1841), 7a.
25. *Guardian* (6 April 1985), 10.
26. *Guardian* (6 April 1985), 10.
27. *Regatta* magazine (Aug. 1987), p. 12.

Appendix 1

It is often said that one picture is worth a thousand words and it is with this in mind that the list below has been compiled so that readers may complement the bibliography with contemporary illustrations which will help communicate the atmosphere of events. Unless stated they appear in the *Illustrated London News* and only the date of publication will be given but where the event took place outside London a small 'p' will indicate 'provincial'.

1840s 11.6.42   8.7.43   19.8.43(p)   31.8.44(p)   29.11.45(p)   11.4.46   4.7.46
14.8.47   27.10.47   14.7.49   3.11.49

1850s 24.5.51   12.7.51   10.4.52   7.7.55   23.8.56   23.5.57   4.7.57   3.4.58
29.9.59

1860s 27.9.62(p)   11.4.63   27.6.63(p)   11.6.64(p)   8.4.65   22.4.65   19.8.65
26.8.65(p)   17.3.66(p)   31.3.66   12.5.66   14.7.66(p)   20.4.67
18.5.67(p)   4.4.68   11.4.68   28.11.68   27.3.69   7.8.69   28.8.69   4.9.69

1870s 2.4.70   16.4.70   11.6.70   1.4.71   8.4.71   9.9.71(p)   3.2.72
23.3.72(×5)   30.3.72(×5)   11.5.72   1.6.72   15.6.72(×3)   22.6.72
19.10.72   29.3.73   5.4.73   5.7.73   20.9.73   28.3.74   4.4.74   25.4.74
27.6.74   24.10.74   20.3.75(×5)   15.5.75   8.4.76   1.7.76   8.7.76
24.3.77(×3)   31.3.77(×3)   16.6.77(p)   20.4.78   27.7.78   5.4.79
28.6.79(p)   20.8.79

1880s 20.3.80   27.3.80   19.6.80   20.11.80   27.11.80   19.2.81   9.4.81(×4)
2.7.82   8.4.82   15.4.82   23.9.82   17.3.83(×5)   24.3.83   10.11.83(p)
5.1.84 (*Boys' Own Paper*)   12.7.84   28.3.85   10.4.86   3.9.87
8.10.87(p)   11.8.88(p)   30.3.89   6.4.89   15.6.89

1890s 22.3.90   29.3.90   23.5.91   11.7.91   16.4.92   21.5.92(p)   18.3.93
17.3.94   6.4.95   28.3.96   4.4.96   27.3.97   26.3.98   2.4.98   25.3.99
15.7.99(p)   19.8.99(p)

1900s 31.3.00   16.3.01   13.3.01   6.4.01   13.7.01   15.3.02   22.3.02
29.3.02   16.3.07   23.3.07   30.3.12   5.4.12   13.9.24

During the 1920s and 1930s the photograph totally supplanted the old hand-drawn illustrations and the national press became satisfied with rather hackneyed shots of the University Boat Race and Henley Regatta, rarely including any other rowing subjects.

(ii) ROWING BIBLIOGRAPHY BY THE DECADE

	Club records	Instructional	Historical	Diary	Total
1840s	–	5	–	–	5
1850s	–	7	1	6	14
1860s	1	12	2	2	17
1870s	2	16	3	2	23
1880s	4	15	7	2	28
1890s	2	9	2	4	17
1900s	6	20	4*	3	33
1910s	6	16	7	8	37
1920s	13	29	7	8	57
1930s	11	3	2	10	26
1940s	3	–	–	1	4
1950s	9	14	4**	2	29
1960s	5	9	1	1	16
1970s	5	8	4***	7	24
1980s	5	2	8	3	18

Notes (a) It is worth noting that some 90% of the above were penned by Oxbridge graduates which might account for the fact that only 7% of the texts mention rowing outside London, Henley, Oxford and Cambridge.

(b) Bibliographical trends, not surprisingly, mirror the trends in the sport, particularly the boating boom of the Edwardian and post-Edwardian eras and the post-WW2 resurgence; also the greater emphasis placed on purely historical writing during recent times.

(c) Only three attempts have been made to cover the subject from the earliest times, viz. *Lord Desborough's *Story of the Oar*, **Hylton Cleaver's *History of Rowing* and more recently ***Keith Osborne's *Boat Racing, 1715–1975*, of which only the first places much emphasis on non-racing activities and none makes more than passing reference to provincial matters.

(iii) REFERENCES TO ROWING IN *THE TIMES*

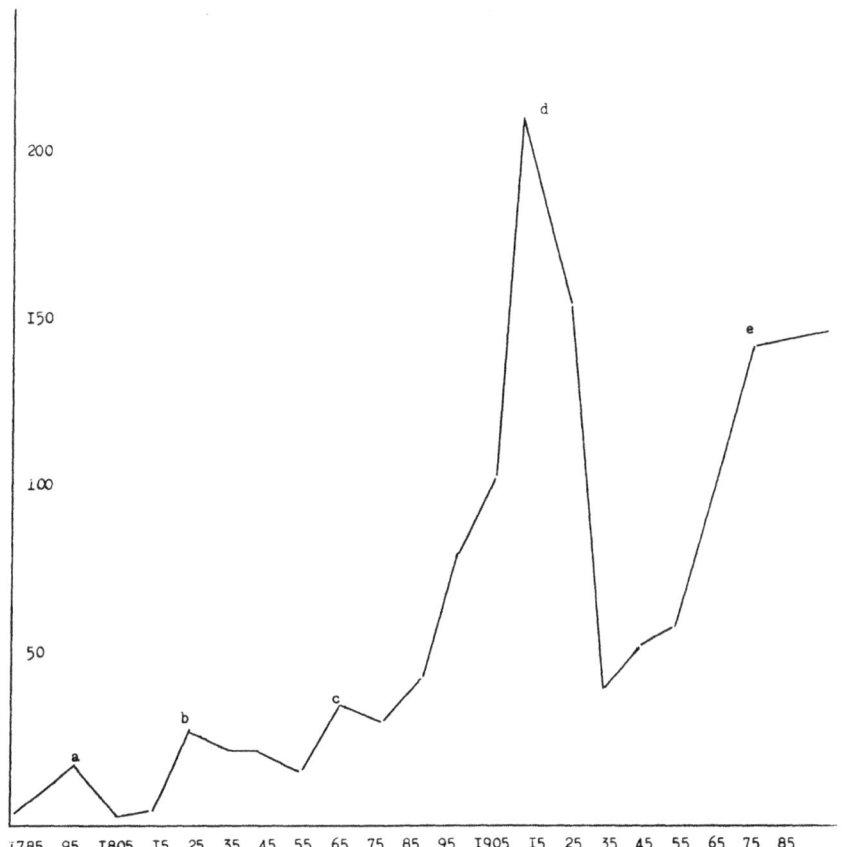

Notes   (a) represents the height of watermen's wager racing;
        (b) represents the new popularity of rowing among gentlemen at colleges and the advent of the Boat Race and Henley Regatta;
        (c) represents the growth of professional sculling and rowing matches throughout the world;
        (d) represents the huge expansion of the fashion in boating with Henley, Boat Race and Oxbridge rowing taking up many column inches throughout the year;
        (e) represents the post-WW2 resurgence of activity particularly with reference to international aspects; Henley and the Boat Race continue to form the majority of reports.

Appendix 2

CLUB DEVELOPMENT 1882–1956

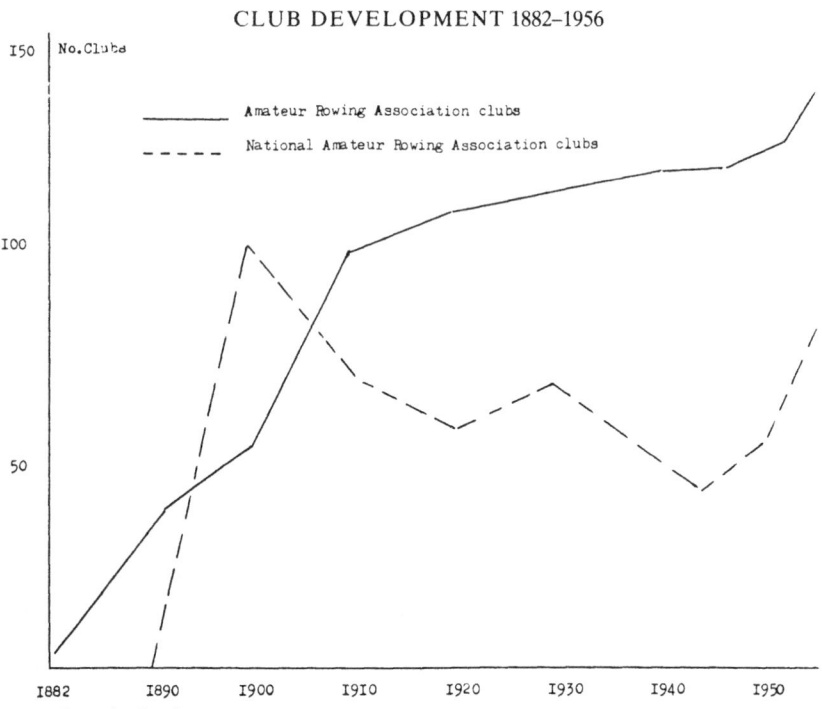

Notes (a) The establishment of the ARA, 1882 encourages the formation of the NARA in 1890 and ensures its initial success.
   (b) From 1900 onwards there were many Coastal Rowing Association clubs which changed allegiance from NARA to ARA.
   (c) NARA's decline was exacerbated by the susceptibilities of its Trade Association members to economic depressions culminating in a low point during the Second World War despite a resurgence during the 1920s.
   (d) It is noticeable that the ARA clubs do not suffer the same knock-on effects from economic fluctuations although their rate of growth is slowed.
   (e) Both associations show a revival after the Second World War but that of the NARA is far more pronounced, due mainly to the efficiency with which this primarily provincial organisation managed to resume operations through its many local branches.
   (f) When the associations amalgamated in 1956 the ARA had 150 town clubs affiliated (with nearly 100 school/college clubs not included here) while the NARA had 100 clubs almost equally divided into town clubs and trade clubs. It was felt that one united body was required to be responsible for the sport nationally at a time when international representation was assuming greater importance.

Appendix 3

CLUBS BY LOCATION AND SOCIO-ECONOMIC ALLEGIANCE
(AB–C–DE) VARIOUSLY TO 1939

Carlisle	Carlisle RC – Talkin Tarn RC
Lancaster	Lancaster RC – John O'Gaunt RC
Preston	Preston RC – Stanley RC – Ribble RC
Rochdale	Hollingworth Lake RC – Littleborough RC (DE)
Manchester	Nemesis RC – Irwell RC – Ellesmere RC/Prince of Wales RC
Salford	Agecroft RC – Broughton RC – Athletic RC
Liverpool	Mersey RC – Liverpool RC – Liverpool Victoria RC
Chester	Royal Chester RC – Grosvenor RC – Museum RC/trades clubs
Shrewsbury	Shrewsbury RC – Pengwern RC – Sabrina RC/trades clubs
Worcester	Vigornia RC – Worcester RC – trades clubs
Bewdley	Bewdley Victoria RC – Bewdley RC
Tewskesbury	Tewkesbury RC – Avon RC – Severn RC
Bristol	Bristol Ariel RC – Avon RC – Bristol RC
Exeter	Isca RC – Exeter RC – Port Royal RC
Poole	Poole RC – Red Star RC (DE)
Southampton	Itchen RC – Coalporters RC – St Mary's RC/trades clubs
I.o.Wight	Ryde RC/Shanklin RC – Vectis RC (DE)
Worthing	Worthing BC – Britannia RC – Worthing RC
Brighton	Leander RC – Cruising Club – Avon RC
Folkestone	Folkestone RC – Excelsior RC
Greenwich	Curlew RC – Poplar RC (DE)
Putney	London RC – Thames RC/Vesta RC
Hammersmith	Kensington RC – Auriol RC – Hammersmith Sculling Club/ trades clubs
Kingston	Kingston RC – Kingston Town RC (DE)
Eton	Eton Excelsior RC – Eton Mission RC (DE)
Henley	Henley RC – Henley United RC – Henley Town RC
Reading	Reading RC – Reading Working Men's Club (DE)
Wallingford	Wallingford RC – Albion RC (DE)
Oxford	Falcon RC – Neptune RC/Hannington RC – trades clubs
Huntingdon	Huntingdon BC – Huntingdon Artisans RC (DE)
Cambridge	Cambridge RC – Cambridge '99 RC – Rob Roy RC/trades clubs
Ipswich	Ipswich RC – Orwell RC – Ipswich Working Men's RC
Lincoln	Lincoln BC – Peregrine RC – Phoenix RC
Nottingham	Nottingham RC – Nottingham Britannia RC – Trent RC
Derby	Derwent RC – Derby RC/Derby Artisans RC (DE)

Burton	Burton Leander RC – Burton RC – Trent RC
Hull	Kingston RC – St George's RC – Humber RC
York	York City RC – White Rose RC – Ouse RC/trades clubs
Middlesbrough	Middlesbrough BC – Tees ARC – Tees RC
Newcastle	Tyne RC – Newcastle RC – Northern RC/trades clubs
Berwick	Berwick RC – Tweed RC (DE)
Whitby	Whitby RC – Friendship RC/Fisherman's RC (DE)

Appendix 4

12 *Devolution* etc., Mike Jolly on being asked to say a few words replied that he had really come to listen and he had been considerably impressed on what he had heard so far on efficient administration, lively activities and numerous projects. Regrettably, he could not say the West Midlands were as advanced or as keen as the North West. They had just received a hammer blow with a proposal to develop the upper Severn which would effectively eliminate Stourport, Bewdley, Bridgnorth and Ironbridge clubs and regattas. As an example he quoted the fact that they had tried to hold two R.I.A.'s but were not able to come up with the instructors and would have to rely on the A.R.A. In general the West Midlands were more interested in individual clubs (27 as against 29 in the N. West) and not so willing to co-operate as a Council to work for the common good. There was smouldering resentment on the rise of the A.R.A. levy, understandably, and the divisional representative was not a particularly popular figure having become 'one of them' and not 'one of us'. The A.R.A. was considered to have produced bad results and bad publicity with little to show for the benefit of individual clubs. As a relatively new divisional representative, the subject of regionalisation/devolution was virtually new to him but he could see numerous advantages. His opinion after one year was that the A.R.A. was baroque in the extreme with not only an inquiry needed into last year's squad results but an inquiry into its administration where Parkinson's Law seemed to rule. Ian Fisher supported Mike Jolly's comments on the A.R.A. in that the administration seemed to get worse, they were snowed under with work (a large percentage of which was unnecessary) and too much use of the answering machine. The Thames Rowing Council was using the Hammersmith office as their headquarters and the squad had become the 'A.R.A. Rowing Club'. Numerous things could be pushed into the regions and dealt with more effectively. N.R.L. Thomas asked W.L.C. Todd as the originator of the document on devolution, to take the meeting through the paper. Todd said that the paper was exploratory and put down to start people's minds working. D.K. Barber estimated that divisions 3a and 3b paid approximately £6,500 p.a. into the coffers of the A.R.A. thus much of the finance needed for independent action already existed. The fact that the N. West Rowing Council had a modern constitution gave us guidelines and it seemed that the constitution of the A.R.A. was more than somewhat out of date. A vigorous discussion ensued mainly being in favour of U.D.I. following the lead of the Welsh devolvement – Mike Jolly felt that the present N. West Council could virtually run itself, as the majority of the head office circulars were unneeded, but was unsure if other regions were as strong or as active. N.R.L. Thomas in thanking Todd and Jolly, suggested that a Special Executive Meeting of the Council was held to investigate in general on how to divert resources from the A.R.A., on what use could be made of the Sports Council and how to divert part of the A.R.A. funding to the regions and if possible produce a paper suitable for distribution to other regional councils. This was agreed.

Appendix 5

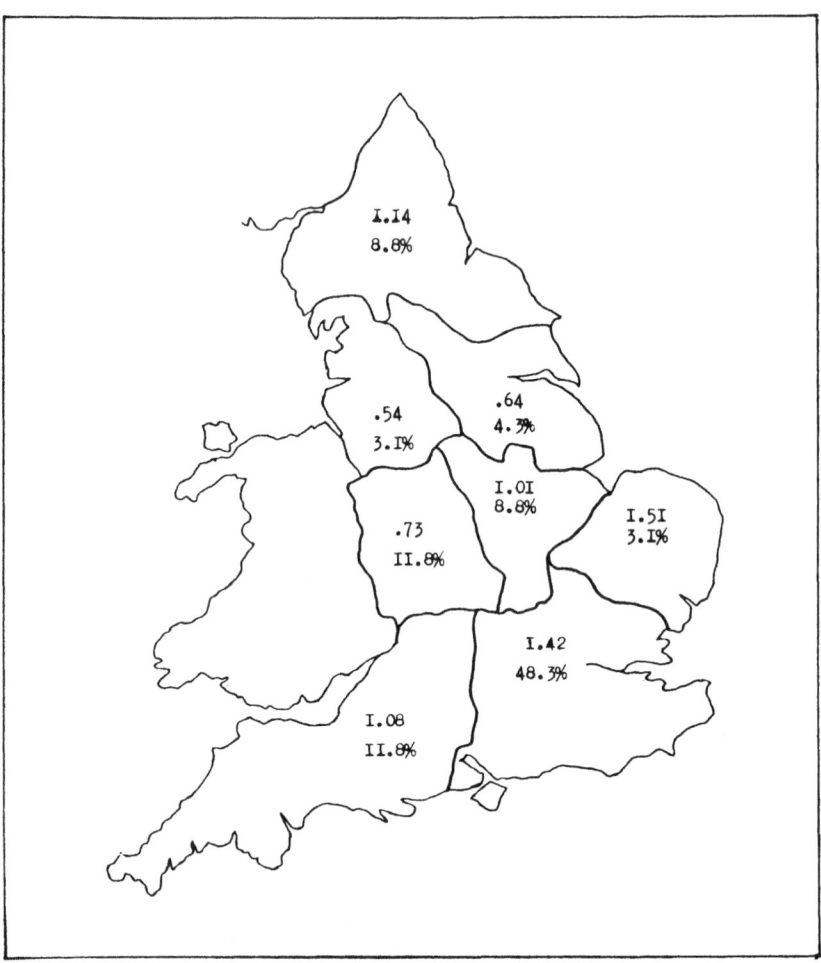

Notes *The first set* of figures indicate the accessibility of rowing water, region by region, as a factor of population. It can be seen that the *south-east* scores highly due to the extent of the River Thames and its proximity to large conurbations. *East Anglia* also scores highly due to the sheer quantity of water (much of it, nevertheless, inaccessible) while the *Severn, Humber* and *Mersey* basins score low as much of the regions' water is unrowable due to the effects of tide, flood and silt.

The second set of figures represent the area percentage of total national participation.

Appendix 6

Place	Trade/Recreation	Organised Activity	Amateur Regatta	Amateur club
London	Every water trade, pleasure boating	17th c. rural sport 18th c. pageant	1866	1865
Greenwich	Ferrying, pleasure boating	18th c. pageant	1866	1866
Gravesend	Lightering, piloting, ferrying	17th c. rural sport	1878	1878
Dover	Fishing, ferrying, freight shipping	18th c. fisherman's racing	1846	1846
Folkestone	Fishing, ferrying, freight shipping	18th c. fisherman's racing	1852	1852
Brighton	Fishing, pleasure boating	18th c. fisherman's racing	1892	1923
Bristol	Every water trade	Harbour sports	1870	1870
Plymouth	Every water trade	18th c. Tamar estuary sports	1949	1949
Gloucester	Freight shipping, pleasure boating		1846	1846
Worcester	Freight, fishing, pleasure boating	Rural sports	1874	1874
Bridgnorth	Freight	Cheltenham vs. Shrewsbury schools	1868	1867
Ironbridge	Freight, fishing	Ironbridge Fêtes	1870	1870
Shrewsbury	Pleasure boating	School races	1871	1871
Southampton	Every water trade	18th c. sports and pageant	1935	1945
Falmouth	Ferrying, fishing, piloting	18th c. fishermen's racing		1971
Newquay	Ferrying, fishing, piloting	18th c. fishermen's racing	1946	1946
Dartmouth	Ferrying, fishing, piloting	18th c. fishermen's racing	1834	1869
Evesham	Ferrying, pleasure boating		1863	1863
Oxford	Freight, ferrying, fishing	18th c. aquatic sports/racing	1856	1869
Reading	Freight, fishing	19th c. aquatic sports	1867	1867
Henley	Ferrying, fishing	University Boat Race 1829	1839	1839
Peterborough	Ferrying, pleasure boating, fishing		1947	1947
St Ives	Freight	Pleasure boating	1874	1860
St Neots	Freight, fishing		1845	1865
Kings Lynn	Every water trade	18th c. aquatic sports 19th c. professional races		

Place	Trade/Recreation	Organised Activity	Amateur Regatta	Amateur Club
Boston	Every water trade	19th c. fishermen's racing	1856	1860
Norwich	Freight, fishing, ferrying, pleasure boating	18th c. fishermen's races	1905	1905
Bedford	Freight, ferrying, pleasure boating	19th c. aquatic sports	1853	1853
Cambridge	Freight, ferrying, pleasure boating	18th c. Fair and sports	1863	1863
Lincoln	Freight, pleasure boating	19th c. aquatic sports	1861	1847
Nottingham	Pleasure boating, freight	Professional racing	1850	1862
Burton	Freight, fishing, pleasure boating	Professional racing	1855	1847
Derby	Freight, pleasure boating	Professional racing	1857	1857
Bradford	Freight, pleasure boating	Recreational boating	1954	1867
York	Every water trade	18th c. pleasure boating/pageant	1865	1863
Durham	Ferrying, fishing	19th c. aquatic carnival	1834	1860
Whitby	Every water trade	18th c. pleasure boating, 19th c. carnival	1849	1879
Newcastle	Every water trade	18th c. aquatic sports/carnival, 19th c. professional racing	1869	1869
Carlisle (Talkin Tarn)	18th c. pleasure boating	19th c. aquatic sports, professional racing	1850	1859
Lancaster	Every water trade	18th c. aquatic sports	1842	1842
Preston	Fishing, ferrying, pleasure boating	Recreational boating	1845	1863
Hollingworth Lake	Fishing, pleasure boating	Aquatic sports, recreational boating	1872	1872
Salford	Freight, fishing, ferrying, pleasure boating	Recreational boating, professional racing	1842	1861
Liverpool	Every water trade, pleasure boating	Recreational boating, 19th c. professional racing	1840	1840
Warrington	Every water trade	18th c. aquatic sports, 19th c. professional racing	1841	1841
Chester	Every water trade	18th c. aquatic sports	1838	1838

APPENDICES

Notes

(a) This review, which is by no means exhaustive, indicates the continuity of aquatic tradition from trade to amateur club in areas where the process of evolution was made possible by the quality of water. In some places, e.g. Lincoln, Preston, Kings Lynn, fluctuations in the access to or quality of water have caused major disruptions in this process while in others, e.g. Warrington, Salford, Liverpool, rowing activity is being revived by clean-up campaigns and urban re-developments.

(b) It is instructive to note the almost total coincidence of the establishment of amateur clubs and regattas. The explanation lies in the fact that either the success of an event inspired the local gentry to consolidate their position by inaugurating a club (e.g. Henley RC) or that, once having formed a club, they considered it to be a prime function to hold an event as an alternative to existing 'sports' (e.g. Lancaster RC).

(c) Indigenous aquatic sports were not always regulated into amateur activities and this is most noticeable at the coastal venues particularly those in the south-west. Most, if not all, the coastal clubs (where they existed at all) either remained unaffiliated to any organisation or joined the NARA.

Bibliography

NEWSPAPERS

Aquatic Register, 1765–1846
Barrow Herald, Sept. 1867–Jan. 1879
Bath Herald, 1855
Bedfordshire Times, Aug. 1853–July 1963
Berkshire Chronicle, 1842–77
Berwick Advertiser, 1869
Bideford Gazette, 1923–33
Blyth Weekly News, 1892
Bolton Chronicle, 1969
Bolton Journal, 1872–82
Bradford Observer, 1883
Bridgnorth Journal, 1868–74
Bristol Evening News, 22 March 1954, 22 May 1954, 17 July 1954
Burnley Advertiser, 1859
Burnley Express, 1980–82
Burnley News, 1923–30
Burton Chronicle, 1874–80
Burton Daily Mail, 1920–30
Burton Observer and Chronicle, 1977
Burton-on-Trent Times, 1857
Bury Times, 1870
Cambridge Chronicle, 1904
Cambridge Gazette, 1884
Cambridge Journal, 1931
Chester Chronicle, 1838–70
Chester Gazette, 1838
Cumberland News, 1891–1978
Daily Telegraph, 1908
Derby Daily Express, 1930
Derby Mercury, 1781–1879
Derby Telegraph, 1903
Eastern Daily Press, 1936
Eddowes Shrewsbury Journal, 1794–1880
Evesham Journal, 1863–1947
Folkestone Chronicle, 1852–74
Folkestone Express, 1906
Gainsborough News, 1862–1902

Gloucester Journal, 1946
Goole Times, 1868
Gravesend Reporter, 1903–21
Hereford Times, 1898–1920
Huntingdonshire County News, 1885–91
Isle of Wight Observer, 1877
Kentish Gazette, 1828–44
Kent Mercury, 1833–39
Lancaster Guardian, 1854–83
Leeds Mercury, 1874, 1900–22
Lincoln Gazette, 1862–74
Lincoln Journal, 1869–79
Liverpool Albion, 1840
Lock to Lock Times, Sept. 1888
Lynn Advertiser, 1865
Manchester City News, 1897
Manchester Guardian/Guardian, 1907–87
Newcastle Courant, 1852–59
Newcastle Daily Chronicle, 1852–1909
Newcastle Daily Journal, 1934–95
Norfolk News, 1803–94
Northern Examiner, 1854–60
Northwich Chronicle, 1921
Northwich Guardian, 1908
Nottingham Journal, 1769–1852
Oxford Chronicle, 1891
Oxford Guardian, 1891
Oxford Mail, 1919–67
Oxford Times, 1841–1920
Poole and Dorset Herald, 1873–1904
Preston Chronicle and Lancashire Advertiser, 1842–65
Preston Guardian, 1865–91
Preston Herald, 1863–75
Rochdale Observer, 1861–72
Runcorn Weekly News, 1904
Salford Chronicle, 1871

Shrewsbury Chronicle, 1876–1953
Southampton Times, 1893
South Coast Mercury, 1892
Southeast London Mercury, 1966
South Kent Gazette, 1935–87
Southport Visitor, 1844–93
Stratford-on-Avon Herald, 1866–76
Surrey Comet, 1876–1904
The Times, 1785–1985
Wellington Journal, 1865–1964
Whitby Times, 1864–1906
Wigan Observer, 1872–1922
Williamsons Liverpool Advertiser,
    1768
Wiltshire Times, 1892–99
Worcester Guardian, 1841–45
Worcester Herald, 1879–95
Worcester Journal, 1845–81
Worthing Gazette, 1885–1966
Worthing Intelligence, 1888
Yorkshire Gazette, 1828–80
Yorkshire Observer, 1923

PERIODICALS

A.R.A News, 1956–86
The Athlete, 1875
*Baileys Monthly Magazine of Sports
    and Pastimes*, 1868
Bedfordshire Magazine, Summer
    1983
Bell's Life in London, 1846–70
Blackwoods Edinburgh Review,
    vol. xvi (1810), vol. xxvii (1830)
Blackwoods Magazine, Jan. 1938
Cornhill Magazine, vol. 65 (1892)
Fortnightly Review, vol. 40 (1883),
    vol. xv (1874)
Gloucester Countryside Magazine,
    Jan. 1965
Golden Penny, 1898
Illustrated Bristol News, July 1961
Illustrated London News, 1844–
    1924
Illustrated Times (Bedford), Aug.
    1861
Lincoln Fireside Magazine, vol. 9,
    no. 10, July 1972
Lincolnshire Life, July 1980
New Review, vol. 7, 1892

Nineteenth Century Journal, 1881–
    1903
North East Labour History Bulletin,
    no. 16, 1982
North East Rowing News, no. 22,
    1985
Punch, 1869–1923
Quest, Summer 1973
Railway Magazine, 1900
Regatta Magazine, 1987, 1988
Rowing Magazine, 1954–88
Rowntree Cocoa Works Magazine,
    Summer 1956
Saturday Review, 1862–67
The Spectator, 1712–16
Staffordshire Magazine, Dec. 1977
T & G Record, April 1987
*Tewkesbury Yearly Register and
    Magazine*, 1834–36

PARLIAMENTARY PAPERS

3rd series

30 July 1833, vol. 22, cc. 139–74
5 Feb. 1844, vol. 72, cc. 216–20
26 April 1866, vol. 182, cc. 2077–
    2176
6 May 1864, vol. 175, cc. 105–43
17 Feb. 1870, vol. 199, cc. 438–98

4th series

20 April 1911, vol. 24, cc. 1053–1241
18 Nov. 1926, vol. 199, cc. 1950–1

5th series

7 April 1937, vol. 322, cc. 193–285

CLUB MINUTES

Agecroft RC, 1861 to the present
Alpha Ladies RC, 1927–76 (and
    accounts)
Ancholme RC, 1873 to the present
Bath ARC, 1875, 1876
Bedford Ladies RC, constitution
    for 1955
Bedford RC, 1886 to the present
    (and accounts)
Berwick RC, boat books, 1890–

1921; cash books, 1872–91

Bewdley RC, report and accounts, for 1899

Bideford ARC, 1896 to the present

Birmingham and Edgbaston RC, rules for 1872

Boston RC, 1860 to the present

Bradford ARC, 1868 to the present (and accounts)

Bradford-on-Avon RC, 1880–1906

Burton Leander RC, 1865 to the present

Burton RC, 1865 to the present

Cambois RC, 1911 to the present

Cambridge Town RC, 1863–1925 (and accounts)

Cambridge University BC, 1829–39

Cambridge '99 RC, 1899–47

City of Cambridge RC, July 1844–Oct. 1844

Clifton RC, Rules for 1877

Curlew RC, 1879 to the present (and accounts, diary, boat books)

Cygnet RC, 1890 to the present (and accounts)

Derwent RC, 1857 to the present (and accounts)

District Line RC, 1911 to the present (and accounts)

Eton Excelsior RC, 1851 to the present

Falcon RC, 1869 to the present

Folkestone RC, rules for 1867, 1900; minutes 1936 to the present

Gravesend RC, 1878 to the present (and accounts)

Hannington RC, 1904–68

Hereford RC, rules for 1970

Hollingworth Lake RC, 1872 to the present

Huntingdon BC, for 1889

Ironbridge RC, 1940 to the present (accounts, 1889–1932)

John O'Gaunt RCm 1880 to the present (and accounts)

Kingston-on-Hull RC, 1885 to the present

Lancaster RC, 1842–1936 (and accounts)

London RC, 1856 to the present

(and accounts)

Merchant Taylors School BC, 1958 to the present

Middlesbrough BC, 1866–1946

Midland Bank RC, 1911 to the present (and accounts)

Nautilus RC (Nottingham), 1855–58

Nelson RC, rules for 1896

Neptune RC, 1863–1968

Norfolk and Norwich RC, rules for 1867

Northwich RC, 1875 to the present

Norwich Union RC, 1936 to the present

Nottingham RC, 1862–1922

Pengwern BC, rules for 1846

Pilkington Blades RC, 1966–70

Poole RC, 1873 to the present

Poplar and Blackwall and District RC, 1955 to the present

Royal Chester RC, 1929–43

Runcorn BC, 1926 to the present

Ryde RC, 1877 to the present

St Ives RC, 1865 to the present

St Neots RC, 1873 to the present

Shrewsbury RC, 1870–89

Star Club (Bedford), 1958 to the present

Stratford-on-Avon RC, 1874 to the present

Talkin Tarn RC, 1912 to the present

Tees ABC, 1864–1946

Tees ARC, 1946 to the present

Third Trinity RC, for 1832

Tynemouth RC, 1867 to the present (and accounts)

Warwick BC, 1861–1923

Westminster Bank BC, 1907–57 (and accounts)

Weybridge Ladies RC, 1919 to the present

Whitby Friendship RC, 1950 to the present

REGATTA MINUTES

Durham Regatta, 1919–47

Henley Regatta, 1867 to the present

National Dock Labour Board

BIBLIOGRAPHY

Regatta reports, 1953–77
Ports Rowing Regatta Committee, 1969–76
Quayside Aquatic Sports (Lancaster), 1884–98
Tideway Charity Regatta, 1910–70
Tyne Regatta, 1887 to the present (and accounts, 1872–1986)
Warrington Regatta, 1841–45
Wingfield Sculls, 1848 to the present (Race Book 1830–97)

REGATTA PROGRAMMES

Bath Rowing Club Regatta, 27 Aug. 1927
Bedford Regatta, 1861–68
Berwick Regatta, 1870, 1872
Chester Regatta poster, 1832
City of Norwich Regatta, 1949

Derby Amateur Regatta, July 1884
Folkestone Regatta, 1946–55
Hereford Regatta, 1875, 1903, 1904, 1909, 1920
Lancaster Regatta, July 1888
Leeds Regatta Club, July 1868
Morecambe Bay Regatta, Aug. 1844
Norwich Church of England Youngmen's Society Regatta, 1897
Nottingham Regatta, Aug. 1858
Putney Town Regatta, May 1984
Snatchems Sports, July 1841
Warrington Regatta, July 1841
Whitby Regatta, 1849
Worthing Regatta, 1873, 1881, 1939
Worthing Regatta subscribers leaflet, Aug. 1859
York Regatta, 1888, 1913, 1922

ASSOCIATION MINUTES

Amateur Rowing Association, 1953–71
Amateur Rowing Association Provincial Committee, 1938
Cambridgeshire Rowing Association, 1928–70
Northwest Rowing Council, 1980–87
Norwich Amateur Rowing Association, members book, 1898

INTERVIEWS

Peter Finney	Ex-president, Bradford RC
Dennis Barker	Ex-chairman, City of Cambridge RC
Mike Stephenson	Secretary, St Ives RC
John Partridge	President, Derwent RC
Len Rey	President, Exeter RC
Harry Read	Ex-chairman, Poplar, Blackwall and District RC
John Eden	Secretary, Guildford RC
Jacka Stevens	Ex-chairman, Curlew RC
John Bishop	Secretary, Hexham BC
Ralp Bird	Boatbuilder and secretary, Truro RC
J.K. Newman	Chairman, Greenback Falmouth RC
R. Cooper	Secretary, Shanklin Sandown RC
David Wheeler	Chairman, Ryde RC
Monty Collins	Ex-president, Evesham RC
Chris Kenyon	Secretary, Tees RC
Richard Moseley	Secretary, Rob Roy RC

Jim Forey	Secretary, Alpha Ladies RC
Mike Fox	Master i/c Rowing, Kings School, Chester
Charles Dimont	Vice-president, Putney Town Regatta
Bill Colley	Secretary, Hammersmith Borough Regatta
Doug Melvin	Secretary, Wingfield Sculls
Keith Osborne	Editor, *British Rowing Almanack*
Neil Thomas	President, Amateur Rowing Association
Martin Spencer	Archivist, Watermen's Hall
Miss Beaumont	Archivist, Fishmongers' Hall
L. Marsh	Lodge keeper, Haigh Country Park, Wigan

ROWING TEXTS

Club histories

The Agecroft Story 1861–1960 (ARC, 1960).

Ainslie, M., *A History of Falcon Rowing Club* (Falcon RC, 1969).

Applebee, L.G., *Vesta Rowing Club, 1870–1920* (McAllen, 1920).

Armytage, H., *The Records of Jesus College B.C.* (Spalding, 1885).

Atchinson and Brown, *A History of Christ Church College B.C.* (Bowes, 1922).

Ball, W.W.R., *A History of First Trinity B.C.* (Bowes, 1908).

Barton, W., *Bewdley Rowing Club – A Short History* (Bewdley RC, 1985).

Burnell and Rickett, *A Short History of Leander Club 1818–1968* (Leander Club, 1968).

Byrne and Churchill, *The Eton Book of the River* (Blackwell, 1952).

Collins, W., *A Short History of Stratford-on-Avon R.C.* (Boyden, 1974).

Curlew Rowing Club, *Centenary History* (Curlew RC, 1966).

Derby Rowing Club, *Centenary History 1879–1979* (Derby RC, 1979).

Derwent Rowing Club, *Centenary History, 1857–1957* (Derby RC, 1957).

Dutton, J.P., *A Short History of Loughborough B.C.* (Loughborough BC, 1982).

Glass and Patrick, *The Royal Chester Rowing Club Centenary History* (Laver, 1939).

Henry Meoles School BC, *Diamond Jubilee History* (Henry Meoles School, 1985).

Henthorne, F., *A History of Ancholme Rowing Club 1868–1976* (Humberside CC, 1980).

Hold, C., *100 years of Bideford R.C.* (Hold, Devon, 1982).

Hunt, F.J., *Deal Walmer and Kingsdown R.C. 1927–1977* (Kent Printers, 1977).

King, P.A., *125 years on at Kingston R.C.* (Kingston RC, 1983).

Kings School Chester Boat Club Centenary (Kings School, 1985).

Lady Margaret Boat Club, 1825–1926 (Johnian Society, 1926).

London Rowing Club 1856–1981 (London RC, 1981).

Magdalen Boat Club, 1828–1928 (Cambridge University Press, 1930).

Mark, R., *Talkin Tarn Amateur Rowing Club, 125 years* (TTARC, 1984).

Oxford University and College Servants R.C. 1850–1950 (College Servants RC, 1950).

Pembroke College B.C. 1831–1981 (Pembroke College, 1981).

BIBLIOGRAPHY

Puckering and Dawber, *A Short History of Gainsborough R.C.* (Bellows, 1923).
Rowing at Westminster, 1813–1883 (Kegan Paul, 1890).
Royal Engineers Rowing Club – an History (Royal Engineers RC, 1980).
St. Philip and St. James Rowing Club, 1889–1909 (Blackwell, 1910).
Smith, H.R., *Dark Blue and White, the History of Evesham R.C.* (Evesham Journal, 1948).
Tarbuck, K., *Liverpool Victoria R.C. 1884–1934* (Dabbel Buck, 1934).
Trinity Hall Boat Club – a History (Heffer, 1930).
Walker, W.J., *Friendship* (Horne & Son, Whitby, 1954).
Wells, H.B., *Vesta Rowing Club, Centenary History* (Vesta RC, 1970).
Wigglesworth, N.D., *A Short History of Rowing in Lancaster* (John O'Gaunt RC, 1980).

Regatta histories

Allen, J., *Reading Regattas* (British Rowing Almanack, 1970).
Aquatic Oracle or Record of Rowing, 1835–1851 (Simpkin, Marshall, 1852).
Boden, H., *Marlowes and the Regatta* (Brockhampton Press, 1961).
Burnell, R., *Henley Regatta* (Oxford University Press, 1957).
Burnell, R., *The Boat Race, 1829–1953* (Oxford University Press, 1954).
Cook, T.A., *Rowing at Henley* (Oxford University Press, 1919).
Dodd, C., *Henley Royal Regatta* (Stanley Paul, 1981).
Dodd, C., *The Oxford and Cambridge Boat Race* (Stanley Paul, 1983).
Doggett's Coat and Badge Race Book, 1715 to the present (Fishmongers Hall).
Drinkwaters and Sanders, *The Boat Race* (Cassell & Co., 1929).
Heavisides, J., *Notes on Durham Regatta* (Durham RC, 1971).
Macmichael, W.F., *The Oxford and Cambridge Boat Races* (Bell & Daldy, 1870).
Nickalls, G., *The Race for Doggett's Coat and Badge* (Longman Green, 1908).
Osborne, K., *Walton Regatta 1862–1977* (British Rowing Almanack, 1977).
Steward, C.T., *Records of Henley Regatta 1919–1939* (Hamilton, 1939).
Steward, H.T., *Records of Henley Regatta 1839–1902* (Hutchinson, 1903).
Sunbury Regatta, 1877–1977 (Sunbury Regatta Committee, 1977).
Topolski, D., *The Boat Race, the Oxford Revival* (Willow Books, 1985).
Treherne and Goldie, *Record of the Boat Race, 1829–1888* (Bickers & Son, 1888).

Local histories

Aquatic Notes, Sketches on the Rise of Rowing at Cambridge (Deighton, 1852).
Armytage, H., *The Cam and Cambridge Rowing* (W. Kent & Co., 1889).
Crump, A., *A History of Amateur Rowing on the River Lee* (Graham, 1919).
Davis, R.J., *A History of Boating in Worcester* (Pershore Press, 1978).
Douglas, J., *Rowing on the Cam* (Birds Farm Publications, 1977).
Grieve, A.A.M., *A History of Durham Rowing* (Andrew Reid, 1922).
Langfield, J., *The Eton Book of the River* (Eton College, 1988).
Sherwood, W.E., *Oxford Rowing* (Frowde, 1900).
Smith, L., *Annals of Public School Rowing* (Oxford University Press, 1920).
Snelson, B.G.A., *63 Years on the Cam* (Cambridge Chronicle, 1931).
Wigglesworth, N.D., *A History of Rowing in the North West of England* (Manchester University, 1982; repr., *British Journal of Sports History*

(Sept. 1986), pp. 145–58).
Woodgate, W.B., *Boating Life at Oxford* (Hogg and Sons, 1868).

General histories

Cleaver, H., *A History of Rowing* (Jenkins, 1957).
Desborough, *The Story of the Oar* (Horace Cox, 1910).
Dodd, C., *Centenary Pageant Souvenir* (ARA, 1982).
Markham, V., 'Boats for Women' (BA thesis Newnham College, Cambridge, 1975).
Osborne, K., *Boat Racing in Britain, 1917–1975* (ARA, 1975).
Ueberhorst, H., *A Hundred Years of the German Rowing Association* (Albrecht Philler Verlag, 1975, trans. P. Payne).

Social commentary

Haberstaum, A., *The Amateurs* (Morrow, NY, 1985).
Halladay, E., 'The Amateur Question in English Nineteenth Century Rowing', *International Journal of the History of Sport* (May 1987), 39–56.
Kiesling, S., *The Shell Game* (Morrow, NY, 1983).
Mangan, J.A., 'Oars and the Man', *British Journal of Sports History* (March 1984).
Wigglesworth, N.D., *Victorian and Edwardian Boating* (Batsford, 1987).

Technical

Aquatics by a Rower of Thirty Matches (Whittaker & Co., 1851).
Beddington, F., *Boating and Boat Racing* (Spedding, 1909).
Brickwood, E.D., *Boat Racing or the Art of Rowing and Training* (Cox, 1876).
East, W.G., *Rowing* (Arthur Pearson, 1904).
Fairbairn, S., *Chats on Rowing* (Heffer & Sons, 1934).
Furnivall, F.J., *Sculls or Oars* (privately printed, 1886).
Grenfell, W.H., *Rowing and Punting* (Macmillan, 1898).
Jeffrey, J., *Rowing* (Dean & Co., 1897).
Lehmann, R.C., *Rowing* (Innes, 1898).
Nickalls, G.E. and P.C. Mallam, *Rowing* (Pitman, 1939).
Pitman and Rowe, *Rowing* (Longman Green, 1903).
Principles of Rowing by an Oarsman (Westley, 1846).
Ransom, A., *Aquatics* (Dawson, 1908).
Shadwell, H.T., *The Principles of Rowing and Steering* (Slatter & Rose, 1857).
Treatise on the Art of Rowing as Practised at Cambridge (J. Hall, 1842).
Woodgate, W.B., *Boating* (Longman Green, 1889).
Woodgate, W.B., *Oars and Sculls* (Bell & Sons, 1875).

Miscellaneous

An Oarsman's Guide to the Thames and Other Rivers (Searle, 1857).
A Rowing Holiday by Canal in 1873 by a Pleasure Boater (Oakwood Press, 1977).
Bolland, R.R., *Victorians on the Thames* (Evans Bros, 1983).
British Rowing Almanack (1860 to the present).
Canals of Great Britain and Ireland (Philip and Son, 1896).
Crossley, S., *Pleasure and Leisure Boating* (Innes, 1899).

Diary of a Rowing Tour from Oxford to London in 1875 (Sutton, Gloucester, 1982).

Dodd C., *Boating* (Oxford University Press, 1983).

Edwards, H.R.A., *The Way of a Man with a Blade* (Routledge, 1963).

Foster, R.H., *Down by the River, a Rowing Man's Miscellany* (Johnson, 1901).

Nickalls, G.E., *A Rainbow in the Sky* (Chatto & Windus, 1974).

Morgan, J., *University Oars* (Macmillan, 1873).

Protheroe and Clark, *A New Oarsman's Guide to the Rivers and Canals of Great Britain and Ireland* (Philip and Son, 1896).

Rees, G.T., *The Rowing Club Directory of Great Britain* (Lock to Lock Times, 1898).

Swartout, R.E., *Rhymes of the River* (Heffer & Sons, 1927).

Vine, P.A.L., *Pleasure Boating in the Victorian Era* (Phillmore, 1983).

Winn, W., *The Boating Man's Vade Mecum* (Swan Sonneschein, 1891).

Woodgate, W.B., *Reminiscences of an Old Sportsman* (Eveleigh Nash, 1909).

Readers who wish to explore the bibliography of rowing in more detail should consult F. Brittain's *Oar, Scull and Rudder: A Bibliography of Rowing* (Oxford University Press, 1930) in which 1,000 references are recorded.

COMPARATIVE TEXTS

Individual sports

Lord Aberdare, *The Book of Tennis and Rackets* (Stanley Paul, 1980).

Altham and Swanton, *A History of Cricket* (Allen & Unwin, 1962).

Ascham, R., *Toxophilus* (1545; repr. Scholar Press, 1971).

Batchelor, D., *British Boxing* (Faber, 1949).

Bellamy, R., *The Story of Squash* (Cassell, 1976).

Bird, D., *Our Skating Heritage* (NSA, 1979).

Brookes, C., *English Cricket* (Weidenfeld & Nicolson, 1978).

Brownrigg, R., *A History of Golf* (Dent, 1955).

Burke, E., *The History of Archery* (Fawcett Muller, 1958).

Cardus and Arlott, *The Noblest Game* (Longman, 1969).

De Beaumont, R., *Fencing, Ancient Art and Modern Sport* (Kaye Ward, 1970).

Downer, A.R., *Running Recollections 1902* (Blairgowrie Books, 1982).

Fleischer, N., *An Informal History of Heavyweight Boxing from 1719 to the Present* (Putnam, NY, 1949).

Fleischer, N., *A Pictorial History of Boxing* (Hamlyn, 1975).

Fleischer, N., *The Ring Record Book* (Hamlyn, 1971).

Grimsley, W., *Tennis, Its History, People and Events* (Prentice Hall, 1971).

Harris, H.A., *Greek Athletes and Athletics* (Hutchinson, 1964).

Hawkes, J., *The Meynellian Science* (Leicester, 1932).

Lake and Wright, *Bibliography of Archery* (Simon Foundation, Manchester University, 1974).

Longrigg, R., *A History of Horse Racing* (Macmillan, 1972).

Lunn, A., *A Century of Mountaineering 1857–1957* (Allen & Unwin, 1957).

Lunn, A., *The Story of Skiing* (Eyre and Spottiswoode, 1952).

Lyttleton and Padwick, *A Bibliography of Cricket* (Clarke, 1977).

Macklin, K., *The History of Rugby League Football* (Stanley Paul, 1974).

McNab, T., 'A History of Professional Athletics', *Athletics Weekly,* nos 26, 37, 38 (1972).

Malherbe, W., *A Chronological Bibliography of Hockey* (Hockey Assoc., 1965).

Moorhouse, G., *Lords* (Hodder & Stoughton, 1983).

Mortimer, R., *A History of the Derby Stakes* (Joseph, 1962).

Mortimer, R., *The Jockey Club* (Cassell, 1958).

Owen, O.L., *The History of the Rugby Football Union* (Playfair, 1955).

Phillips-Birt, D., *The Cumberland Fleet* (David & Charles, 1975).

Rowley, P., *The Book of Hockey* (Batsford, 1963).

Scott, J., *The Athletic Revolution* (Free Press, 1971).

Shearman, M., *Athletics* (Longman Green, 1889).

Solomon, J.W., *Croquet* (Batsford, 1966).

Steele and Lyttleton, *Cricket* (Longman Green, 1893).

Thomas, P., *The Northern Cross Country Association Centenary History* (NCCA, 1982).

Whyte, J., *A History of the British Turf* (Longman Green, 1840).

Collective sports

Arlott, J., *The Oxford Companion to Sports and Games* (Paladin, 1977).

Bale, J., *Sport and Place – A Geography of Sport in England, Scotland and Wales* (Hurst & Co., 1982).

Briggs, A., *Essays in the History of Publishing*, esp. 'The View from Badminton' (Longman, 1974).

Burke, P., *Popular Culture in Early Modern Europe* (Temple Smith, 1978).

Burrows, H. and L. Wood, *Sports and Pastimes in English Literature* (Nelson, 1925).

Cone, C. (ed.), *Sunday Sports of Merry England* (University of Kentucky, 1981).

Cox, R., *Sport – A Guide to Historical Sources in the U.K.* (Sports Council Information Series, No. 9, 1983).

Ford, J., *This Sporting Land* (New England Library, 1977).

Goodman, P., *Sporting Life – An Anthology of British Sporting Prints* (British Museum, 1983).

Lady Grenville, *The Gentlemen's Book of Sports* (Spalding, 1880).

Harris, H.A., *Sports in Britain* (Stanley Paul, 1975).

Lennox, W., *Pictures of Sporting Life and Character* (Hurst, 1860).

Longrigg, R., *The English Squire and His Sport* (Joseph, 1977).

McCrone, K., 'Sport at the Oxbridge Women's Colleges from Foundation to 1914', *British Journal of Sports History* (Sept. 1986), 191.

Maclaren, A., *Training in Theory and Practice* (Macmillan, 1866).

Nickalls, G.E., *With the Skin of their Teeth* (Country Life, 1951).

Peeks, H., *The Poetry of Sport* (Longman, 1986).

Reekie, H.M., 'A History of Sport and Recreation for Women in Great Britain, 1700–1850' (Ph.D Ohio State University, 1982).

Rodgers, H.B., *Pilot National Recreation Survey* (Keele University, 1966).

Trollope, A., *British Sports and Pastimes* (Virtue, 1868).

Vale, M., *The Gentleman's Recreations 1580–1630* (Brewer, 1977).

Walsh, J.H., *A Manual of British Rural Sports* (Routledge, 1856).

Whitney, C., *A Sporting Pilgrimage to Oxford, Cambridge and the Shires* (Osgood McIlvaine, 1894).

Social commentary

Arnold, J., 'The Influence of Pilkington Brothers on the Growth of Sport and Community Recreation in St. Helens' (M. Ed., Liverpool University, 1977).

Aspin, D., 'On the Nature and Purpose of a Sporting Activity: the Connection between Sport, Life and Politics', *Physical Education Review* (Spring 1986), 5–14.

Bailey, P., *Leisure and Class in Victorian England 1830–1885* (Routledge, 1978).

Ball, D. and J. Loy, *Sport and Social Order* (Addison-Wesley, 1975).

Bent, C. and C. Scott, *Borrowed Time – Social History of Running* (45 Brosscroft, Hadfield, Cheshire, c. 1978).

Berryman, J.W., 'Sport History as Social History?' *Quest* (Summer 1973).

Brailsford, D., *Some Factors in the Evolution of Sports and Games* (Shenstone New College, Bromsgrove, 1971).

Brooke-Smith, M., 'The Growth and Development of Popular Entertainment in Lancashire Cotton Towns 1830–1870' (M. Litt., Lancaster, 1971).

Cardus, N., *Cardus on Cricket* (Souvenir Press, 1977).

Cashman and McKernan (ed.), *Sport in History* (University of Queensland, 1979).

Chataway, C. and G. Goodhart, *War without Weapons* (Allen, 1968).

Cunningham, H., *Leisure in the Industrial Revolution* (Croom Helm, 1980).

Dobbs, B., *Edwardians at Play* (Pelham, 1973).

Dunning, E. and K. Sheard, *Barbarians, Gentlemen and Players* (Robertson, 1979).

Ensor, E., 'The Football Madness', *Contemporary Review*, lxxiv (1898).

Ford, J., *Cricket – A Social History 1700–1835* (David & Charles, 1972).

Golby, J.M. and A.W. Purdue, *The Civilisation of the Crowd – Popular Culture in England, 1750–1900* (Batsford, 1984).

Griffiths, I., 'Gentlemen Suppliers and "with it" consumers', *International Review of Sport Sociology* (1970), 59.

Haley, B., 'Sports and the Victorian World', *Western Humanities Review*, 22 (1968).

Haley, B., *The Healthy Body and Victorian Culture* (Harvard University, 1978).

Itzkovitz, D., *Peculiar Privilege – A Social History of English Fox Hunting 1735–1885* (Harvester Press, 1977).

James, C.L.R., *Beyond a Boundary* (Hutchinson, 1963).

Krawczyk, B., 'Social Origin and Ambivalent Character of Ideology of Amateur Sport', *International Review of Sport Sociology* (1977), 35.

Lowerson and Myerscough, *Time to Spare in Victorian England* (Harvester, 1977).

McCrone, K., *Sport and the Physical Emancipation of English Women, 1870–1914* (Routledge, 1988).

McIntosh, P.C., 'An Historical View of Sport and Social Control',

International Review of Sport Sociology (1971), 5.

McIntosh, P.C., *Fair Pl y – Ethics in Sport and Education* (Heinemann, 1979).

McIntosh, P.C., *Sport in Society* (Watts, 1963).

Malcolmson, R., *Popular Recreations in English Society 1700–1850* (Cambridge University Press, 1973).

Mangan, J.A., *Athleticism in the Victorian and Edwardian Public School* (Cambridge University Press, 1981).

Mason, A., *Association Football and English Society* (Harvester Press, 1980).

Mellor, H., *Leisure and the Changing City 1870–1914* (Routledge, 1976).

Metcalfe, A., 'Sport in Nineteenth Century England' (Ph.D Wisconsin, 1968).

Murray, B., *The Old Firm – Sectarianism, Sport and Society* (Donald, 1984).

Natan, A., *Sport and Society* (Bowes & Bowes, 1958).

Pimlott, J.A.R., *An Englishman's Holiday: A Social History* (Harvester, 1977).

Pimlott, J.A.R., *Recreations* (Studio Vista, 1968).

Plumb, J.H., *The Growth of Leisure 1630–1830* (Cambridge University Press, 1972).

Rees, R., 'The Development of Physical Recreation in Liverpool during the Nineteenth Century' (MA Liverpool, 1968).

Smith, M.B., 'Popular Leisure and the Music Hall in Nineteenth Century Bolton' (Centre for N. West Studies, Lancaster University, Paper 12, 1982).

Smith, R., *A Social History of the Bicycle* (American Heritage, 1972).

Strutt, J., *Sports and Pastimes of the People of England* (White, 1801 and repr. Kelly, NY, 1970).

Vamplew, W., *The Turf – A Social and Economic History of Horse Racing* (Allen Lane, 1976).

Walton, J., *The English Seaside Resort. A Social History 1750–1914* (Leicester University Press, 1983).

Walvin, J., *Football and the Decline of Britain* (Macmillan, 1986).

Walvin, J., and J. Walton, *Leisure in Britain 1780–1939* (Manchester University Press, 1983).

Walvin, J., *Beside the Sea* (Allen Lane, 1978).

Walvin, J., *Leisure and Society 1830–1950* (Longman, 1978).

Walvin, J., *The People's Game: A Social History of British Football* (Arrow, 1975).

Waszack, P., 'The Development of Leisure and Cultural Facilities in Peterborough, 1850–1900' (B.A. Huddersfield Polytechnic, 1972).

GENERAL TEXTS

Directories and Guides

Alkin, A., *Four Miles around Manchester* (Manchester, 1795).

Baines, *History, Directory and Gazetteer of Lancashire* (Preston, 1825).

'Barrow Almanack and Tide Tables' 1889 and 1903, *Barrow News*.

Beaty's Guide to Brampton (Beaty & Sons, Carlisle, 1905).

Brennan, F. (trans.) *Puckler's Progress – Tour around Britain in 1826* (Collins).

Colligan, A., *The Weighvers Seaport* (Kelsall, Littleborough, 1977).

Cudworth, W., *Round about Bradford* (1876; repr. Mountain Press, 1968).

Davenport's Guide to Hollingworth Lake (Stockport, 1860).

Defoe, D., *A Tour through the Whole Island of Great Britain, 1722* (Dent, 1962).

de Saussure, C., *A Foreign View of England in the Reigns of George I and George II, 1725–1729* (Murray, 1902).

Dickens, C. Jnr., *Dictionary of the Thames* (Macmillan, 1887).

Directory of Barrow and North Lonsdale 1871 and 1876 (Mannix, Barrow).

Directory of Lancaster (Barrett & Co., 1866).

Health Giving Huntingdon (Huntingdon Chamber of Commerce, 1906).

Hickman and Kinch, *A Guide to Henley and Its Vicinity* (Simpkin & Marshall, 1838).

Huntingdon (Huntingdon District Council, 1985).

Huntingdon and the Great Ouse (Homeland Handbooks, 1905).

Huntingdon Official Guides, 1922 and 1950 (Hunts. Chamber of Commerce).

Kelly's Directory of Bradford (Temple Bar, 1936).

Kelly's Directory of Cambridgeshire (Temple Bar, 1847).

Kelly's Directory of Hampshire and the Isle of Wight (Temple Bar, 1875).

Kelly's Directory of Huntingdonshire (Temple Bar, 1906).

Kelly's Directory of South Devon (Temple Bar, 1902).

Kirkland, T., *A Guide to Southport and North Meoles* (Rivington, 1826).

Lancaster, Morecambe and District Directory (Cook, Derby, 1899).

Mission, M., *Memoirs and Observations* (London, 1719; repr. Collins, 1975).

Parsons Directory of Kent (Folkestone Herald, 1920).

Pidgeon, H., *A Memorial of Shrewsbury, A General Guide* (Eddowes, 1837).

Robertson, W., *Guide to Rochdale* (Rochdale, 1875).

St Neots (Huntingdon District Council, 1985).

Slaters Directory of Shropshire (Shrewsbury, 1850).

Staffordshire Waterways (Staffs. Education Department, 1969).

Ward's Directory of Newcastle (Newcastle, 1850).

Whitby Illustrated Almanack and Diary (Whitby Times, 1908).

Local histories

Anderson, J., *Anchor and Hope* (Hodder & Stoughton, 1980).

Avery, E., *The London Stage, 1600–1800* (Southern Illinois University Press, 1960).

Bellavitis, G., *Itinerari per Venezia* (L'Espresso, Roma, 1980).

Bennett, M., 'Late Mediaeval Society in North West England' (Ph.D Lancaster, 1975).

Birkenhead, 1877–1974 (Borough of Birkenhead, 1974).

Birkenhead Improvement Commission, minutes for 1844 and 1845.

Bourne, G.C., *Memories of an Eton Wet Bob of the '70's* (Oxford University Press, 1933).

Bracey, D., *The Book of Peterborough* (Barracuda Books, 1984).

'Bradford Antiquary', *Journal of Bradford Historical Society*, vol. 1 (1912).

Bradford Book of Dates (Bradford City Council, 1910).

Burn, P., *Brampton as I Have Known It* (Hodgson, Brampton, 1893).

Burnley, J., 'Busy Bradford', *Our Magazine* (Holborn, 1903).

Burnley, J., *Phases of Bradford Life* (Simpkin & Marshall, 1897).

Burstall, P., *The Golden Age of the Thames* (David & Charles, 1981).

Century's Progress – Yorkshire (London Printing Company, 1893).

Chambers, J.D., *Modern Nottingham in the Making* (Oxford University Press, 1945).

Christian, R., *Derby* (Derby Cathedral, 1983).

Church, R., *Economic and Social Change in a Midland Town – Victorian Nottingham, 1815–1900* (Cass, 1966).

Cohen, B., *The Thames, 1580–1980, A General Bibliography* (Anchor Brendan, 1985).

Company of Watermen and Lightermen on the River Thames (Watermen's Hall, 1978).

Corbett, J., *The River Irwell* (Haywood, Manchester, 1907).

Cowe, F.M., *Berwick on Tweed* (Cowe, Berwick, 1972).

Cunningham, T.A., 'The Growth of Peterborough, 1850–1900' (M. Litt., Cambridge, 1972).

Dane, R., *Peterborough Papers*, no. 2. (Peterborough Arts Council, 1978).

Davison, J., *Social Life in Whitby in the Nineteenth Century* (Waingate, 1977).

Dore, G., and B. Jerrold, *London, A Pilgrimage* (Grant & Co., 1872).

Feinstein, C.H., *York, 1831–1981* (British Association, 1981).

Fletcher, H., *A Life on the Humber* (Faber & Faber, 1975).

Frangopolo, N.J., *The Historical Evolution of the G.M.C.* (E.P. Publishing, 1977).

Gooderson, P.J., *A History of Lancashire* (Batsford, 1980).

Gravesend Chronology (Gravesend Library, 1980).

Gray, N., *The Worst of Times – Depression Years in Salford, Rochdale, Lancaster and South Shields* (Wildwood House, 1985).

Greaves, R.W., *The Corporation of Leicester* (Longman, 1939).

Greenhough, G.J., 'The Present Use of the River Cam' (M. Litt., Cambridge, 1972).

Heron, M., *Ferry Path – The Story of a Cambridge River Street* (Cockayne, 1974).

Hewins, A., *Mary after the Queen* (Oxford University Press, 1985).

Hewins, A., *The Dillen, Memories of a Stratford-on-Avon Man* (Oxford University Press, 1981).

Hibbert, C., *London, Biography of a City* (Penguin, 1969).

Hibbert, C., *The London Encyclopaedia* (Macmillan, 1983).

Hughes, H., *Chronicles of Chester 1715–1975* (Macdonald, 1976).

Illiffe and Baguley, *Edwardian Nottingham* (Nottingham Library, 1981).

Jolley, R., *Edmund Sharpe, a Lancaster Architect* (Lancaster University, 1977).

Kennerley, E., *The Old Fishing Community of Poulton le Sands* (Lancaster Museum, 1982).

Kingman, M.J., 'Chester 1801–1861' (MA, Leicester, 1972).

Lambert, R.S., *The Cobbett of the West* (Faber, 1939).

Laws and Constitution of the Masters, Wardens and Commonalty of Watermen and Lightermen of the River Thames (Philanthropic Society, 1828).

Lawson, W., *Tyneside Celebrities* (Lawson, Newcastle, 1873).

Lincoln (Lincoln City Hall, 1985).

Little, B., *The City and County of Bristol* (Werner Lauries, 1954).

Lloyd, L.C., *The Inns of Shrewsbury* (Shropshire Library, 1976).

Maitland, J., *A History of London* (London, 1739).

Makepeace, C., *The Manchester Ship Canal* (Hendon Publishing, 1983).

Manson, D.J., 'Brampton in the 1870's', *Cumberland Antiquarian Society*, vol. lxxiii (1973).

Marshall, J.D., *Life in Victorian Lancashire* (David & Charles, 1974).

Middlebrook, S., *Newcastle on Tyne, Its Growth and Achievements* (Kemsley, 1950).

Morgan, H., 'Social and Political Leadership in Preston 1800–1865' (MA, Lancaster, 1980).

Morley, F.V., *The River Thames* (Methuen, 1926).

Paige, R.T., *The Tamar Valley at Work* (Dartington Trust, 1978).

Partington, S., *The Danes in Lancashire and Yorkshire* (Sherratt & Hughes, 1909).

Phillips, J.F.C., *Shephers London* (Cassell, 1976).

Prior, M., *Fisher Row – Fishermen, Bargemen and Canal Boatmen in Oxford, 1500–1900* (Oxford University Press, 1982).

Pudney, J., *Crossing London's River* (Dent, 1972).

Report of the Lancaster Bribery Commission (HMSO, April 1867).

Robertson, H.R., *Life on the Upper Thames* (Hutchinson, 1875).

Sands, M., *An Invitation to Ranelagh* (Westhouse, 1946).

Shotter, D., *Romans in Lancashire* (Dalesman Books, 1974).

Southport Council Proceedings: Minutes of the Improvements and Foreshore Committee for 1893.

Spencer, K.M., 'Social and Economic Geography of Preston 1800–1865' (MA, Liverpool, 1968).

Summers, D., *The Great Ouse* (David & Charles, 1973).

Sutton, J.H., 'Early Fleetwood' (M. Litt., Lancaster, 1968).

Tomlinson, J., *Victorian and Edwardian Chester* (Deesider, 1976).

Trafford Park 1896–1939 (Manchester Polytechnic, 1979).

Victoria County History of Bedford, vol. II (Dawson, 1908).

Wedgwood, I., *Fenland Rivers* (Rick & Cowan, 1937).

Wynne, M.E., 'The Role of the River Mersey in the Bronze Age' (MA, Liverpool University, 1959).

Social commentary

Adams, R., *Paradoxical Harvest: Energy and Explanation in British History, 1870–1914* (Cambridge University Press, 1982).

Baumann, Z., *Memories of Class* (Routledge, 1982).

Beeton, Mrs, *The Book of Household Management* (1888; repr., Cape, 1968).

Bell, Lady, *At the Works, A Study of a Manufacturing Town* (Arnold, 1907).

Benson, J.R. (ed.), *The Working Class in England 1875–1914* (Croom Helm, 1985).

Briggs, A., *Victorian Cities* (Oldhams, 1963).

Campbell, R., *The London Tradesman, 1747* (repr. Augustus Kelly, NY 1969).

Cannadine, D. (ed.), *Patricians, Power and Politics in Nineteenth Century Towns* (Leicester University Press, 1982).

Cannon, J., *Aristocratic Century, the Peerage of Eighteenth Century England* (Oxford University Press, 1984).

Christie, I., *Stress and Stability in Late Eighteenth Century Britain* (Oxford University Press, 1985).

Cole and Postgate, *The Common People* (Methuen, 1961).

Crouch, C., *The Scope for Socialism, A Pessimistic View* (Fabian Soc., 1985).
Daverson, J. and K. Lindsay, *Voices from the Middle Class* (Hutchinson, 1975).
Davidoff, L., *The Best Circles* (Croom Helm, 1973).
Davidoff, L. and C. Hall, *Family Fortunes, Men and Women of the English Middle Class 1780–1850* (Hutchinson, 1987).
Davis, I.M., *The Harlot and the Statesman* (Kensal Press, 1987).
Donajgrodski, D. (ed.), *Social Control in Nineteenth Century Britain* (Croom Helm, 1977).
Dunkerley, D., *Occupations and Society* (Routledge, 1975).
Dyson, A. and J. Lovelock (eds.), *Education and Democracy* (Routledge, 1975).
Escott, T.H.S., *Social Transformations of the Victorian Age* (Seeley & Co., 1897).
Evans, E., *Social Policy, 1830–1914* (Routledge, 1975).
Fried and Elman (eds.), *Charles Booth's London* (Hutchinson, 1969).
Fulford, R. (ed.), *The Greville Memoirs* (Batsford, 1963).
Gash, N., *Aristocracy and People* (Arnold, 1985).
Gay, J., *Rowlandson the Caricaturist* (Chatto, 1880).
Hampden, J., *An Eighteenth Century Journal 1774–1776* (Macmillan, 1940).
Harrison, B., *Drink and the Victorians* (Faber, 1971).
Harrison, B., *Peaceable Kingdom* (Clarendon Press, 1982).
Hayes, J., *Rowlandson – Watercolours and Drawings* (Phaidon, 1972).
Heald, T., *Networks* (Hodder & Stoughton, 1983).
Hecht, J., *The Domestic Servant Class in Eighteenth Century England* (Routledge and Kegan Paul, 1956).
Henisch, B.A., *Cakes and Characters* (Prospect Books, 1984).
Heward, C., *Making a Man of Him – Parents and Their Sons' Education at an English Public School 1929–1950* (Routledge, 1988).
Hibbert, C., *The English – A Social History* (Grafton, 1986).
Himmlefarb, G., *The Idea of Poverty* (Faber, 1984).
Jeffreys, S., *The Spinster and Her Enemies 1880–1930* (Pandora, 1985).
Jenkins, P., *The Making of a Ruling Class, 1640–1790* (Cambridge University Press, 1983).
Lansdell, A., 'Costume for Oarswomen, 1919–1979', *Costume*, no. 13 (1979).
Lauwerys, J., 'The Philosophical Approach to Comparative Education', *International Review of Education*, vol. 5 (1959).
Lorimer, D., *Colour, Class and the Victorians* (Leicester University Press, 1978).
Lovelock and Stanley (eds.), *The Diaries of Hannah Cullwick: Victorian Maidservant* (Virago, 1984).
Mann, M., *Country Life: A Social History of Rural England* (Weidenfeld, 1987).
Mantoux, P., *The Industrial Revolution in the Eighteenth Century* (Methuen, 1964).
Marsh, D., *The Changing Social Structure of England and Wales* (Routledge, 1965).
Marx, K., *Capital* (Penguin, 1976).
Mingay, C.E., *The Transformation of Britain, 1830–1939* (Routledge, 1986).
Munsche, P.B., *Gentlemen and Poachers: The English Game Laws, 1671–1831*

(Cambridge University Press, 1981).

Neale, R.S., *Class and Ideology in the Nineteenth Century* (Routledge, 1972).

d'Ormesson, J., *Grand Hotel* (Dent, 1984).

Owen, C., *Social Stratification* (Routledge, 1968).

Paulson, R., *Hogarth, His Life and Times* (Yale University Press, 1971).

Payne, P., *British Entrepreneurship in the Nineteenth Century* (Routledge, 1974).

Penn, R., *Skilled Workers in the Class Struggle* (Cambridge University Press, 1983).

Pepys' Diary (Bell & Hyman, 1973).

Perkin, H., *The Origins of Modern English Society 1780–1880* (Routledge, 1969).

Perkin, H., 'The Origins of the Popular Press', *History Today*, vol. 7 (1957) 425–35.

Perkin, H., *Professionalism, Property and English Society since 1800* (Reading University Press, 1981).

Perkin, H., *The Social Tone of Victorian Seaside Resorts in North West England* (University of Lancaster, 1976).

Perkin, H., *The Structured Crowd* (Harvester Press, 1981).

Philips, K.C., *Language and Class in Victorian England* (Blackwell, 1984).

Pick, J., *The West End – Mismanagement and Snobbery* (Offerd, Eastbourne, 1984).

Plumb, J.H., *The Birth of a Consumer Society: The Commercialisation of Eighteenth Century England* (Hutchinson, 1983).

Read, D., *The English Provinces 1760–1960* (Arnold, 1964).

Reed, M.B., *The Georgian Triumph 1700–1830* (Routledge, 1983).

Richards, J. and J. Mackenzie (eds.), *A Social History of the Railway Station* (Oxford University Press, 1986).

Roberts, E., *A Woman's Place 1890–1940* (Blackwell, 1984).

Robinson, J.M., *The Latest Country Houses, 1945–1983* (Bodley Head, 1983).

Robson, B., *Where Is the North?* (City of Manchester, 1985).

Sanderson, M. (ed.), *The Universities in the Nineteenth Century* (Routledge, 1975).

Scott, A.F., *The Early Hanoverian Age 1714–1760* (Croom Helm, 1980).

Sharpe, J.W., *Crime in Early Modern England 1550–1750* (Longman, 1984).

Stevenson, J., *English Urban History 1500–1780* (Open University Press, 1982).

Stone, L. and J., *An Open Elite* (Oxford University Press, 1986).

Trollope, A., *The Newzealander* (Clarendon, 1972).

Victorian Poacher – James Hawker's Journal (Oxford University Press, 1961).

Walker, S., *Sporting Art, 1740–1900* (Studio Vista, 1972).

Wigley, J., *The Rise and Fall of the Victorian Sunday* (Manchester University Press, 1980).

Wingfield-Stratford, P., *Victorian Sunset* (Murray, 1932).

Worsley, T.C., *Barbarians and Philistines* (Hale, 1940).

Worsley, T.C., *The End of the Old School Tie* (Secker & Warburg, 1941).

Wright, T., *Some Habits and Customs of the Working Classes by a Journeyman Engineer, 1867* (repr., Augustus Kelly, NY, 1967).

Yeo, E. & S., *Popular Culture and Class Conflict 1590–1914* (Harvester, 1981).

Technical

Atterbury, P., *English Rivers and Canals* (Weidenfeld & Nicolson, 1983).
Burton, A., *The Changing River* (Gollancz, 1984).
Davis, R., *The Rise of the English Shipping Industry* (Macmillan, 1962).
Hornell, H., *Water Transport – Origins and Early Evolution* (David and Charles, 1970).
Kipling, R., *Rescue by Sail and Oar* (Tops'l Books, 1982).
Morrison, J., *Greek Oared Ships* (Cambridge University Press, 1968).
Roman Shipping and Trade in Britain and the Rhine Provinces (Council for British Archaeology, Research Report no. 24, 1978).

Biographical

Constable, W.G., *Canaletto* (Clarendon, 1976).
Cook, T. and G. Nickalls, *Thomas Doggett Deceased* (Constable, 1908).
Frederick James Furnivall – A Record (Frowde, 1911).
Green, P., *Kenneth Grahame* (Murray, 1959).
Harris, H., *Under Oars* (Stepney Books, 1978).
Hudson, D., *Munby – A Man of Two Worlds* (Abacus, 1974).
Leon, W., *Thomas Doggett Pictured* (Watermen's Company, 1980).
Nickalls, G., *Life's a Pudding – An Autobiography* (Faber, 1939).
Nickalls, V., *Oars, Wars and Horses* (Hurst & Blackett, 1932).
Trollope, A., *An Autobiography* (Blackwood & Sons, 1883).
Woodgate, W.B., *Reminiscences of an Old Sportsman* (Eveleigh Nash, 1909).

Index

Lowe, Robert, 119
Lower Tideway Trades Rowing
    Association, 163
Lupton, Eric, 139

Macgregor, J. ('Rob Roy'), 100, 104
Maclaren, Archibald, 121
Manchester, 10, 36, 97, 190
Manchester, Duke of, 44
Manchester and Salford Regatta, 72, 122,
    149, 152, 160
Mangan, J.A., 196
Mantoux, Paul, 147
manual ban, the, 131
Marlow Ferry, 20
Marlow RC, 189
Marshall, Major, 150
Mason, A., 191
Maurice, F.D., 97
Maurice RC, 97
Melvin, D.V., 180
Mersey Docks and Harbour Board, 145
Mersey RC, 149
Metropolitan Rowing Association, 124–5,
    130, 168, 193
Metropolitan Vickers RC, 136
middle class, the, 13
Middlesbrough BC, 158, 160
minute books, 9
Mitchell, James, 139
modern sporting journalism, origins of, 47
Molesey RC, 153, 158
Monarch BC, 61, 120
Morecambe, 53
Morecambe Bay, 10
muscular Christianity, 97, 101, 114

Nadin, Harry, 124
National Amateur Rowing Association,
    132–3, 152, 163, 168, 188, 194, 195,
    200
National Dock Labour Board, 175
National Fitness Council, 115
National Lifeboat Committee, 22
National Rowing Squad, 169
Nemesis RC, 147, 148, 149
Neptune RC, 108, 139, 156, 158, 170
Newcastle, 4, 11, 37, 190, 206
Newcastle Amateur RC, 129
Newcastle Commission, The (1861), 119
Newcastle Regatta, 48
Newquay, 205
Newquay RC, 18
News Chronicle, 135
Nil Desperandum RC, 159
Norfolk and Norwich RC, 131

Norman, John, 12
Northern RC, 129
North–South divide, 189–90, 193
Northumberland, Duke of, 26
Northwest Rowing Council, 170, 203
Northwich RC, 136, 147
Norwich, 69, 99, 101, 206
Norwich Regatta, 48
Norwich RC, 103, 153
Nottingham, 95, 206
Nottingham and Union RC, 110
Nottingham BC, 102
Nottingham Britannia RC, 130
Nottingham Regatta, 40, 145
Nottingham RC, 64, 102, 129, 151, 156,
    160
Nottinghamshire Rowing Association,
    170, 195
Noulton, John, 63, 64

Oarsmen,
    amateur, 17, 89, 178
    classification of, 66, 75, 128
    professional, 71, 77, 79
occupational rowing, 10–31
octuple sculling boat, 98
Olympic Regattas, 166, 167, 169, 173
'one boat clubs', 67, 149
Osborne, K.L., 1
outriggers, 4, 83
Owston Ferry, 21
Oxbridge influence, 124, 184, 188, 192,
    193, 198
Oxford, 22, 45, 205
Oxford City Regatta, 129
Oxford University BC, 44, 84, 130, 169,
    179, 181
Oxford University Women's BC, 107
Oxford watermen, 20, 23, 129, 137

parish boatmen, 23
patriotism, 156
Pengwern RC, 131, 160
Penwortham Ferry, 22
Pepys, Samuel, 92
Peterborough, 205
Peters of St Mawes, 18, 83
Phelps, E., 139
Phelps family, 14
Phelps, J., 61, 122
Phoenician rowing, 11
Pier Head, Liverpool, 68
pilot gig, 19
Players' Company (Nottingham), 151
Playford, F.L., 80, 123
pleasure boating, 112–13, 117

CPSIA information can be obtained at www.ICGtesting.com
Printed in the USA
LVOW04s0755091014

408013LV00002B/12/P